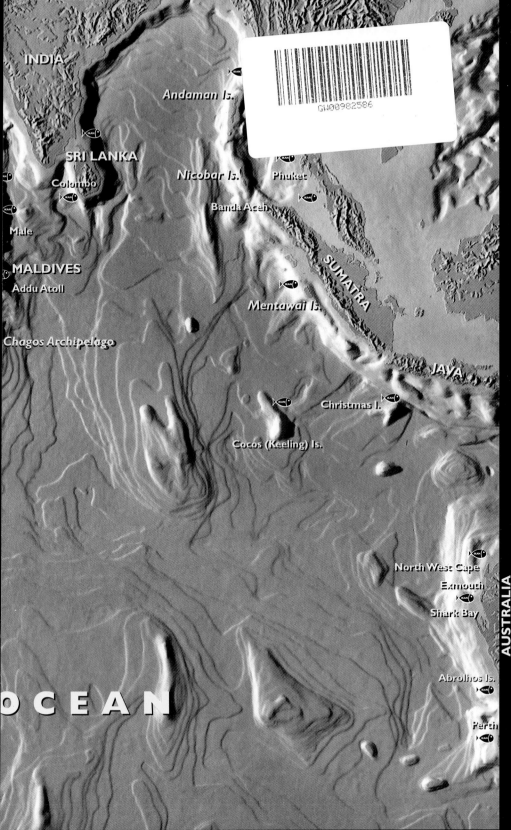

Fifth edition published in Germany 2013
and to be ordered directly from

ConchBooks
Bahnhofstrasse 117, 55296 Harxheim, Germany
www.conchbooks.de

e-mail: conchbooks@conchbooks.de

Copyright: IKAN-Unterwasserarchiv D-65933 Frankfurt
All rights reserved. No part of this publication may be reproduced,
stored in a retrieval system, or transmitted in any form or by any means,
electronic, mechanical, photocopying, recording or otherwise, without
prior permission of the publisher. Such permission, if granted, is subject
to a fee depending on the nature of the use.

Layout: Helmut Debelius
Print & Production: Tesinska tiskarna, a. s., Czech Republic

Helmut Debelius

INDIAN OCEAN REEF GUIDE

**Maldives • Sri Lanka • Thailand
South Africa • Mauritius • Madagascar
East Africa • Seychelles**

Over 1,000 photographs
of coral reef animals
taken in their natural habitat

ConchBooks

TABLE OF CONTENTS

4

PICTURE STORIES

A newly discovered species of angelshark *Squatina* sp. from the Andaman Sea, eastern Indian Ocean.

MARK STRICKLAND

FOREWORD

It is a pleasure to write the foreword for Helmut Debelius' revised edition of his Indian Ocean Tropical Fish Guide, the new INDIAN OCEAN REEF GUIDE. I have used the first edition of this field guide on several field trips (to Mozambique, Madagascar, Mauritius, and the Red Sea) and found it informative and very useful for identifying fishes. The new REEF GUIDE features two main changes: 1) it comprises not only fishes, but includes other vertebrates, living in or depending on the marine environment, and also many invertebrate reef species from diverse groups such as corals, molluscs, and crustaceans; 2) some short stories serve to learn about the interesting behaviour of selected species, others portray remote and barely known diving places, mainly oceanic island groups, to which the author has a personal relationship in one way or the other.

Except for war photography, nature photography is probably the most difficult type of photographic work. And underwater fish photography is undoubtedly the most demanding field of nature photography. Underwater, the photographer is out of his element. Just to breathe and move about safely underwater requires several hundreds of dollars worth of heavy cumbersome equipment. Next, to operate the camera and get good pictures usually requires two hands and lots of concentration. At the same time you don't want to kick or damage the coral reef, stir up the sediment, land on a long-spine sea urchin, run out of air, put your hand on a stonefish, ignore your buddy (who just might need your help), and lose sight of the anchor or whatever other landmark you need to keep from getting lost. When I am trying to do underwater photography, I always wish that I had a few extra arms and hands. If there is a patron saint of underwater photographers, she would look like a mermaid with eight arms and eyes in the back of her head. Every diver, who has attempted underwater photography will appreciate the many hours of work that has gone into assembling this wonderful collection of photographs.

Books like Helmut Debelius' INDIAN OCEAN REEF GUIDE are important and valuable because they help us to learn more about fishes and the ecosystems, of which they are a major component. As we increase our knowledge and appreciation (which comes from observation and understanding) of the wonderful world of tropical fish diversity, we will be better able to enjoy and protect this beautiful and fascinating "other world" beneath the sea.

Dr. Phillip C. Heemstra
J.L.B. Smith Institute of Ichthyology
Grahamstown, South Africa, November 1998

Phil Heemstra ready to dive off Mauritius.

INTRODUCTION

HELMUT DEBELIUS

Most of the Indian Ocean islands are coral atolls, here an example from the Maldives.

The Indian Ocean is the smallest of the three great oceans on our planet. Nevertheless, it has always been the most important one for me, considering that I started diving in the tropical waters off the coast of Sri Lanka back in 1974. At that time I got to know the coral-fish collector Rodney Jonklaas, whom I later accompanied in the course of his meetings with German customers. I had just done a few dives in the Mediterranean and Atlantic and seen a couple of colourless fishes here and there when Rodney introduced me to the larger fish dealerships in the greater Frankfurt area. Fascinated by the brilliant colours of the fishes swimming around in rows and rows of aquariums, I naively asked where in the world one could see beautiful fishes such as these. The answer - "right in my back yard" - was to have permanent consequences. Three weeks later I was standing in his garden full of aquariums located on the outskirts of the small city of Negombo, along the western coast of Sri Lanka. Starting from the very first day, I accompanied Rodney on collecting expeditions to his "back yard" and the then still accessible eastern coast around Trincomalee. He had a lot of patience with this curious novice of the tropical seas and answered each and every one of his questions, even those (from a contemporary standpoint) that were undoubtedly somewhat silly. In subsequent visits with Rodney, the studied biologist, I learned much of what I know today about the biological processes taking place in the marine environment. Rodney Jonklaas has since passed away, but I am certain that he would have been pleased with my development up until the publication of this book.

In contrast to the tropical Pacific, there are relatively few islands in the Indian Ocean. More than 2,000 islands, out of an estimated total of 3,000, make up the flat coral atolls of the Laccadives and Maldives. The other groups of islands, such as the Mascarenes or the Seychelles, as well as many small islands lying off the coasts of Africa and Arabia, differ markedly from the atolls in their topography: rolling hills or jagged mountains break up

HELMUT DEBELIUS

Rodney Jonklaas on his estate in Negombo, Sri Lanka. He was also well-known for his extensive collection of shells.

the coastline here. The southern part of the Indian Ocean is under the constant influence of the southern equatorial current. When it reaches Madagascar along its westerly course, it branches off in two directions. One arm continues south along the Mozambique Canal to the Agulhas Strait, which makes it possible for tropical fishes to exist as far down as the South African coast. The other arm flows along the East African coast, before turning eastward once again at the equator. The direction of the currents in the northern Indian Ocean varies with the seasonally changing winds: due to the northeasterly monsoon winds, the northern equatorial current dominates from November until April. Beginning in April, the winds change direction radically and the southwest monsoon drives the water masses in the opposite direction. Carrying colder water, the northerly Somalian

Just snorkelling on an Indian Ocean coral reef is an unforgettable experience.

current influences the coast of Africa and the Arabian Sea.

So where are the coral reefs that form the natural habitat for most of the fishes included in this book located? The most impressive reef formations in the Indian Ocean are found in the archipelagos of the Laccadives and Maldives, which are entirely composed of corals. Both groups lie along the Laccadive-Chagos Ridge, which is considered to form a part of the submerged shelf of the Mid Indian Rise and extends southward for more than 2,300 km, all the way to the Chagos Archipelago. I found well-developed reefs round Sri Lanka, which is also located on the Mid Indian Rise. Farther west, the Mascarene Ridge, which occasionally rises up to the surface from a depth of 4,000 m, runs for approximately 2,500 km in a north-south direction. To the north rise the ten granite islands of the Seychelles (with offshore reefs), and southwest from these are the Amirantes (with atolls). The coral islands of Cargados, or St. Brandon, which now belong to Mauritius, as well as the volcanic islands of Mauritius and Réunion, rise to the surface of the Indian Ocean along the southern ridge. The huge island of Madagascar only has a few smaller offshore reefs, whereas the volcanic Comoros are entirely surrounded by them.

There are also some reef formations in the eastern Indian Ocean, such as those in the Andaman Sea. Not so much along the coast of Thailand, but surrounding that country's offshore islands. A week's tour on a live-aboard is the ideal way to see the Similan Islands. Not only the myriad of anemones covering the reefs there left a lasting impression on me: at Richelieu Rock and along the Burma Banks I had some of the most spectacular shark sightings of the past 25 years! Not everyone has the opportunity to dive at "the end" of the Indian Ocean in places like the west coast of Sumatra, around Christmas Island, or the Abrolhos Islands off the west coast of Australia: I took advantage of mine.

Up until now the most common threats to the coral reefs have been overfishing, dynamite or cyanide fishing, and oil spills. But a new menace has emerged recently: the global rise in temperature. During a visit to the Seychelles in November of 1998, I was able to observe the results of a rise in temperature of about 7°C over a period of two months: almost all of the hard corals within the 10 m depth range had died and were covered with ugly blue-green algae. Without a doubt, my photographs of an octopus wedding on page 196 would have turned out much better on a healthy reef....

Basically, the bleaching of corals is a natural process. It can be observed regularly wherever the climatic phenomenon known as El Nino takes effect. In 1982-83, for instance, hard corals all over the world bleached out because of the rising temperatures. However, more overheated surface areas, or so-called hot spots, were registered during the first half of 1998 than ever before. In May the water temperature in the Maldives ranged around 30°C down to a depth of 50 m; the sur-

The author watches a field of anemones and its inhabitants in the Andaman Sea.

Diving from a live-aboard is the ideal way to explore the coasts of Thailand and Myanmar.

face temperature off the island of Mahé (Seychelles) was 36°C in April. At the same time, cold waters welled up from the deep in the Andaman Sea and flowed to the coasts of Myanmar and Thailand, where experienced divers suddenly encountered fishes they had never seen in this area before.

The present bleaching of corals, which has also been registered in the Pacific, has shocked the scientific community. Even centuries-old coral blocks died out in 1998. Experts have expressed their concern because the global rise in temperature has caused El Nino to appear more frequently and with greater force. Sad prospects for the coral environment: the US-based National Oceanic and Atmospheric Administration (NOAA) predicts that, unless the current

Algae now cover the stony corals that have been killed by global warming in 1998.

development is stopped, approximately 40% of the coral reefs worldwide will cease to exist by the year 2028.

It has been my endeavour to reveal, through selected underwater photographs, as much of the beauty of the INDIAN OCEAN coral reefs and their inhabitants as the 320 pages of this book will permit. I have also included a few picture stories to illustrate the fascinating habits of marine

Due to a surplus of food the number of algae eaters like these juvenile Striped bristletooth tangs Ctenochaetus striatus has rapidly multiplied.

animals. I can only hope that the diving community will be able to observe such submarine wonders for many years to come.

Frankfurt, 25 years later, spring of 1999   Helmut Debelius

HELMUT CORNELI

Impressions from the Maldives of the special kind.

PHOTO CREDITS

t = top, c = centre, b = bottom, w = whole page)

CHARLES ANDERSON: 81 t c 98 t 102 t b 113 c b
122 b 126 c 137 c 164 t b 187 b 203 t 205 b 206 c
207 t 208 b 221 c 223 c 232 c 263 t 268 c 272 t 305 c
WALTRAUD BINANZER: 19 t 28 t 117 c 162 t
HELMUT CORNELI: 35 b 47 c 52 c 253 t
HELMUT DEBELIUS: 20 b 21 t c b 22 c b 26 t b 28 b
30 t b 32 t c b 34 t 35 t 41 t b 42 c 44 t b 45 c b
46 t c b 47 t b 48 c b 52 b 53 t c b 54 t c b 56 t c
57 t 58 b 66 t b 67 c 68 c 70 t c b 71 t 74 b 76 t
77 c b 78 b 79 c b 80 b 81 b 82 t 83 t c 84 c b
86 t b 87 b 88 c 89 c 90 t c b 91 t c b 96 b 97 t
98 c b 99 t c b 102 c 103 b 104 c b 106 t c b 107 t c
108 b 109 t b 110 b 111 c b 112 t c b 113 t 114 c b
115 t b 116 t c b 117 t b 122 t c 123 t 124 t c b
125 c 126 t b 127 t c b 130 c b 131 c b 132 t b
133 b 134 t c 135 t 136 c b 137 t 138 b 140 c b
141 t c b 142 t b 143 c b 144 t c b 145 t c b 146 t c b
147 t 148 b 154 t c 155 c b 156 t c 157 t 158 c b
159 t 160 t c b 162 c b 163 t b 165 c b 166 t b 167 t c b
168 t c b 169 t b 174 t c b 175 b 176 t 177 t b 178 b
179 t b 180 t c b 181 t b 182 t c b 183 c b 184 t c b
185 t c b 186 t c b 187 t 188 c b 189 t b 190 c b
192 t c b 193 t c b 198 t c b 200 t c b 201 t c 202 c
203 c 204 b 206 t 208 t c 209 c b 210 t c b 211 t b
212 t c b 213 c 214 t 215 t c b 216 t c b 217 t c b
218 c b 219 t b 220 t c b 221 t 222 t c 223 t 227 t c
228 t c b 229 b 230 c b 232 t b 233 t 234 c b 235 t b
236 t c 237 b 238 c b 239 b 240 t c 241 t b 242 t c b
243 t 250 b 251 t b 252 t c b 253 b 255 c 257 w
258 c 259 t 262 t c 266 t 267 t b 269 t c b 270 t
271 t 272 c 275 t b 276 b 277 c b 278 c b 279 t b
282 c b 284 c 285 c 288 c b 289 c b 290 t b 291 t b
293 t c 294 t c b 295 t 296 t b 297 t c 298 t c b
299 t 300 t c b 301 t c b 302 t b 303 t c 305 b
306 t c b 307 t c b 308 t c b 310 b 311 t c 313 t 316 b
STEVE DROGIN: 13 b
KARIN ELGERT: 214 b
KIYOSHI ENDOH: 129 w
TOM HAIGHT: 19 b
JOHANN HINTERKIRCHER: 33 b 89 b 110 c 158 t
169 c 218 t 261 t c
HARALD JANUSCHKE: 205 t
GARRY JEAN-BAPTISTE: 80 c 143 t
RODNEY JONKLAAS: 312 b
DENNIS KING: 82 b 83 b 84 t 85 c b 87 c 95 w

96 t c 100 c b 110 t 132 c 133 t 134 b 135 c b
136 t 148 t c 183 t 188 t 213 t 233 c b
MICHAEL MOXTER: 131 t
PAUL MUNZINGER: 42 b 77 t 292 b
JOHN NEUSCHWANDER: 29 b 207 c
WINFRIED PERSINGER: 63 c 71 c 137 b 239 c 284 t
JAN POST: 68 t 74 t 76 c 86 c 88 t 130 t 159 b
176 c 178 t 199 b 202 t b 204 c 213 b 222 b 250 c
272 b 274 c 278 t 289 t 297 b
NORBERT PROBST: 73 t 103 t 178 c 199 c 223 b
255 t 256 c 261 b 262 b 276 t 282 t 285 t 299 b
303 b 313 c
JACK RANDALL: 201 b
JÜRGEN SCHAUER: 18 b
FRANK SCHNEIDEWIND: 236 b 239 t
MARK STRICKLAND: 13 t c 17 t 18 t 22 t 26 c
27 t 30 c 31 b 40 w 42 t 45 t 52 t 58 c 59 t b 61 w
62 t b 63 b 67 t b 68 b 69 w 72 c b 75 w 78 t 79 t
80 t 85 t 87 t 97 b 104 t 105 t 107 b 111 t 114 t
123 t 125 t 128 t c b 138 t 147 b 155 t 159 c 190 t
199 t 203 b 204 t 205 c 206 b 209 t 219 c 221 b
227 b 230 t 234 t 235 t 237 c b 243 c b 250 t 251 c
254 c b 255 b 256 t 258 t 259 c b 268 b 270 c b
275 c 276 c 277 t 283 b 310 t c 316 t
HERWARTH VOIGTMANN: 11 w 17 b 19 c 20 c
27 b 29 t 31 t 34 c b 41 c 43 t b 48 t 55 w 57 c b
58 t 60 c b 63 t 71 b 72 t 73 b 76 b 82 c 88 b 89 t
100 t 101 w 105 b 108 t 109 b 121 w 125 b 140 t
142 c 153 w 154 b 156 b 157 b 161 w 175 t 176 b
177 c 179 c 188 t 191 t b 197 w 207 b 214 c
229 t c 231 w 238 t 241 c 247 t b 260 t b 263 c b
267 c 268 t 271 c 273 w 274 t 279 c 285 b 292 t
295 b 311 b 312 t
LAWSON WOOD: 256 b 271 b 274 t 283 t 284 b
PHIL WOODHEAD: 33 t 316 c

PHOTO CREDITS COVER, left to right:
Carcharhinus albimarginatus - Mark Strickland
Scarus rubroviolaceus - Helmut Debelius
Lysmata debelius - Herwarth Voigtmann
Sepia pharaonis - Mark Strickland
Acanthurus leucosternon - Helmut Debelius
Amphiprion ephippium - Mark Strickland

BACK COVER:
Hymenocera picta - Herwarth Voigtmann

The more diving as a sport has developed, the more frequent are the encounters between people and elasmobranchs, commonly known as the sharks and rays. Nowadays diving does not take place just in coastal waters, but hotel ships for divers, so-called 'liveaboards,' make it possible to dive in places well away from the shore and to encounter the creatures of the open ocean. Moreover, there are islands and atolls in the Indian Ocean, which remain relatively undisturbed, and where the totally unexpected lies hidden beneath the surface. These developments have led to many divers becoming interested in identifying the species of elasmobranch fishes they have seen or photographed, and in learning more about their behaviour. In this book spectacular underwater photographs of sharks and rays from locations throughout the Indian Ocean are presented with special emphasis on aspects of biology and behaviour of the species wherever possible. Also, it encompasses not only large species like Whale shark and Manta ray, which can easily be seen in the right locations, but includes shy or secretive species, which have to be approached carefully or even searched for in their benthic habitat. However, one cannot expect to correctly identify each species after a first glimpse. In some cases it is difficult even for elasmobranch specialists to identify sharks and rays from only one photograph. But top illustrations are still the best way of finding out how to identify a creature by its correct name, and names are important for communication.

The skeleton of sharks and rays (elasmobranchs) is composed of calcified cartilage (hence cartilaginous fishes, which also include the chimaeras, mainly deep water dwellers). Their spinal column consists of 60 to 420 vertebrae, depending on the species. Firmly attached to it by connective tissue is the body musculature that provides forward propulsion. Earliest fossils of shark species still extant today are the extremely durable teeth of Mako and White sharks (age 100, resp. 65 million years). That means some shark species roam the seas virtually unchanged by evolution since the beginning of the Tertiary period, when huge mountain chains like the Alps, the Himalayas, and the Andes were folded up! How modest in comparison is a span of 120,000 years, when the precursor of man stood upright as Homo erectus. Cartilaginous fishes are carnivorous. But among many opportunists, feeding on everything they can devour, there are also specialists preferring certain food stuff. Grey reef sharks feed mainly on fish, Nurse sharks eat sea urchins, Eagle and Cownose rays prefer mussels. However, food preference depends not only on the species, but also on the age of the individual. Young Eagle rays search for mussels on the surface of the substrate, while adults dig for them in the sediment with their 'duck-billed' snout. Guitarfishes and stingrays have flat, strong, interlocked crushing dentitions to crack open the shells of crabs, mussels, clams, gastropods, and sea urchins. To get their preferred prey, sharks and rays have evolved interesting hunting strategies. Stingrays and young nurse sharks have been observed to rest motionless propped up on their pectoral fins, leaving a space beneath the body. A fish or crab seeking shelter there has no chance. Sharks rely on their speed to catch fast and agile prey. Grey reef sharks attack schools of snappers to isolate single individuals, and seize them in a dash of speed when they try to escape towards the sheltering reef. Some Hammerhead shark species specialise on buried stingrays. Like in all species of cartilaginous fishes, their peculiar head is equipped with many electro-sensitive pores with a sensitivity as high as that of the best man-made equipment. Sweeping the head from side to side while swimming forward, they are especially apt to detect the electric potentials of muscular activity of animals buried in the substrate. When the prey is localised, the head also serves as hydrofoil ('canard wing') in executing very tight turns at considerable speed to finally catch a stingray on the run.

The modes of elasmobranch reproduction are diverse: many species lay yolk-rich eggs (oviparous), while most species shown in this book give birth to live young (ovoviviparous) after long development periods of several months and with placental supply (placental viviparous) in many species. Litter sizes range from one or two to several hundred. It has to be emphasised that all elasmobranchs - compared to bony fishes - reproduce slowly with only relatively few young per reproduction cycle, which makes them susceptible to overfishing. Numerous species can still be observed in the Indian Ocean. But many of them are endangered - at least locally - by uncontrolled catching in drift-nets, which drown millions of these important members of the food chain each year. Sharks are often just finned alive for expensive (= commercially successful) shark fin soup, and then thrown back to the sea to die a slow death. Diverse societies all around the world try to cope with this unwise policy by informing the consumers about the victims and responsibilities. Artisan fisheries usually take from the sea only what the local people need to survive. This policy leaves enough time for regeneration of stocks. But as soon as 'exports' start to play a role, stocks are easily overfished, which may lead to the extinction of species. So think twice before you buy any elasmobranch products.

Whale shark

Length: up to 12 m; there are questionable, unconfirmed reports of sightings of specimens up to 18 m in length.
Distribution: circumtropical, found in the entire area covered by this book.
Depth: 1 - 130 m.
General: the largest living fish species is easily recognised by its immense size and a two-tone pattern of light spots and lines on a dark brown dorsal surface. Unlike that of most other sharks its enormous mouth is terminal in position and can be opened wide to filter large amounts of water for small fish, squid, crustaceans, and other plankton organisms.

The Whale shark is ovoviviparous and not oviparous as has been thought previously for a long time. In 1995 an 8 m long female was harpooned off Taiwan, which contained hundreds of embryos in different stages of development. Some had already hatched from their egg shells: they were about 70 cm long, which most probably is the size at birth. Thus the largest shark species also has the largest litter size of all sharks.

Only very little is known about the habits of the Whale shark. Subadults live in small groups, but these are seen only very rarely. Adults are usually solitary and nothing is known about the way these giants find each other, or how and where they mate.

Whale sharks are very popular with divers and in spite of their general scarcity encounters are guaranteed off the Seychelles, Thailand (Similan Islands), Christmas Island, and tropical West Australia (Ningaloo Reef). Meeting the largest fish in one of these areas, however, strongly depends on the season of the year and one should ask the diving travel agent about the best time.

Richelieu Rock, Thailand

Richelieu Rock, Thailand

Rhincodon typus   **Ningaloo Reef, West Australia**

DISCOVERED IN THE INDIAN OCEAN: THE LARGEST FISH IN THE WORLD!

It is the largest fish, but we still know very little about it because this open-ocean-dweller is rarely ever seen whenever there are divers in the water. And yet, we have learned a lot during the past few years about its behaviour and anatomy. Just how does the Whale shark, the largest living fish in the world today, measuring some 12 m in length and weighing up to 11 tons, live, feed, and reproduce?

A rare sight: an unsually large group of Cobia can be seen hitchhiking with this adult Whale shark of about 9 m in length.

The first Whale shark that became known to science was caught in 1828 near the Cape of Good Hope. This southernmost distribution of the tropical shark species is the result of the warm Mozambique current that runs southward along the east coast of Africa. The relatively small fish measuring only 4.6 m in length was harpooned. The dead animal was then preserved, its scientific description published in the South African Zoological Journal in the same year, and the specimen finally sent to the Musée National d'Histoire Naturelle (National Natural History Museum) in Paris, where it is still on display today! The longest Whale shark, the length of which was determined exactly, was netted 1983 off the coast of Bombay. The male shark was 1218 cm (12.18 metres) long and weighed 11 metric tons. An impression of just how scarce the largest fish in the world is can be gleaned from a list of all Whale shark encounters between 1828 and 1987: a biologist listed 320 sightings - an average of only two per year. In November of 1994, the pilot of an airborne helicopter sighted several whale sharks together directly off Mahe, Seychelles, and very close to a diving centre. He radioed his discovery to the centre. The result was a unique documentary, in which up to four feeding Whale sharks are to be seen simultaneously.

In contrast to most other shark species, the Whale shark's wide mouth is not located on the lower surface, but at the front end of the head. The nasal openings are visible directly above the mouth and their barbels remind one of the Whale shark's kin, the nurse sharks. How do the eyes of this giant work? Compared to the bulky body they are quite small, and serve only in close-range perception as in the case of all sharks. The

Whale sharks can rotate their eyes in almost any direction, even inwards to assure their protection.

unusually shaped, strongly flattened head contains eye sockets of far greater volume than the eyes themselves. This results in an omni-directional mobility unmatched by other sharks. For protection the eyes can even be rotated inwards, which looks like they sink into the head. Nictitating membranes, the optional means for protecting many sharks' eyes, are lacking in the Whale shark. When filter-feeding, it swims straight without the side-to-side-movement of the head typical for other sharks, which in that way gather sensory and visual information. The Whale shark simply collects its prey while swimming through the surface layer of plankton organisms. Its eyes then serve in determining plankton density, and also guide the animal towards a school of anchovies as soon as it has discovered one. It is not a problem if the Whale shark ingests air while skimming the surface: it simply leaves the gills' sieving apparatus via the long gill slits.

To investigate the way of life of an animal, it has to be

A Whale shark skims the surface for plankton and other food.

After the full moon in March veils of sperm and eggs rise from *Favia* coral polyps at Ningaloo Reef, West Australia.

observed in its natural surroundings, preferably without disturbance. One elegant method of observing wildlife, namely the attachment of a transmitter with diverse sensors and a recorder, has unfortunately failed when applied to the largest of all cold-blooded marine animals. Hence all Whale shark observations will remain lucky encounters as long as we do not know their favourite feeding places in the ocean. In the 1980s an Australian Whale shark researcher noticed the coincidence of corals spawning in March and the subsequent, more frequent appearance of Whale sharks off the West Australian Ningaloo Reef. After the full moon in the local autumn season the sea is soon covered with vast pink and lilac veils of the corals' spawn. This protein mass is the beginning of an interesting food chain: huge swarms of the tropical krill species *Pseudeuphausia latifrons* rise from the depths and also spawn. While the shrimp-like krill are usually seen close to the surface only by night, they are found there during the plankton bloom also by day. The Whale sharks, whose favourite food is crustaceans, also make their appearance then. Naturally, also schools of anchovies appear to devour the coral eggs, which in turn attracts pelagic fish species like tuna and mackerel. They herd the anchovies into huge spheres, only to dash into these fish masses from below and feed on them. This is also appreciated by the Whale sharks and they readily help to decimate the swarms.

For a long time scientists could only speculate about the reproduction of Whale sharks. After the discovery of a large egg case enclosing a living Whale shark embryo in 1953, it was generally assumed that their mode of reproduction was oviparity (laying egg capsules) as with the related Zebra shark. It was not until a few years ago, however, that the whole truth was found out (see p. 13). Juvenile Whale sharks have been caught all around the world, but only small ones of up to one metre in length, or somewhat larger ones from a length of 3 m and up. Unlike the adults, they swim in groups. It is yet unknown just where the intermediate sizes are to be found.

Mating in the natural habitat has been observed only in a few shark species. Unfortunately, this is not the case with Whale sharks. Nevertheless, Whale sharks, like all cartilaginous fishes, practice internal fertilisation. In contrast to the bony fishes, energy is invested in a few well protected and at birth highly developed, independent juveniles, which have a high rate

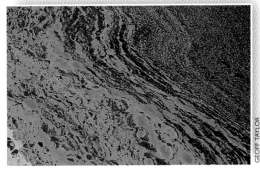

The reddish patterns created by the corals' spawn on the water resemble modern art.

Freshly caught tropical krill *Pseudeuphausia latifrons* that spawn simultaneously with the corals

of survival. Like in all shark species, the male Whale shark has a pair of claspers (long, cylindrical intromittant organs), which develop at the inner margin of the ventral fins when it reaches sexual maturity. Their presence or absence is a definite external indicator for the sex of a shark that has reached a certain degree of maturity. During copulation (probably in a belly-to-belly position) one of the two claspers is inserted into the female genital opening (the cloaca). In the case of male Whale sharks that have not yet reached full sexual maturity, the penis-like claspers are short and soft. In adult specimens, however, they are substantially longer than the ventral fins, and stiffened by the calcification of their cartilaginous skeletal elements. Scratches and scars on a Whale shark's claspers clearly indicate that they have already been functional. Connected to the claspers are two muscular sacs that

The crescent-shaped gap in the trailing edge of this Whale shark's caudal fin very probably has been inflicted by a large predatory shark.

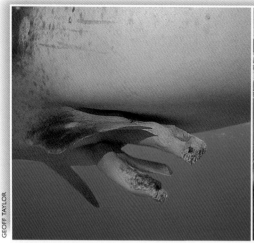

Wounds on the claspers of an adult male Whale shark are evidence for recent sexual activity.

View of a female Whale shark's ventral fins with the slit-like cloacal opening, an attached remora, and a juvenile pilot jack.

lie anteriorly beneath the belly's skin, and are filled with seawater prior to copulation. During copulation the water is squeezed out, which simultaneously washes sperm into the internal reproduction organs of the female.

Even a huge animal like the Whale shark obviously has enemies, as wounds and missing fin parts prove. Whether these were inflicted by other large shark species or boat propellers, can only be guessed. There is no evidence for such a duel of giants yet. The Whale shark's steady companions are harmless, though: species of bony fish from different families seek its company for several reasons. The giant is always looking for food and thus sufficient remains are guaranteed also for commensals. Furthermore, it saves energy to swim in the wake of a Whale shark.

The most frequent hitchhikers are jacks and remoras. Highly conspicuous are the juveniles of the Golden pilot jack *Gnathanodon speciosus*, which swim near the head of the Whale shark in groups of up to 150 individuals. Very frequently Striped remoras *Echeneis naucrates* can be seen accompanying the Whale shark. They cling to various parts of the shark - below the mouth, on the head, in the spiracle, on the fins, or even in the cloaca of the female - with an oblong sucking disc (a modified dorsal fin) that looks similar to the relief of a shoe's sole and is located on the remora's head. The Striped remora reaches a length of 80 cm. The largest fish in the

A 45 cm long Whale shark embryo already fully resembles the adult.

company of the Whale shark is the Cobia *Rachycentrum canadum*. It reaches a length of 200 cm, but those seen together with Whale sharks so far were merely 100 cm long. The distinct white longitudinal stripes of the juveniles become dark grey in adults, like the rest of the body. Unfortunately, there is another hitchhiker: man, totally possessed by the urge to touch everything, even under water. The best advice is: photographing and swimming alongside permitted, but do not touch!

This subadult Whale shark of about 5 m length was photographed in Thai waters at Richelieu Rock, and is accompanied by remoras of various sizes.

Zebra shark

Length: up to 350 cm.

Distribution: entire area.

Depth: 5 - 65 m.

General: this unmistakable shark is frequently encountered singly in coral reefs and lagoons. Its caudal fin is almost as long as its body. There are characteristic ridges along its back. The juvenile coloration (dark and light vertical bars, popular name!) is completely different from the adult pattern seen in the photos.

During the day the Zebra shark is usually seen resting motionless on the bottom (large photo), during the night the nocturnal hunter swims close to the substrate in order to find its prey of crustaceans, other shelled invertebrates, also fish, and even sea snakes. Occasionally it ventures off the ground even by day (photo below).

Ridges and coloration remind of the Whale shark and some scientists believe both species to be closely related. The main differences lie in the Whale shark's highly specialised pelagic way of life.

Stegostoma fasciatum   Similan Islands, Thailand

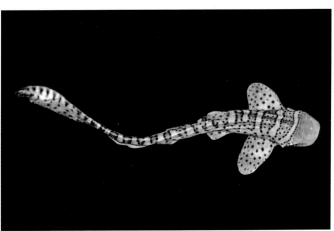

Indian Ocean nurse shark

Length: up to 300 cm.
Distribution: entire area.
Depth: 1 - 70 m.
General: a nocturnally active, bottom-dwelling shark species, hiding in caves by day, often seen in groups (see large photos). Its coloration is uniformly brownish yellow without any pattern.
  The two nominal species of the genus *Nebrius* are united by some shark taxonomists, who argue that *N. ferrugineus* are just larger *N. concolor*.

Nebrius ferrugineus   **Mulaku Atoll, Maldives**

A pair of barbels extending from the inner margins of the nasal openings above the mouth (small photo) serve in locating and identifying the Nurse shark's prey of crustaceans, sea urchins, cephalopods, reef fishes, which are literally sucked from crevices.

Myanmar

Comoros cat shark

Length: up to 60 cm.
Distribution: until now known only from the Comoros.
Depth: 40 - 300 m.
General: this is the first photo showing this species in its natural habitat. All shallow water cat shark species have camouflaging patterns of stripes or blotches and dots suiting them for a benthic life. All are oviparous, and mainly feed on benthic invertebrates. They themselves are eaten by larger sharks and predatory bony fishes.

Scyliorhinus comoroensis   **Comoros**

Sandtiger shark

Le: up to 330 cm. Di: Mozambique to South Africa, also Red
Sea. De: 1 - 200 m.
Ge: encountered singly or in
groups in coastal areas. The
aggressiveness of Sandtiger
sharks is still under debate.
There are reports of timid
specimens not attacking even
when cornered, and reports of
attacks on humans, especially
from South African waters and
under murky conditions.
  Sandtiger sharks are well
known for their special mode
of reproduction: basically they
are ovoviviparous, giving birth
to two large young (one from
each uterus, they have about
one third of the mother's
length), which previously have
eaten all siblings (adelphopha-
gy) and unfertilised eggs in the
uterus. Adults feed on teleosts, sharks, rays, and crabs.

Carcharias taurus   all photos: Aliwal Shoal, South Africa

Megamouth shark

Le: up to 520 cm. Di: Atlantic,
Pacific, and Indian Ocean. De:
50 - 1500 m. Ge: discovered in
1976 this large plankton feeder
is known from only 10 accidental drift net catches and
strandings, one of them in the
Indian Ocean near Perth, West
Australia. All were subadult
males except for a 470 cm
female. Very little is known of
this most unusual pelagic shark
and although there is only a
slight chance to meet one in
the sea, everyone should be
able to recognise it in order to
gather more information.

Megachasma pelagios   East Pacific

THRESHER SHARKS   ALOPIIDAE

Alopias vulpinus   **Amirantes, Seychelles**

Common thresher shark

Length: up to 330 cm.
Distribution: entire area.
Depth: I - 150 m.
General: an unmistakable
species with a very long caudal
fin that is used to stun schooling fishes, the main prey of this
timid shark. It also feeds on
schooling shrimp and squid.
The Thresher shark lives
pelagically and is only rarely
encountered in coastal waters.
Reproduction is ovoviviparous
with a litter size of two. The
family Thresher sharks comprises three species, all of
which occur in our area. They
are not easy to distinguish.

REQUIEM SHARKS   CARCHARHINIDAE

Ari Atoll, Maldives

Carcharhinus amblyrhynchos   **Lhaviyani Atoll, Maldives**

Grey reef shark

Le: up to 180 cm. Di: entire
area including Red Sea. De: 5 -
280 m. Ge: one of the most
popular and well-known sharks
in general. This is THE shark
species most often encountered near Indian Ocean and
Red Sea coral reefs. It is curious, and readily approaches
divers. The Grey reef shark
has been filmed and photographed many times. All reef
sharks are placental viviparous,
which means that before they
are born the embryos are connected for an extended period
of time to the inner wall of
their mother's uterus via an
umbilical chord and a placenta
derived from their yolk-sac.
Up to 6 young are born at the
end of each reproductive
cycle that lasts about 2 years.
The species feeds on a wide
variety of bony fishes mainly
during dusk and dawn. Live
observations in the Pacific
showed it to be territorial and
behave like a fenced dog.
When disturbed, it displays a
typical agonistic swimming
behaviour: hunching the body,
lowering the pectoral fins,
swimming in an exaggerated
manner. Indian Ocean specimens are much less aggressive
and may become commercially
important for local diving
resorts when fed by hand
under water. See also p.11.

Silky shark

Le: up to 330 cm. Di: northern Indian Ocean, southernmost record from Mozambique. De: 1 - 500 m. Ge: usually this species is living pelagically in the open ocean, but it is also seen near the coast. It is not aggressive and docile encounters are possible in the open water off reefs. The Silky shark heavily feeds on tuna and is thus feared by fishermen. It is No. 3 in the hierarchy of oceanic sharks behind Oceanic whitetip and Blue shark. Its name refers to the silken sheen created by millions of dermal denticles on the skin.

Carcharhinus falciformis   Aldabra, Seychelles

Blacktip reef shark

Length: up to 180 cm. Distribution: entire area. Depth: 1 - 30 m. General: a common shark on Indo-Pacific reef tops, where it is usually seen in small groups hunting for fish. It readily enters very shallow and sometimes even brackish waters. The species is easily identified by its distinct fin tips, which often protrude from the shallow water.

Some marine aquaria display the lively species, which should not be kept together with larger (dominant) sharks. See also GOING TERRESTRIAL, p.49-51.

Carcharhinus melanopterus   Mauritius

Oceanic white-tip shark

Le: up to 350 cm. Di: entire area. De: 1 - 150 m. Ge: pelagic species, only sometimes venturing close to coral reef areas. One of the largest species of the family, it is easily distinguished by its large, rounded dorsal and pectoral fins with broad white tips. The elegant and fast swimmer lacks the hectic movements typical of many requiem sharks. Often accompanied by Pilot fishes *Naucrates ductor* or other sharks. Said to be one of the four sharks most dangerous to humans, but there are no confirmed reports on attacks!

Carcharhinus longimanus   Cocos Keeling Islands, West Australia

21

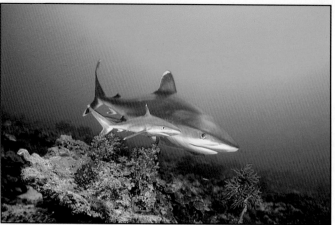

Silvertip reef shark

Le: up to 300 cm. Di: western Indian Ocean southward to South Africa. De: 30 - 150 m. Ge: encountered in the open water near coral reef drop-offs, mainly below 30 m. Usually singly or in pairs, also in small schools. A shy species that is difficult to catch on film. Reproduction - as in all genus members - is placental viviparous, litters of up to 11 live young (number depending on size and age of mother) are born about every two years. The species feeds on bony fishes and was described from the Red Sea over 150 years ago.

Carcharhinus albimarginatus   **Burma Banks, Thailand**

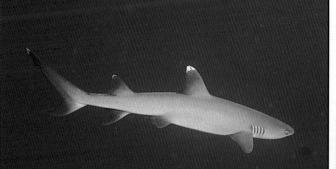

White-tip reef shark

Le: up to 210 cm. Di: entire area. De: 1 - 40 m. Ge: the common species is seen singly or in small groups in the reef, resting on the bottom or in caves by day, hunting fishes among the corals at night. Likely the first shark encountered on reefs in our area.

Triaenodon obesus   **Praslin, Seychelles**

Scalloped hammerhead shark

Length: up to 420 cm. Distribution: entire area. Depth: 3 - 280 m. General: the most common of the peculiar hammerhead sharks. The non-aggressive species is encountered singly or in large migrating schools. Like in the closely related Requiem shark family the reproduction of hammerhead sharks is placental viviparous. This species may have at least up to 31 young per litter, and feeds on rays, sharks, and teleosts, e.g. mackerels.

Sphyrna lewini   **Aldabra, Seychelles**

SHARKS SIGNIFICANT FOR THE MALDIVES

What do divers and maritime tourists expect to find in the Maldives? Big fish like sharks and rays, as well as snappers, sweetlips, mackerels and tunas, all of which can still be encountered there in huge schools. Maldivian fishermen are primarily after the bony fishes mentioned above, but they have also been catching an increasing number of sharks recently.

Several methods of catching sharks are known in the Maldives. Three important ones are: targeted deepwater angling of spiny dogfishes, specifically Gulper shark (Centrophorus spp., family Squalidae), for their valuable liver oil; offshore angling of pelagic shark species like Oceanic whitetip shark (Carcharhinus longimanus) and Tiger shark (Galeocerdo cuvier) for their fins and meat; and coastal fishing of reef associated species like Silvertip shark (Carcharhinus albimarginatus) and Grey reef shark (Carcharhinus amblyrhynchos) for the same products using nets and handlines. All shark products are exported. For several years now the activities of the reef shark fisheries have been in conflict with the tourism industry of the Maldives. "Shark watching" is one of the main attractions for divers. According to rough estimates the sharkmania of divers alone earns the government of the Maldives US $ 2.3 million per year. If one accepts further stipulations, a living Grey reef shark is worth a hundred times more than a dead one in a fishing boat.

In the Maldives sharks do not have the false reputation of being maneaters as is common in other countries. Although there are a few cases in which fishermen at work have been bitten by sharks, there is no confirmed unprovoked attack on divers or snorkellers in the Maldives. Thus an unbelievable shark boom has developed there. The guarantee for an underwater shark encounter has become an important argument in the tourism business. Naturally, sharks are only part of the Maldives package in which white sand, palm trees, clear water and colourful coral reef fishes are likewise important. But a questionnaire submitted to 32 experienced diving instructors in the Maldives resulted in a list of 35 diving sites frequented only to meet sharks there. These include Fish Head, Maaya

Shark fins drying in the sun aboard a fishing boat.

Tila, and Lion's Head, as well as Madivaru and Kuda Faru. It is hard to estimate the number of "sharks only" dives per year. Season, periods of absence of sharks, and the obvious lack of interest in sharks among some divers taken into account, there are still 77,000 pure "shark watching dives," which make up or about 15% of half a million tourist dives in the Maldives per year. If one dive costs US $ 30, then shark watching dives alone yield the yearly amount of US $ 2.3 million mentioned above.

However one choses to interpret these figures, it becomes clear that travel agents must have a great (financial) interest in healthy reefs. So the loud protests following the arrest of Maldivian shark fishermen at Fish Head and Lions's Head were no surprise. When the sharks did not show up at all at Fish Head between February and June 1992 consternation spread among the diving base operators. Today we know that this was only an extraordinarily long period of an annually recurring phenomenon whereby the sharks (mainly Grey reef sharks) simply disappear in the deep for several weeks. After all, who wants to be observed during love games? Yet travel agents have already urged the Maldivian government several times to totally ban shark nets and lines inside the atolls. The following calculation was used to reinforce the demand: about 20 adult sharks are regularly to be seen at Fish Head. If the US $ 670,000 net income from shark observations is divided by the number of sharks, each one at Fish Head is worth US $ 33,500. An analog calculation for all 35 shark diving sites still results in the fictitious shark value of US $ 3,300 per year. Naturally, also the value of a dead Grey reef shark can be calculated: if one adds the proceeds from dried meat and fins, jaws and liver oil the sum is about US $ 32. Altogether, a living Grey reef shark at the diving site is approxi-

Finned reef shark left behind to die a slow death.

A much better way to 'use' them: living sharks, every uw-photographer's delight.

mately a hundred times more valuable than a dead one. This is true for the period of one year, but if one takes into account that a Grey reef shark reaches 18 years of age and is stationary, this sum has to be multiplied several times.

It is not only important to reason how much profit there will be, but also who will benefit from it. The Maldivian fishermen directly depend on the income from their catch. They would not profit from any catching prohibition. This does not mean that they do not profit indirectly from diving tourism as about US $ 8 of the charge for one dive are for the boat's rent, including the dhoni's crew, who otherwise would be fishing. To give an example: between July 1991 and August 1992, seven out of nineteen shark fishing dhoni crews of Dungati accepted the offer to work for a newly opened diving resort nearby. In addition, the diving bases themselves offer work to Maldivians and indirectly increase their well-being as they pay taxes for all imports and guests. The government passes on these taxes for use in health and education programs.

Even today the Maldives still have a big competitive advantage over other diving destinations. Especially in neighbouring areas like South East Asia, there is the threat of overfishing the reefs due to the high food demands of a growing population. If fishing in the Maldives is continued sensibly, the advantages will prevail. Most of the diving base managers, however, are convinced that the numbers of visitors will decrease drastically if there are no more sharks to be seen in the Maldives.

Hit list of Maldives' sharks

Twenty-six shark species have been identified in a scientifically correct way in the Maldives until now. Three species of spiny dogfish from the depths of the Indian Ocean are frequently caught there, but have not yet been correctly identified. Four additional species are represented by dried jaws alone. Consequently, there are 33 species of shark reported from the islands. Furthermore, Maldivian fishermen regard Bowmouth guitarfish *(Rhina ancylostoma)* and White-spotted shovelnose ray *(Rhynchobatus djiddensis)* as sharks! Those five species which every diver - almost guaranteed, depending on the season - can observe in the Maldives, are presented in order of their abundance.

GREY REEF SHARK *Carcharhinus amblyrhynchos*   Maldivian name: thila miyaru

This stout, impressive shark of up to 180 cm in length often appears in groups. An encounter with 10 or more of these animals is THE Maldivian experience for most divers. Generally this species is quite shy, but some diving instructors - at least in the past - have fed them in order to make them approach people. Those who approach are females, while males and juveniles live in deeper regions. Because they can be seen there throughout the year, the best diving sites for Grey reef sharks are Fish Head (Mushimasmingili Thila) in the Ari Atoll and Lion's Head in the North Male Atoll. At Miyaru Kandu, Guraidhoo and the Embudu Channel they are seen only during the Northeast monsoon (November to April), while around Kuda Boli and Rasfari they occur during the Southwest monsoon. With the monsoons the currents also change. The species can always be found at the channel mouths, which are exposed to the current. Between March and May the female Grey reef sharks also retreat to

Another kind of uw-photography. Even coloured lights do not hurt!

mate. A 144-cm female caught in August in the Ari Atoll is known to have carried two young of a length of 48 cm each. The species is preferred by Maldivian fishermen and caught with standing gillnets, bottom longlines and handlines.

Most divers visit the Maldives mainly to see living sharks. What will be in the future for the sharks and the tourists?

WHITETIP REEF SHARK *Triaenodon obesus*   Maldivian name: faana miyaru
Compared to the Grey reef shark this species is much less impressive even though it grows larger (up to 210 cm).
Sighting a Whitetip reef shark is guaranteed in the Maldives as it is not very shy with divers. This is true throughout the year, including both monsoon seasons. During the day the species is often encountered resting in caves
or under table corals, frequently also on open sand patches and in water so shallow that even snorkellers can
observe it. The nocturnally active species hunts in groups and feeds on parrotfish, goatfish and triggerfish. Each
individual is stationary and returns to its resting place. Maldivian fishermen catch the Whitetip reef shark at night
using standing gillnets and handlines.

COMMON NURSE SHARK *Nebrius ferrugineus*   Maldivian name: nidhan miyaru
The Maldivian name means "sleeping shark." This is exactly what this nocturnally active shark does during the day
in caves along the reef where it can be seen more often by divers than the Leopard shark, which has similar habits.
The bottom-dweller reaches a length of 320 cm and specialises in catching octopus and other cephalopods. With
its barbels it also probes coral thickets and crevices for crabs and small fish which are sucked into its mouth. One
female reportedly carried 8 embryos. Some time ago the fishermen also sold living specimens to the tourist
resorts where they were presented to the guests in so-called "shark pools." Fishermen catch this nurse shark at
night using standing gillnets and handlines.

SILVERTIP SHARK *Carcharhinus albimarginatus*   Maldivian name: kattafulhi miyaru
This species is widespread in the Maldives and can be seen frequently. The local name refers to the clearly visible
white-edged fins. The Silvertip shark swims in a much more majestic way than the often hectic Grey reef shark.
This is also due to the former species' greater length, which may reach 300 cm. However, large Silvertip sharks
can only be seen along outer reefs, which also is where the fishermen catch individuals up to 230 cm in size. Juveniles of 75 to 125 cm have been caught inside the Maldives atolls. Stomach content analysis revealed that the
species feeds on bony fishes and cephalopods. In the Maldives it also occurs singly in shallow water (around 10
m).

WHALE SHARK *Rhincodon typus*   Maldivian name: fehurihi
The largest living fish species (length up to 12 m) is a harmless plankton feeder. The massive fish - in the Maldives
mainly 5- to 7-m-long specimens are encountered - often swims in shallow depth and can easily be identified by
the white spots on the back. For filter-feeding the huge terminal mouth is opened wide. It has to be pointed out
that Whale sharks cannot be observed regularly everywhere in the Maldives. During the northeast monsoon the
currents run from east to west, and vice versa during the southwest monsoon. Every time the currents change
direction lots of sediment is stirred up in the Maldives. This results in plankton blooms which attract the Whale
sharks, especially in the north, where the water around the two atoll chains is more thoroughly mixed and the
monsoon change is more pronounced than in the south. It needs to be mentioned that Whale sharks are also
caught in the Maldives. According to questionnaires, the catch is about 30 specimens per year, which in the long
run is far too many of this relatively rare species, especially if they are meant to attract tourists. Meat and fins are
not utilised; they die only for 100 to 200 litres of oil yielded per individual. Thirty dead Whale sharks net no more
than US $ 4000!

South Male Atoll, Maldives

Spotted shovelnose ray

Length: up to 310 cm.
Distribution: entire area.
Depth: 2 - 50 m.
General: similar to the following species, but slimmer and more flattened like a typical ray. It retains the lower caudal fin lobe, although it is usually swimming close to the ground unlike its bulkier relative *Rhina*. Largest guitarfish, common on sand, sometimes seen in extremely shallow water. It is ovoviviparous with litters of up to 10 young, which are born in estuaries or mangrove areas. Feeds on benthic fishes and invertebrates.

Although the centre photo has been taken under less than ideal conditions, it is unusual in showing a pair of the species swimming together, very probably displaying courtship behaviour; the male is the smaller specimen below the female.

The small photo below shows a juvenile, which has distinct white spots on the upper surface. Most of these spots disappear in adults as can be seen on the top photo.

Rhynchobatus djiddensis   Myanmar

Bowmouth guitarfish

Le: up to 240 cm. Di: entire area. De: 3 - 90 m. Ge: the caudal fin of this transient form between sharks and rays has a distinct lower lobe, usually a feature of genuine sharks, but all members of this and the following families of cartilaginous fishes are true rays. Local fishermen in the Indian Ocean area often regard sharkfin guitarfishes as sharks. In rays, however, the gill slits are located on the underside of the head. The species lives over coral rubble, and swims off the ground as can be seen in the large photo next page.

Rhina ancylostoma   Mauritius

SHARKFIN GUITARFISHES   RHYNCHOBATIDAE

Bowmouth guitarfish
continued

Both sexes look similar at first glance, but like in all cartilaginous fishes adult females are usually larger and lack the male's intromittant organs, the claspers, visible at the inner margin of the ventral fins. The small photo below depicts the unusually long claspers of a male guitarfish. Those of stingrays are much shorter, as shown in *Himantura undulata* on the next page.
 All species of guitarfishes are ovoviviparous with a litter size of about four, and mainly feed on crustaceans and other shelled invertebrates.

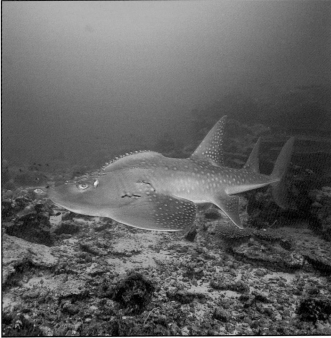

Rhina ancylostoma   Burma Banks, Thailand

TORPEDO RAYS   TORPEDINIDAE

Black-spotted torpedo ray

Length: up to 64 cm.
Distribution: Sri Lanka to South Africa, but absent from around the Arabian peninsula.
Depth: 3 - 500 m.
General: like almost all species of torpedo rays this one too lives close to the bottom. While resting, it is perfectly camouflaged by its dark reticulate pattern on a lighter background, and often covered with sand (see small photo below). Torpedo rays hunt for benthic fishes and invertebrates, which are stunned by discharging two kidney-shaped electric organs (over 200 Volts and several Amperes!).

Torpedo fuscomaculata   Ari Atoll, Maldives

27

TORPEDO RAYS   TORPEDINIDAE

Marbled torpedo ray

Length: up to 100 cm.
Distribution: entire area.
Depth: 2 - 200 m.
General: found in lagoon reefs
around coral bommies and
rocks. Aggregating in schools
during the mating season. The
small photo below from Oman
shows a colour variant.

Torpedo sinuspersici   **Pemba, Tanzania**

STINGRAYS   DASYATIDIDAE

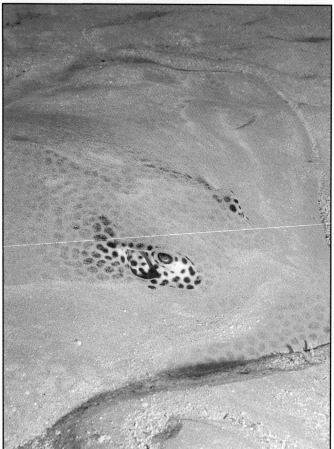

Leopard whipray

Width: up to 140 cm.
Distribution: entire area.
Depth: 3 - 80 m.
General: a moderately common species that mainly lives
on the inner continental shelf,
occasionally entering shallow
depths. It can best be distinguished from similar species by
its pattern of variously shaped
dark spots (compare photos)
on a lighter background, which
are more close-set in adults
and do not fuse to form a
maze-like pattern as in the
more common Honeycomb
whipray *Himantura uarnak*.
   Note the claspers and tail
spine depicted in the bottom
photo (same male specimen as
shown in the large photo).

Himantura undulata   **Aldabra, Seychelles**

Honeycomb whipray

Width: up to 150 cm.
Distribution: entire area.
Depth: 3 - 175 m.
General: the (unbroken) whip-like tail of this species has more than twice the length of the body disc. The snout is pointed, the pectoral tips are bluntly rounded. The distinct reticulate pattern is slowly disappearing with age. This stingray inhabits sandy bottoms near reefs; usually only parts of the animal such as eyes and tail are visible when it is hiding in sandy substrate. The species heavily feeds on crustaceans, molluscs, squid, and jellyfish.

Himantura uarnak   Punto d'Oro, Mozambique

Mangrove whipray

Width: up to 100 cm.
Distribution: entire area.
Depth: 5 - 10 m.
General: as its name implies this stingray lives in the shallow water of mangrove areas, estuaries, and sheltered coastal bays of corals reefs. The species can best be recognised by its partly white tail (including the spine), which looks like having been dipped in white paint. The base of the tail and the upper surface of the body disc are dark slate grey in colour with irregularly distributed, widely spaced white spots. The distinct colour pattern can clearly be seen in the photos (small one at bottom from Similan Islands, Thailand). Like many stingray species the Mangrove whipray feeds on a great variety of shelled benthic invertebrates, which are covered by the bluntly rounded snout and sucked from the substrate to be crushed between the teeth. The latter form bands of blunt tips, but are not fused to form dental crushing plates like in the Eagle ray family (see below).

Himantura granulata   Gaafu Atoll, Maldives

Himantura jenkinsi

Ari Atoll, Maldives

Jenkins' whipray

Wi: up to 100 cm. Di: entire area. De: 5 - 55 m. Ge: margin of disc distinctly white, disc and tail yellowish brown. Seen singly, sometimes in groups.

Pink whipray

Width: up to 150 cm. Distribution: entire area. Depth: 20 - 200 m. General: a large species of stingray with a very long tail: if the tail is unbroken, total length may exceed 500 cm! The coloration of the upper surface is a uniform brownish pink mottled with darker blotches. This whipray is mainly encountered in offshore habitats, usually around atolls in deep water. It feeds on crustaceans, and may have a taste for shrimps and prawns as it is often caught in the nets of shrimp-trawlers.

Himantura fai

Surin Island, Thailand

Bluespotted stingray

Wi: up to 100 cm. Di: entire area. De: 2 - 20 m. Ge: the common species can easily be identified by many large, brilliantly blue spots on its body disc. Sting (often two) set well back on the tail, which also has a small, fringe-like caudal fin. It is encountered in reefs, resting on (rarely buried in) sand under corals and in crevices by day, swimming about and hunting for prey at night. Feeds on worms, shrimps, and hermit crabs. *Dasyatis kuhlii* (see p.32) is similar, but has fewer and dark-ringed blue spots, also a white tip of the tail.

Taeniura lymma

Sri Lanka

Blotched fantail ray

Width: up to 180 cm.
Distribution: entire area.
Depth: 6 - 100+ m.
General: a large ray, reaching 300 cm in length, if the tail is unbroken. Most common stingray species in our area. Its coloration is highly variable, from pale grey to almost black with many irregular dark blotches. The tail usually carries one sting, which is set well away from the base of the tail.

The species is encountered along the base of drop-offs or on sand flats in or near coral reefs. It often excavates large holes (see large photo at the right) by blowing water from the mouth, previously taken in through the spiracles. The latter are vestigial gill slit openings located behind the eyes that enable all benthic rays to ingest water for breathing, even when resting on the ground. By blowing into the substrate, the ray dislodges molluscs and crustaceans from the sand, which are taken up and eaten. The large photo at the bottom shows a specimen of *Himantura fai* "riding" a larger *Taeniura meyeni*. This association can be seen quite often in our area, and also includes other species of *Himantura*. Its significance has not yet been investigated, but probably the smaller stingrays profit from the food-providing substrate digging of the large one.

Small photos below: the species is not shy, and has been a photo model on many occasions; three juvenile *Gnathanodon speciosus* swimming near the spiracle.

Punto d'Oro, Mozambique

Taeniura meyeni   Myanmar

31

Feathertail stingray

Width: up to 180 cm.
Distribution: entire area.
Depth: 1 - 60 m.
General: this species is found near coral reefs and in lagoons, also in freshwater streams. It is of uniformly brown coloration except for a clearly distinct large lobe of skin on the underside of the posterior half of the tail, which is much darker. A sting is located on the tail at about the beginning of the tail fin lobe. Feeds on shelled molluscs and crustaceans. Inquisitive, investigating divers' activities, and often accompanied by pilot fish.

Pastinachus sephen   Thailand

Kuhl's stingray

Wi: up to 40 cm. Di: entire area. De: 3 - 90 m. Ge: similar to *T. lymma* (see p.30), but often buried in sand by day, and less frequent in reefs, rather living on vast sand flats. It has a caudal fin fold, and usually two stings set midway on the tail. Tip of tail distinct.

Dasyatis kuhlii   Sri Lanka

Porcupine ray

Wi: up to 100 cm. Di: entire area. De: 1 - 30 m. Ge: distinct by oval to circular outline and numerous thorn-like spines on the back, without tail spine. Found on coral rubble, in shallow sand flats, and seagrass beds. Feeds on fishes (wrasses sleeping in the sand) and crabs.

Urogymnus asperrimus   Ari Atoll, Maldives

BUTTERFLY STINGRAYS   GYMNURIDAE

Butterfly stingray

Width: up to 250 cm.
Distribution: entire area,
around the Arabian peninsula,
not in the Red Sea.
Depth: 1 - 50 m.
General: this species is mainly
encountered singly. It inhabits
lagoons, but also occurs in
sandy areas well away from the
coral reef. Butterfly stingrays
are fast swimmers, which hunt
in small groups; the main prey
are small schooling fishes.
  All species of this distinct
stingray family have a body disc
and pectoral fins much wider
than long, giving them a but-
terfly-like appearance when
swimming. Their tail is short,
and usually carries two barbed
stinging spines at its base,
which are - like in all stingrays
- only used in defense. Reproduction is ovoviviparous with a
litter size of up to 8 and a gestation period of about half a
year. Unborn embryos are
already equipped with tail
spines.

Gymnura poecilura   Oman

EAGLE RAYS   MYLIOBATIDIDAE

Patterned eagle ray

Width: up to 160 cm.
Distribution: the small photo
below (Kuredu, Maldives) is
the first record of this species
from the Indian Ocean, which
otherwise is widely distributed
in the western Pacific (Taiwan,
Indonesia, North Australia).
Depth: 5 - 50 m.
General: this very attractive
eagle ray is clearly distinct by a
reticulate pattern of dark lines
and rings on its back (compare
both photos). It has an
extremely long tail, which - if
unbroken - considerably adds
to the maximum total length
of almost 400 cm. The massive
head of the shell-eater has sev-
en tooth rows in each jaw.

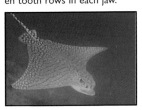

Aetomylaeus vespertilio   Felidhoo Atoll, Maldives

Aldabra, Seychelles

Spotted eagle ray

Width: up to 350 cm.
Distribution: entire area.
Depth: 1 - 45 m.
General: most common 'flying' ray observed in the Indian Ocean including the Red and Arabian Sea. It is found mainly in open water of coastal coral reef areas as well as around atolls. It is clearly distinct by a dark dorsal surface of the body disc, which carries small white spots in a quite regular arrangement (compare to the previous species *Aetomylaeus vespertilio*). It is encountered singly or in small groups as can be seen in the photos. The specimen on the centre photo is searching the substrate for shelled molluscs, its favourite prey. The shells are cracked open between two flat dental plates consisting of interlocked rows of crushing teeth.

Sometimes huge schools of eagle rays travel over long distances, swimming near the surface. The schools are probably mating aggregations on their way to the mating grounds, but these large-scale movements of rays are yet poorly understood. Eagle rays mate in midwater or on the ground. The male gets a tight hold of the female by biting her pectoral. It then inserts one clasper into the female's cloaca in a belly-to belly position. After a gestation period of one year up to four young are born (ovoviviparous).

Aetobatus narinari   Ari Atoll, Maldives

Manta ray

Wi: up to 670 cm, usually max. 400 cm. Di: entire area.
De: 1 - 40 m. Ge: the largest ray lives pelagically in the open sea, but is also observed near reefs (photo left). Below: Manta used for food (Sri Lanka).

Manta birostris   Ari Atoll, Maldives

Manta ray
continued

Despite its numerous small teeth, the huge Manta ray is a filter feeder. It feeds on plankton and small fishes, and sometimes can be encountered singly or in small groups close above the corals (see large photos at the right) or even over seagrass beds, engulfing small organisms close to the bottom. The prey organisms are guided into the enormous mouth by a fleshy lobe (cephalic fin) on each side of the head. Most often, however, Manta rays feed close to the surface, where plankton has accumulated. In the process the rays execute somersaults and even break the surface. Jumping high in the air can sometimes be observed, and seems to be playing or dominance behaviour. Getting rid of dermal ectoparasites may also play a role, much like in the case of breeching whales. Manta rays frequently visit reef-side cleaning stations to let cleaner wrasses remove skin parasites and old skin from healed wounds. In the Maldives the wrasse *Thalassoma amblycephalum* is often involved in this process.

Manta rays are ovoviviparous, and give birth to two young after a gestation period of thirteen months. It has been observed that pregnant females perform spectacular jumps out of the water, during which they eject their offspring.

The small photo below from Pemba shows the almost entirely white lower surface of the pectoral fins and body disc. In most specimens there are several scattered dark spots, which become more numerous with age. These patterns are well suited to distinguish individuals underwater, even at a distance (compare photos).

Ari Atoll, Maldives

Manta birostris   **Ari Atoll, Maldives**

For a long time phylogenetic research inclined to the opinion that originally there were only cartilaginous fishes and that the bony fishes evolved from them. More recently we have learned otherwise. Nowadays the majority view is that bony fishes were present right from the start - 440 million years ago - and the cartilaginous fishes followed, perhaps 15 million years later. Several facts lead us to the supposition that the early phases of the evolution of bony fishes took place in brackish and fresh water. It was only later that some of these "new models" found their way into the sea whence their ancestors had come and where the close relatives of those ancestors had remained. As far as the cartilaginous fishes are concerned, it is certain that they are an offshoot of those creatures which never left the sea. Although they have the same primeval ancestry both major classes have quite distinct characteristics. The bony fishes show an appreciably greater number of innovative features, which has led to explosive speciation: there are at least 36 species of bony fishes for every cartilaginous one!

Among other features, bony fishes evolved the swim bladder, an extremely useful piece of equipment which enables its owner to maintain a horizontal position without any energy expenditure, and at any chosen depth. In order to rise or sink the fish has only to point its head up or down and bring its locomotive muscles into play. The swim bladder registers the change in pressure and automatically decreases or increases the amount of gas required to maintain the specific consistency of the entire organism against the water pressure at a selected depth. Only the gas pressure is altered; the swim bladder remains the same size. It is thought to have originated as an organ for breathing atmospheric air, necessary in oxygen-depleted, warm, brackish waters. Cartilaginous fishes were not involved in this evolutionary process and to the present day have to make do without this buoyancy aid. A few bony fishes have dispensed with a swim bladder because it was superfluous to their bottom-oriented life-style. There are also major differences in the metabolic processes of the two classes, with only the latter resembling the vertebrates with a secondary marine ancestry: reptiles, birds, and mammals. The advanced evolution of the bony fishes has enabled them to occupy all ecological systems with new forms.

There are interesting examples of this in the Indian Ocean, where bony fishes have formed symbiotic relationships with cartilaginous ones: one often sees cleaner wrasses of the genus *Labroides* removing parasites from bottom-oriented elasmobranchs such as nurse sharks and blue-spotted rays. The wrasse species *Thalassoma amblycephalum* has specialised on Manta rays, and swims in and out of the immobile gills of its willing customer. Whale and requiem sharks, long distance swimmers, are often surrounded by remoras, which not only remove parasites, but also snap up the leavings of these large fishes. The main benefit to the bony fishes is, however, transport without energy expenditure and protection by their cartilaginous host. The Cobia *Rachycentrum canadum,* is always found in association with Whale sharks, eagle, and sting rays. When the rays feed on the bottom the Cobia circles round them in order to seize any fishes they put to flight. Many trevallies of the genera *Caranx* and *Seriola* accompany large sharks or turtles, using them as cover from which to surprise their prey. The same family includes the pilot fish *Naucrates ductor* and the Golden pilot jack *Gnathanodon speciosus,* which swim very close to the body of a shark or immediately in front of its snout, without being harmed in any way. It is now known that they do not pilot the shark, but utilise its pressure wave to save energy. They also have been seen to remove ectoparasites from their host.

The first bony fish shown on the following pages is an outstanding example of this group in several ways...

LATIMERIA

The ancient oceans are the cradle of all life - and conservators of old life-forms. The list of the so-called living fossils, of species that survived the extinction of their next relatives, has become quite long until today, at the end of a century of scientific investigation. An absolute highlight for evolutionists was the discovery of a new marine fish species in the southern Indian Ocean.

Some 400 million years ago a unique event took place in the evolutionary history of the vertebrates: the first fish-like amphibians evolved from a group of primeval fishes, the Crossopterygians - the evolution of terrestrial vertebrates was under way. But about 60 million years ago the Crossopterygians or Coelacanths vanished. Extinct, was the general opinion of scientists who only knew Crossopterygians as fossils. None have been found in younger deposits.

Lateral view of a living coelacanth in its natural habitat in a depth of 200 m.

In 1938 a sensational discovery was made when a trawler netted a one-and-a-half-metre long fish off the Indian Ocean coast of South Africa: the ichthyologist James L. B. Smith identified the fish and named it *Latimeria chalumnae* after its discoverer, Marjorie Courtnay Latimer, and the locality, the Chalumna River. In the hope of obtaining additional specimens, Smith then offered a reward for further finds and distributed a "Wanted" notice in three languages along the East African coast. Yet he had to wait until 1952 until another specimen of this living fossil was captured - this time off the Comoro Islands. New theories about the habitat and behaviour of Coelacanths were formulated.

The behaviourist Hans Fricke, like many of his colleagues, was fascinated by this primitive fish from the Indian Ocean, and considered it a privilege to be able to study a creature with such a celebrated early history. During the course of the years he and his colleagues at the Max-Planck-Institut für Verhaltensforschung (behavioural research) in Seewiesen/Bavaria collected many facts about the coelacanth and even had a research submersible built in order to study the fish in its natural habitat at an estimated depth of 200 m. In January of 1987, during a night dive off the Comoros, the researchers sighted the first living coelacanth: Smith's theory about "old fourlegs" was immediately refuted, as the primeval fish does not use its paired fins to move along the bottom, but it turns out to be a slow and sluggish swimmer which uses its fins as hydrofoil for gliding and keeping balance. But Fricke was able to detect a similarity to quadrupeds: like a trotting horse, the coelacanth moves its pectoral and pelvic fins in lateral opposition - as the left pectoral fin moves downward, the right travels up. The corresponding pelvic fins

The innovative German scientist Hans Fricke in front of his submersible Jago.

simultaneously move in opposite directions. Normally the primeval fish swims with almost stoical serenity, but when a prey animal comes into sight its behaviour changes: in a burst of speed it is able to accelerate to 26 m/sec!

Since 1991, thanks to a new submersible suited for greater depths, more information about the behaviour of the coelacanth has come to light. Over a period of five years about 70 individuals of *Latimeria chalumnae* were identified by their individual white blotch patterns and observed along a 10-km-long coastline off the island of Grande Comore. The movements of the animals were tracked by video camera and painlessly applied miniature ultrasonic uw-transmitters twenty-four hours a day. This resulted in a first impression of the home range of the coelacanth: by day it rests in peaceful aggregations of up to 14 individuals in caves in the relatively young lava base of the island which are located between 160 and 210 m of depth. At sunset, however, these unique fishes leave their daytime resting place and descend to greater depths in order to hunt (mainly fairy basslets, also small sharks) mostly between 250 and 300 m, once even in almost 700 m where prey is already very scarce. Their low metabolic rate allows them to live on occasional catches. The coelacanths seem to be in an energy-saving mode during all of their activities. This is probably the reason for their survival as a relic from prehistoric times.

A group of coelacanths resting in a cave by day. Some of the fish swim normal at the bottom of the cave, others have turned their belly towards the ceiling.

Gombesa is the local name of the coelacanth in the Comoros.

Besides the already impressive vertical extension of the home range of such a sluggish animal, tracking of the transmitter signals has also revealed at least 8 km horizontal home range extension. In addition, the high territorial fidelity of the coelacanth became apparent after five years of observation: some individuals could be found in the same territory throughout the entire period. The daytime resting caves, however, were changed and preferences for one or another by different individuals became obvious.

Coelacanths are ovoviviparous. After a gestation period of about one year they give birth to 35 cm long young weighing 0.5 kg each. These grow in eggs of up to 9 cm in diameter and extremely rich in yolk, which are among the largest known fish eggs. There is no additional nourishment inside the mother's body, e.g. via a yolk sac placenta. A female of about 100 cm - a lucky catch in a trawler's net off Mozambique - carried 26 young almost ready to

Portrait of a coelacanth's head.

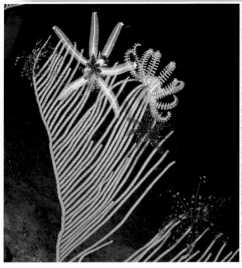
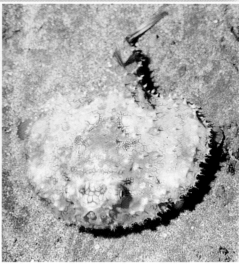

Typical organisms from the deep-sea habitat of the coelacanth: gorgonians, feather stars, and a *Malthopsis* seabat.

hatch. The external yolk sac is absorbed entirely until birth, which probably takes place in depths greater than those usually inhabited by the adults. But part of the yolk reserve is stored inside the coelacanth baby and still available for further development, a kind of starter for independent life, so to speak.

The small population size of only about 500 individuals at the Comoros together with the large territorial size and the high mobility in a topographically narrow habitat point towards a high rate of inbreeding. A genetic analysis of the relationships of some individuals also supports this view. Single individuals caught over untypical substrates in shallow depths were probably taken there by oceanic currents (Mozambique and Agulhas current). At this point questions arise concerning the treatment of such a small but unique and world famous animal stock. The attempt has already been made - luckily without success - to catch a living coelacanth for aquarium display in order to satisfy commercial interests.

But how many coelacanths are taken by Comoran fishermen? Their main target is the oilfish *Ruvettus pretiosus*, which is caught by long-lining from motorised vessels far offshore, well away from the "coelacanth zone." But if the fishermen have no money to repair their engines, they use their traditional canoes to catch oilfish in the "coelacanth zone." Here they cannot avoid catching a coelacanth every now and then. During the first half of the 1990ies the numbers of coelacanths were observed to dwindle. Hastily, in 1994 *Latimeria* was put into category I of the Washington treaty for the conservation of species (CITES) in order to fully protect it. This means that no coelacanth must be killed or traded in any form. Still, education of the Comoran fishermen is most important. Sometimes coelacanths are even killed not for food, but only to retrieve the valuable fishing hooks! On the Comoros and in neighbouring African countries the attempt has already been made to utilise the coelacanth other than for consumption. There are handicraft goods for sale as souvenirs, postage stamps with coelacanth motives, and the like.

What about more coelacanths in different places of the world? Should there really be only the approximately 500 Comoran survivors of an extinct lineage of fishes? In 1964 two handmade silver figurines (see photo) clearly depicting coelacanths were discovered in Bilbao and Toledo, Spain, respectively. They are finely detailed and even show the individual blotch patterns, which can only be seen in living specimens! According to experts they are 17th or 18th century work, have probably been made by Indian silversmiths, and are thus of Mesoamerican origin. Are there still living coelacanths in the Atlantic or even on the Pacific side of Central America?

Since 1997 there have been reports of coelacanths in a certain region of Indonesia, which are very probably identical to *Latimeria chalumnae*. Now it is only a question of time and the political sensitivity of the research groups involved until we know whether one of the most outstanding and rarest animal species in the world is not as rare and vulnerable as has been thought.

Spanish silver figurine of a coelacanth, length about 35 cm. The head can be rotated down at a masterly forged hinge. Note pattern on scales.

Ribbon eel

Le: up to 120 cm. Di: entire area. De: 1 - 55 m. Ge: the most distinct moray of tropical reefs. The secretive species lives hidden in sand or among coral rubble with only the head showing. Head and part of the very long body reach out of the burrow to grab its prey of small fishes (e.g. damselfishes). The species is a protandrous hermaphrodite, and can rapidly change sex and coloration. Caution: males are black, females brilliantly blue with bright yellow fins (see photo left from Similan Islands, Thailand), old females yellow (right).

Rhinomuraena quaesita   Mauritius

Black-spotted moray

Length: up to 180 cm.
Distribution: entire area.
Depth: 10 - 30 m.
General: the species inhabits outer slopes of continental shelf reefs and sheltered atoll reefs. It lives solitarily and is mainly active at night. The Black-spotted moray is relatively rare and very little is known about its specific habits and biology.

Gymnothorax isingteena   Comoros

Honeycomb moray

Le: up to 200 cm. Di: entire area. De: 3 - 40 m. Ge: relatively common in protected coastal bays to deep reefs, one of the largest morays in our area, coloration distinct. Preys on a variety of smaller reef fishes. Right: subadult; the small photo below from Thailand shows a juvenile.

Gymnothorax favagineus   Kenya

41

White-mouth moray

Le: up to 100 cm. Di: entire area. De: 1 - 35 m. Ge: distinct by a white interior of the mouth. Not common in our area, more abundant in the western Pacific. It is found in rich, clear, coastal and protected inner reefs, usually among living corals mixed with algae.

Gymnothorax meleagris   Surin Island, Thailand

Fimbriated moray

Length: up to 80 cm.
Distribution: Mauritius to Sri Lanka, not in the Red Sea.
Depth: 10 - 55 m.
General: the coloration of this moray is variable depending on the size of the dark spots. It inhabits lagoons and seaward reefs. Not very abundant in our area, reportedly common off Bali. Seems to like the steep sand slopes with many isolated outcrops of reef patches and sponges, in which the moray makes its home, especially where shrimps have well-established cleaning stations.

Gymnothorax fimbriatus   Cocos Keeling Islands, West Australia

Yellow-edged moray

Length: up to 120 cm.
Distribution: entire area.
Depth: 3 - 60 m.
General: the relatively common and widespread Yellow-edged moray has a strong dentition which is used to feed on a wide variety of smaller reef fishes at night. It is a very active species, and has a cryptic coloration of yellowish-brown densely mottled with small dark brown spots. There is a black blotch at the gill opening. In the posterior part of the body the long dorsal and ventral fins are edged with yellow-green.

Gymnothorax flavimarginatus   Réunion

Bearded moray

Length: up to 65 cm.
Distribution: Tanzania,
Comoros to Maldives.
Depth: 4 - 30 m.
General: this moray species is
clearly distinct by a dark
blotch extending from the eye
to the edge of the mouth. It
preferably lives near oceanic
islands and in platform reefs
with coral rubble. Said to be
aggressive in the vicinity of its
shelter. High population densi-
ties of this species have been
observed in the Maldives.

Gymnothorax breedeni   Raa Atoll, Maldives

Giant moray

Length: up to 240 cm, possibly
to 300 cm.
Distribution: entire area.
Depth: 10 - 50 m.
General: the Giant moray is
distinguished by a yellow-
brown head with small dark
spots and a large dark patch at
the gill opening. Adults have a
leopard-like spotting all over
the body. This moray has an
impressive dentition: the jaws
bear canine teeth arranged in
one row, which are laterally
compressed and have sharp
edges. The teeth at the front
of the jaws are long and fang-
like, the two longest are in a
median row. Also there are
teeth in one irregular row on
the roof of the mouth. The
species occurs in lagoons as
well as in seaward outer reefs.
Juveniles lead a more secretive
life on reef flats in water as
shallow as 20 cm. This is the
largest moray eel of our area.
It has the potential to inflict
injury to divers. The depicted
specimens are being cleaned
by a cleaner shrimp (large photo) and a cleaner wrasse,
respectively (photo below).

Gymnothorax javanicus   Male Atoll, Maldives

Undulate moray

Length: up to 150 cm.
Distribution: entire area.
Depth: 1 - 30 m.
General: this moray is a common inhabitant of reef flats, and frequently found among coral debris; it also lives in lagoons and seaward reefs. Juveniles may be found in tide pools with a water depth of only 20 cm.

The small photo below from Similan Islands, Thailand, shows the **Golden moray** *Gymnothorax melatremus*. The small and rare moray species is found in the entire Indian Ocean with the exception of the Red Sea, but is known only from a few scattered locations. It is distinct by its bright coloration of orange-yellow, and can be spotted in the reef environment more easily than most of its camouflaged congeners. It mainly lives in coastal bays and reefs among corals and sponges. Its bright coloration may be an adaptation to the likewise coloured invertebrates prevailing around the moray's sheltering crevice in the coral reef habitat.

Gymnothorax undulatus   **Mauritius**

Bar-tail moray

Length: up to 46 cm. Distribution: entire area, but not in Red Sea. Depth: 6 - 40 m.
General: the small species inhabits ledges and rubble of outer reef slopes. Often found deeper than other morays. Distinct by body pattern, fully seen only at night (photo left).

Gymnothorax zonipectis   **Kenya**

White-eyed moray

Length: up to 65 cm.
Distribution: entire area.
Depth: 1 - 35 m.
General: this widespread
moray species inhabits coastal,
often silty habitats, shallow
coral reefs, lagoons, and isolated reef outcrops on muddy or
sandy slopes. It is distinguished
by a light brown or tan
coloured body with very faint
mottling, a white to bluish
snout, and silvery-white eyes.
It is often found in pairs or
even together with other
species of moray eels such as
Gymnomuraena zebra (see
p.46).

Siderea thyrsoidea   Richelieu Rock, Thailand

Peppered moray

Le: up to 38 cm. Di: not as
common in the Indian Ocean
as in the Red Sea. De: 1 - 40 m.
Ge: relatively small, confined
to coral reefs. Juveniles in
groups of up to ten individuals
in their sheltering rock crevice.
Hunts small fishes at night.
Synchronous hermaphrodite.

Siderea grisea   Beau Vallon, Seychelles

Painted moray

Length: up to 68 cm.
Distribution: entire area.
Depth: 0 - 12 m.
General: an indistinct shallow
water moray species that
inhabits reef flats and tide
pools. At low tide it can sometimes be seen entirely out of
the water striking at grapsid
crabs. Like the Peppered
moray this species also is a
synchronous hermaphrodite,
which means it is male and
female at the same time.

Siderea picta   Ari Atoll, Maldives

45

Zebra moray

Length: up to 150 cm.
Distribution: entire area.
Depth: 10 - 50 m.
General: a fairly common but secretive moray that feeds on small reef animals, particularly crustaceans. The entire animal can only be seen at night. Small photo below: Seychelles.

Gymnomuraena zebra   **Ari Atoll, Maldives**

Barred moray

Length: up to 60 cm.
Distribution: entire area including Red Sea.
Depth: 1 - 15 m.
General: the Barred moray is mainly found in the clear shallow water of reef flats and lagoons. It is patterned with indistinct dark bands on a light background, which fade with age. The skin folds in the throat region are pronounced. This moray is mainly active at night when it hunts small prey - preferably crabs - but sometimes also seen during the day, wedged into a crevice.

Echidna polyzona   **Sri Lanka**

Leopard moray

Length: up to 120 cm.
Distribution: entire area, but not around Arabian Peninsula.
Depth: 5 - 20 m.
General: this species of moray is rare throughout its range, and lives in rich coral reefs. Its coloration is pale brown to pale yellowish with numerous large and small dark brown, irregularly rounded spots. Also distinct is the massive rounded head with the comparatively small eyes. The Leopard moray's slender and sharp teeth are perfectly adapted to grab and hold its slippery prey of diverse reef fishes.

Scuticaria tigrina   **Mauritius**

SNAKE EELS   OPHICHTHIDAE

Banded snake eel

Le: up to 88 cm. Di: entire
area. De: 5 - 25 m. Ge: finds
its prey of small sand-dwelling
fishes and crustaceans by an
acute sense of smell, which is
an attribute of most eel-like
fish species. Mimics sea snakes.
Below: **Spotted snake eel**
Myrichthys maculosus, 100 cm.

Myrichthys colubrinus   Kenya

Crocodile snake eel

Le: up to 100 cm. Di: entire
area. De: 3 - 29 m. Ge: jaws
very long, eyes placed forward.
Snake eels are quite common,
but easily overlooked because
they spend most of their time
buried in the sand. Below:
Marbled snake eel *Callechelys
marmoratus*, 57 cm, 9 - 22 m.

Brachysomophis crocodilinus   Baa Atoll, Maldives

GARDEN EELS   HETEROCONGRIDAE

Freckled garden eel

Le: up to 70 cm. Di: Maldives,
Seychelles, Comoros, Mas-
carenes. De: 25 - 90 m. Ge:
the shy fish lives in colonies on
sandy bottoms. Each garden
eel lives solitarily in a vertical
tube-like burrow, which is
longer than its body so it can
rapidly retreat into it completely. The sand grains of the
tube's wall are glued together
with a secretion from a gland
at the end of the tail. A colony
looks like a field of asparagus
curving towards the current,
which brings the plankton food.

Gorgasia maculata   North Male Atoll, Maldives

GARDEN EELS   HETEROCONGRIDAE

Splendid garden eel

Le: up to 33 cm. Di: Maldives
to West Pacific. De: 35 - 80 m.
Ge: a colourful, poorly known
garden eel, found in colonies
on sandy slopes in strong current, also together with *G.
maculata*.
   The photo immediately left
and the small photo below
show the **Spotted garden
eel** *Heteroconger hassi*, found in
all of our area. It attains a
length of up to 40 cm, and
lives between 15 and 40 m.
Like its congeners, the most
common species of garden eel
in the Indian Ocean lives in
colonies, often together with
G. maculata.

Gorgasia preclara   Maldives *Heteroconger hassi*   Maldives

EEL CATFISHES   PLOTOSIDAE

Striped eel catfish

Le: up to 32 cm. Di: entire
area including Red Sea. De: 1 -
30 m. Ge: most catfish species
occur in freshwater, only a few
are marine. Only this one is
commonly seen in coral reefs
and inshore habitats like estuaries and tide pools. Juveniles
occur in dense schools over
sand and seagrass, adults live
solitarily and hide by day. At
night they prey on crustaceans,
molluscs, and fishes. One
should avoid handling catfishes
as their stout fin spines are
venomous and have strong
barbs on their edges that make
removal from a wound difficult.
Often seen in constantly changing group formations (below).

Plotosus lineatus   Mauritius

GOING TERRESTIAL

The idyll at the breakfast table in Mirihi is almost perfect. A slight breeze touches the island restaurant and the eyes wander over the mirror-like surface of the sea that almost reaches the tables. Under a cloudless sky some of the guests' foreheads are already covered in sweat at 7:30 in the morning. Scrambled eggs steam on the plates and when the waiter brings the coffee every diver knows what to do. But this idyll is treacherous. Suddenly there is a frantic splashing on the beach! The guests jump up, and hurry to the restaurant's veranda to get a better view of the scene...

But as quick as the rumble started, the disturbed water surface directly on the shoreline smoothens again. Baffled, everybody watches the small Blacktip reef shark *Carcharhinus melanopterus*, which lies on the beach half-way out of the water and now tries to crawl back in like a seal. The reason for its terrestrial escapade soon becomes

The beachside restaurant in Mirihi, Maldives, as seen from the shallow water on the shore. Here a breakfast was interrupted by a frantic scene...

apparent: many small twisting silvery fish lie on the sand. And they too try to find the way back into their natural habitat. What had happened?

Obviously there had been a much earlier "breakfast." The dark shadows, which cruise in the shallow water, are clearly to be seen through the surface: about ten Bluefin trevallies *Caranx melampygus* are already on patrol again, ready for the next attack. As can be observed repeatedly during the first half of the day, their target - and that of several small Blacktip reef sharks as well - is a huge school of Hardyhead silversides *Atherinomorus lacunosus* that has spread like a long band over the sandy shallow reef just in front of the beach. There is virtually no room left between the mass of bodies of the 8- to 12-cm-long silversides and the sand above the waterline. Surely an unusual place to be for these fish!

From a snorkeller's view, however, one readily understands why the silversides act the way they do. Their bodies, the coloration of which is low in contrast anyway, almost completely melt into the glistening sunlight of the reflecting water above the white sand bottom. Therefore it is extremely difficult for a predator to focus on a single victim. But

A school of Hardyhead silversides *Atherinomorus lacunosus* looks like a cloud in the shallows, and is prey for many.

49

still, mackerels and sharks alike in joint ventures try to prey on the swarm of silversides. Most often a shark leads the group of trevallies that swims parallel to the shoreline and the prey. Around the predators the approximately 150-m-long band of silversides is narrow, in front of and behind them it is wider. The silvery

One of the merciless hunters: a Blacktip reef shark *Carcharhinus melanopterus* cruises in shallow water.

schooling fish also take each snorkeller for a potential predator: if one swims into the band of fish, it splits and leaves a large, circular free space around the observer. Amazingly, the predators are not distracted by tourists standing on the beach even though they patrol just about one metre in front of them. The swimming back and forth goes on for some time until suddenly the hunters speed up and hit the mass of silversides with full power! These burst into panic because there is no space to flee to or hide in the steaming shallow water without any coral growth. Consequently, some silversides jump out of the water and - unintentionally - seek shelter on dry land. And even there they are pursued by the especially greedy small Blacktip reef sharks!

While the Maldivian silversides are forced "to go terrestrial," there are fish in the Gulf of California which do so voluntarily. Again, it is a related species of silverside. Three days after the full moon during the spring months from February to May, thousands, if not millions, of Grunion *Leuresthes sardina* use the high tide to let themselves be washed ashore. An almost unbelievable event! The female digs into the sand, is embraced by a male, and then each pair spawns outside the water. When the next wave approaches, they wriggle back into the sea.

Bluefin trevallies *Caranx melampygus* are usually swimming in open water, but when a meal is waiting, they also penetrate into the shallows to join the sharks in their pursuit of silversides.

A closer look at a school of silversides. Like anchovies and sardines these small fishes fall prey to diverse marine predators..

The frantic hunt for silversides is in full swing: several small Blacktip reef sharks approach from the sea, and force the silversides to jump high into the air at the surfline. Sometimes one of the hunters overshoots the target, and goes terrestrial...

NEEDLEFISHES · BELONIDAE

Crocodile needlefish

Le: up to 130 cm, common to 90 cm. Di: entire area. De: 0.2 - 5 m. Ge: a pelagic species usually inhabiting coastal waters, but also found far offshore. All needlefish species mainly feed on small fishes, which are stalked while keeping close to the reflecting silvery surface of the water for camouflage (see photo). Accidental injuries to humans inflicted by their bony beaks acting like a spearhead have been recorded. Has a wide range of distribution including the tropical to warm-temperate waters of the Indian Ocean.

Tylosurus crocodilus   Thailand

FLYINGFISHES · EXOCOETIDAE

Redchin flyingfish

Le: up to 23 cm. Di: entire area. De: 0.1 - 8 m. Ge: pelagic in neritic surface waters, rare in the open ocean. Can leap out of the water and glide for long distances above the surface to avoid predators.

Cypselurus poecilopterus   Gaafu Atoll, Maldives

LIZARDFISHES · SYNODONTIDAE

Gracile lizardfish

Length: up to 30 cm.
Distribution: southern Indian Ocean.
Depth: 1 - 135 m.
General: a common species usually found in shallow sandy areas adjacent to coral reefs or on the fringes of patch reefs. Lizard fishes mainly feed on fishes. They catch their often relatively large prey by waiting motionless on the ground and suddenly darting forward a short distance to grab it with their numerous small sharp teeth.

Saurida gracilis   Kenya

Variegated lizardfish

Length: up to 25 cm.
Distribution: entire area
including Red Sea. Depth: 3 -
50 m. General: the most common reef-dwelling lizardfish.
On coastal to outer reefs,
resting motionless on hard
substrate. Singly or in pairs. Its
coloration is very variable.

Synodus variegatus   Sri Lanka

Sand lizardfish

Le: up to 22 cm. Di: entire
area including Red Sea. De: 1 -
50 m. Ge: found from coastal
sand flats and sandy slopes to
outer reef lagoons. Often
buried in the sand or rubble
near reefs, encountered singly
or in small groups when males
compete about a female.

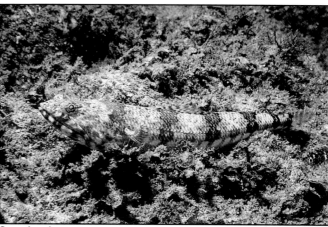

Synodus dermatogenys   Réunion

Blackblotch lizardfish

Length: up to 20 cm.
Distribution: southern India,
Sri Lanka, Maldives to Mauritius.
Depth: 2 - 88 m.
General: the species is usually
associated with coral reefs and
found down to considerable
depths. Like all members of
the family it is mainly piscivo-
rous (feeding on fishes).
  There are about 40 species
of lizardfishes. Their round
body is covered with large
scales. When disturbed, lizardfishes swim a short distance
only to settle again and lie in
ambush without any motion.

Synodus jaculum   Mauritius

53

White-edged soldierfish

Length: up to 22 cm.
Distribution: entire area
including Red Sea.
Depth: 2 - 37 m.
General: one of the most common soldierfish species in our
area. Sometimes in huge aggregations, also swimming far
from the sheltering reef. See
also the photo (Maldives) at
the right: a nice formation of
small individuals seek shelter
under a gorgonarian fan coral.
   Soldierfishes mainly feed on
zooplankton in the open water
above the reef at night. All
family members can produce
sounds for communication.

Myripristis murdjan   **Male Atoll, Maldives**

White-tipped soldierfish

Le: up to 15 cm. Di: East
African coast, Maledives, Seychelles. De: 3 - 80 m. Ge: a
coral reef species hiding in
caves and crevices, also among
staghorn coral branches by
day. Below (Sri Lanka):
Silver soldierfish *M. melano-
sticta,* 30 cm, 15 - 65 m.

Myripristis vittata   **Sri Lanka**

Bronze soldierfish

Length: up to to 25 cm.
Distribution: southern Indian
Ocean, Maldives, not in the
Red Sea.
Depth: 2 - 30 m.
General: a coral reef species
living in relatively shallow
water. Like all soldierfishes it
seeks refuge in caverns and
underneath ledges by day. Easily identified by its unusual coloration.
   The soldierfishes (subfamily
Myripristinae) are generally
smaller than squirrelfishes,
they rarely exceed 25 cm in
length, have very blunt heads,
and overall red bodies.

Myripristis adusta   **Aldabra, Seychelles**

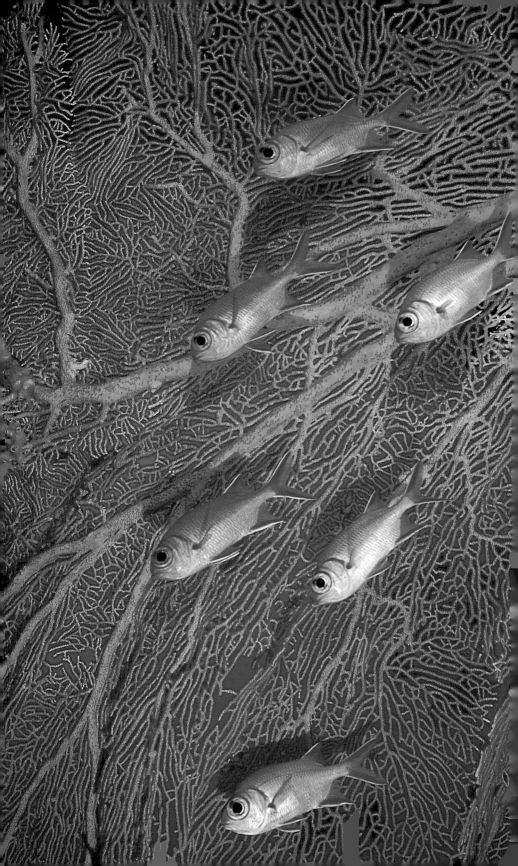

Bloodspot squirrelfish

Length: up to 24 cm.
Distribution: entire area including Red Sea.
Depth: 2 - 46 m.
General: often seen in shallow water of protected lagoons and bays. Among the first fishes to leave their shelter with the advent of darkness.

Neoniphon sammara   **Sri Lanka**

Redcoat squirrelfish

Length: up to 27 cm.
Distribution: entire area including Red Sea.
Depth: 6 - 50 m.
General: the species is found in coastal reefs and large lagoons It is usually seen at moderate depths in pairs (see photo) or small to large aggregations on gentle reef slopes and sand flats with large coral bommies. In some areas, especially near remote oceanic islands, the species is replaced by the similar S. *praslin,* which has darker longitudinal stripes.

Sargocentron rubrum   **Burma Banks, Thailand**

Seychelles squirrelfish

Length: up to 25 cm.
Distribution: Seychelles, Madagascar, Mascarenes, Chagos Archipelago.
Depth: 2 - 18 m.
General: a shallow-water species inhabiting coral reefs and rocky shores. Like the other members of the family it is active mainly at night, but even then always remains in the shelter of the reef.

A main feature separating both subfamilies is the backward-pointing preopercular spine of squirrelfishes. Its painful sting is not as poisonous as that of scorpionfishes.

Sargocentron seychellense   **Praslin, Seychelles**

Crown squirrelfish

Length: up to 25 cm. Distribution: entire area including Red Sea. Depth: 5 - 45 m. General: inhabits subtidal reef flats, lagoons, and seaward reefs. Seen singly or in small groups under ledges and in crevices by day. Feeds on isopods, polychaetes, small crabs.

Sargocentron diadema   Aldabra, Seychelles

Giant squirrelfish

Length: up to 45 cm. Distribution: entire area including Red Sea. Depth: 5 - 122 m. General: this is the largest species of squirrelfishes and the highest-bodied *Sargocentron*. Its long preopercular spine is venomous. In certain areas also its flesh may be poisonous. This is because the fish has eaten organisms that are already poisonous after the uptake and accumulation via the food chain of a toxic compound. The latter is called Ciguatera-toxin and is produced by unicellular algae in the first place. Consumption of such fishes that become poisonous while eating may be fatal. The degree of toxicity depends on many factors such as season of the year, location, and abundance of food items. Thus one never can tell, if a tropical predatory fish is good to eat or not.
By day this nocturnally active species is encountered under ledges in pairs or small groups (see photos, small one below from the Maldives).

Raa Atoll, Maldives

Sargocentron spiniferum   Ari Atoll, Maldives

Ari Atoll, Maldives

Giant anglerfish

Le: up to 33 cm. Di: entire area including Red Sea. De: 1 - 45 m. Ge: a coral reef species, which can be yellow, black, green, brown, or orange. The lower photo shows the giant anglerfish with an extended mouth. The extremely rapid opening movement of the angler's jaws creates a vacuum to suck in the fish prey. This results in a loud noise.

Small photo below: **Sargassum anglerfish** *Histrio histrio.* Le: up to 19 cm. Di: entire area. De: 0 - 10 m. Ge: this "special" anglerfish lives pelagically in floating Sargassum weed patches. It mimics the surrounding plants and is able to change from light to dark very rapidly. Highly voracious and even cannibalistic. When threatened from below it is able to climb out of the water onto the Sargassum . The fish was photographed after it "fell" from its algal float.

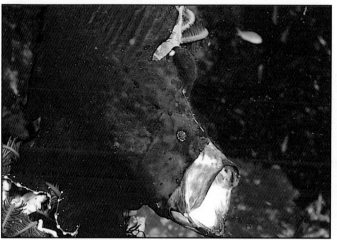

Antennarius commersoni   Similan Islands, Thailand

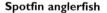

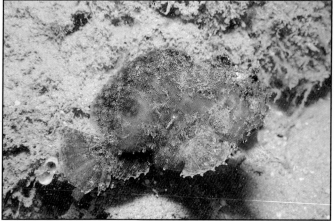

Antennarius nummifer   Kenya

Spotfin anglerfish

Le: up to 13 cm. Di: entire area including Red Sea. De: 3 - 176 m, mainly around 20 m. Ge: found in reefs and estuaries. The first dorsal fin spine of anglerfishes is modified into a "fishing pole" (illicium) with a "lure" (esca) that is flicked enticingly to attract prey fish. Illicium of this species about as long as second dorsal spine. Esca large and variable in form and colour, often resembling a small shrimp. Overall coloration very variable, often with a large ocellated dark spot at the base of the soft dorsal fin (see photo).

Clown anglerfish

Length: up to 10 cm.
Distribution: entire area.
Depth: 2 - 30 m.
General: adults often live in silty inshore habitats with heavy sponge growth. They are usually yellow with red saddle-like blotches and wart-like swellings all over body and fins. Small juveniles are bright yellow or white; they are often found sitting on a dark background, mimicking nudibranchs. The esca resembles a small fish.
All anglerfishes have bulbous bodies, jointed elbow-like pectoral fins that are used like arms, small holes behind the pectorals as gill openings, and large mouths directed upward. Their coloration and habit of sitting motionless make anglerfishes nearly invisible. Their loose prickly skin is often adorned with filamentous appendages. Females spawn thousands of tiny eggs imbedded in a large gelatinous mass.

Antennarius maculatus   Similan Islands, Thailand

Freckled anglerfish

Length: up to 24 cm.
Distribution: entire area.
Depth: 1 - 75 m.
General: a common, variable species found in coral reefs.
The lure of anglers even deceives lionfishes, themselves voracious fish eaters. During an encounter of a Painted anglerfish and *Pterois volitans* the curious lionfish came close enough to inspect the flicking lure. The angler caught its prey by surprise: it darted forward a short distance with unbelievable speed - much too fast even for a regular film camera - and engulfed the lionfish without giving it the slightest chance to escape.

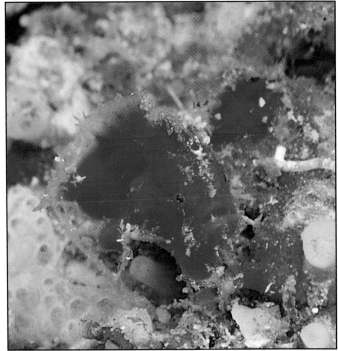

Antennarius coccineus   Hin Daeng, Thailand

FLASHLIGHTFISHES   ANOMALOPIDAE

Photoblepharon palpebratus   Comoros

Flashlightfish

Length: up to 11 cm.
Distribution: entire area.
Depth: 1 - 50 m.
General: there is a light-emitting organ under each eye, which contains bacteria that produce lime-green light. Each organ can be covered by a lid, enabling the fish to produce blinking on-off sequences of light reminding very much of Morse code. Very probably this mechanism is used in communication and to confuse predators. Hidden by day. A very similar species is found in the Red Sea, where it found close to the surface at night.

PEARLFISHES   CARAPIDAE

Carapus homei   Malaku, Maldives

Silver pearlfish
Le: up to 17 cm. Di: entire area incl. Red Sea. De: depending on host. Ge: by day the translucent fish hides inside sea cucumbers *(Stichopus, Thelonota)* and mussels (photo). At night it leaves its host to hunt for small prey (below).

SEAMOTHS   PEGASIDAE

Eurypegasus draconis   Male Atoll, Maldives

Seamoth

Le: up to 10 cm. Di: entire area including Red Sea. De: 1 - 15 m. Ge: this bizarre benthic fish inhabits areas of coarse sediment including sand, gravel, and shell-rubble. Often seen in pairs. Its body is encased by fused bony plates, which are ring-like in the tail region thus leaving the tail flexible for locomotion. It moves slowly on its pelvic fins with the large pectoral fins spread like wings. The long, tube-like rostrum extends well ahead of the small, ventral, toothless mouth.

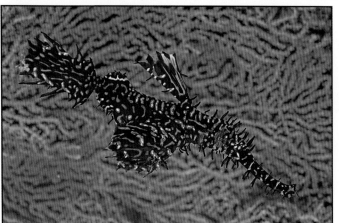

Solenostomus paradoxus   Surin Island, Thailand

Ornate ghost pipefish

Le: up to 12 cm. Di: entire area including Red Sea. De: 1 - 25 m. Ge: lives among the branches of gorgonians, soft corals, and leather corals, where it is almost invisible due to its perfect camouflage (able to change its body coloration). Feeds on minute crustaceans. In pairs or small groups. Ghost pipefishes are a small tropical family with a single genus and five species, closely related to true pipefishes, but the females incubate the fertilised eggs in a brooding pouch, not the males like in pipefishes. See also previous page (Similan Is., Thailand).

Seagrass ghost pipefish

Length: up to 16 cm.
Distribution: entire area including Red Sea.
Depth: 1 - 10 m.
General: the species usually occurs in pairs in sheltered waters among seaweeds or seagrasses, to which it adapts its body coloration (note white spots imitating epizoans).
   The transparent pelagic larvae of ghost pipefishes reach a large size before they metamorphose into the fish form and settle on the ground. Most species swim in a head-down position (see photo), always searching the bottom for their small invertebrate prey (minute crustaceans).

Solenostomus cyanopterus   Koh Racha Yai, Thailand

Halimeda ghost pipefish

Le: up to 16 cm. Di: only Maldives. De: 1 - 10 m. Ge: this only recently described species has been found living in close association with the alga *Halimeda*, which it resembles remarkably closely (alga at the top of the photo). Little is known about its habits.

Solenostomus halimeda   Ari Atoll, Maldives

Slender ghost pipefish

Length: up to 8 cm.
Distribution: Indian Ocean including Red Sea.
Depth: 2 - 18 m.
General: nocturnal, in coral reefs, not in seagrass beds. Feeds on small crustaceans. Photo right: transparent post-larva; small photo below: adult.

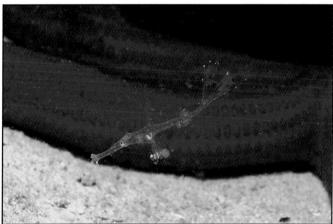

Solenostomus leptosomus   Pemba, Tanzania

TRUMPETFISHES   AULOSTOMIDAE

Trumpetfish

Le: up to 80 cm. Di: entire area, not in Red Sea. De: 1 - 35 m. Ge: vertically among corals, seagrass, or other shelter (see also A TRUMPET SOLO, p.64-65) to stalk fishes and crustaceans. Juvenile below.

Aulostomus chinensis   Andaman Sea

A TRUMPET SOLO

There are many partnerships between different marine animals. Often an advantage in food acquisition or the need for protection leads to the development of these animal communities and ensures the existence of the species involved. However, such partnerships are not always mutually beneficial. In many cases one fish species simply takes advantage of the other. Trumpet- and Cornetfish belong in this category.

ALL PHOTOS: HELMUT DEBELIUS

Right beside a school of Bluestriped snappers, the Trumpetfish stalks its prey without being noticed.

One can simply speak about "the" Trumpetfish, as its family includes only two species: one widespread in the Indo-Pacific, the other distributed in the Atlantic Ocean. The Trumpetfish *Aulostomus chinensis* is found in different colorations from the reefs of South Africa to Hawaii, but not in the Red Sea. It is thus not a strictly tropical species, but also lives at temperatures below 20°C. It swims singly or in pairs, and can easily be identified by the elongated body and the oversized snout. The front part of the dorsal fin consists of short spines, each supporting a triangular piece of skin. The soft-rayed part of the dorsal, however, terminates far back, just in front of the caudal fin. The ventral fins likewise are set far back on the body and the posterior margin of the caudal fin is pointed in the middle.

The yellow colour form of the Trumpetfish. When the photo was taken, this specimen was not hunting.

It is hard to believe, but this fish is one of the most ferocious predators in the coral reef, and it is also cunning: because of its hunting technique, the Trumpetfish likes to roam the reef together with other fishes. In the Indo-Pacific it prefers single, large, camouflaged groupers as partners, or yellow snapper species (family Lutjanidae), in the schools of which its body shape virtually dissolves. Its Atlantic relative *Aulostomus maculatus*, however, associates mainly with diverse species of parrotfish. It is often encountered for example in the Caribbean.

At first sight it certainly is a peculiar pair of animals: a grouper swimming about with an often much longer Trumpetfish trailing it. It almost looks as if it were riding the grouper. But the Trumpetfish does not hold onto the grouper, it simply swims close above its dorsal fin. In that way the trumpetfish adopts the swimming style and the coloration of its percoid partner in order to

Another colour variant of the Trumpetfish in its typical "riding" pose above a grouper.

approach small fish unde-tected. This large predator has no interest in such small prey, which in turn fits perfectly into the fluted mouth of the Trumpetfish. Small damselfishes and shy sand-divers are caught fast as lightning whenever they fall for this ruse. This association is neither beneficial nor disadvantageous for the grouper. While the grouper is

When its "hunting assistant" is resting, the Trumpetfish stays in the immediate vicinity until the grouper moves on. At once it "mounts" the grouper's back again.

resting on a table coral, the Trumpetfish does not remain by its side, but always stays in the vicinity until their joint tour continues.

The same hunting technique is sometimes applied by the similar and even sleeker Cornetfish *Fistularia commersonii* of the closely related family Fistulariidae. This species is not only widespread in the Indo-Pacific, but also common in the Red Sea. It can easily be distinguished from the Trumpetfish by a long tail filament. The Cornetfish hunts singly or in small groups by day. At night it assumes a camouflage coloration of dark vertical bands. Similarities to oversized pipefishes are not accidental: Trumpet- and Cornetfish are related to them, all belong into the order of fishes called Syngnathiformes.

In contrast to the Trumpetfish, the Cornetfish is encountered in groups. A misidentification is unlikely after a second glance.

FLUTEMOUTHS

FISTULARIIDAE

Cornetfish

Length: up to 150 cm.
Distribution: entire area
including Red Sea.
Depth: 1 - 30 m.
General: the elongate, slender
species is seen singly or in
groups over sandy slopes and
coral reefs. Its preferred prey
are small fishes and shrimps. It
is related to the stouter Trumpetfish (see also A TRUMPET
SOLO, p.64-65). The Cornetfish can easily be recognised by
its long tail filament, and has a
distinct nocturnal colour pattern of dark vertical bars
superimposed on the lighter
background coloration.

Fistularia commersonii   Sri Lanka

SHRIMPFISHES

CENTRISCIDAE

Striped shrimpfish

Length: up to 14 cm.
Distribution: East Africa, Seychelles, not in Red Sea.
Depth: 1 - 20 m.
General: the Striped shrimpfish
occurs in groups of up to several dozen individuals. Most of
the time they swim vertically
in a head-down position and
synchronised, all turning at the
same time, in order to mimic
leaves or to enhance camouflage in general. The species
also hides among the spines of
Diadema sea urchins (especially juveniles) or in between the
branches of staghorn corals
(see small photo below from
Mentawai). The suction-feeder
preys on zooplanktonic crustaceans and tiny bottom-
dwelling invertebrates (e.g. 5-
mm-long mysids or possum
shrimps), which are sucked in
through the elongated bony
tube-like snout. The eggs are
probably pelagic like the larvae. Two genera and four
species of this small and peculiar family are recognised in
our area.

Aeoliscus strigatus   Mentawai, Sumatra

Cleaner pipefish

Length: up to 13 cm.
Distribution: eastern Indian
Ocean. Depth: 3 - 35 m.
General: usually a secretive
species in rich coastal reefs
under large plates or in dense
bushy sponges, however an
active cleaner in some areas,
where pairs swim upside down
under large table corals and
specialise in cleaning cardinalfishes, and damselfishes. Often
seen in the background of
caves, where cleaner shrimps
are at work, and without a
doubt the pipefish gets
involved when the right customers arrive for treatment.

Doryrhamphus janssi   Similan Islands, Thailand

Bluestripe pipefish

Le: up to 7 cm. Di: entire area.
De: 9 - 40 m. Ge: lives among
the sea urchin spines, where it
feeds on floating plankton. This
coral pipefish prefers hiding
places in the crevice system of
the coral reef. Small photo
below: a "pregnant" male, carrying young. Juveniles in bottom photo of *D. multiannulatus.*

Doryrhamphus excisus   Kenya

Multibar pipefish

Le: up to 18 cm. Di: entire
area. De: 8 - 45 m. Ge: under
ledges, in deep crevices and
caves, where swimming upside
down. Adults in pairs. Territorial male carries eggs externally
underneath posterior part of
body, partly embedded into
skin, but without dermal cover.

Dunckerocampus multiannulatus   Similan Islands, Thailand

67

Knysna seahorse

Le: up to 7 cm. Di: Cape Province, South Africa. De: 2 - 20 m. Ge: this seahorse is found singly or in pairs mainly in bays and estuaries with plantal growth. Spinules on body rings and the small coronet are present in juveniles (below) only, obsolete in adults (left).

Hippocampus capensis   **Knysna, South Africa**

Borbon seahorse

Length: up to 18 cm.
Distribution: East Africa to West Pacific.
Depth: 1 - 30 m.
General: this seahorse species is mainly found in rocky and coral reef areas with a rich vegetation of algae.
  The seahorse subfamily (Hippocampinae) of the family pipefishes needs taxonomic revision because new species are discovered every year and existing scientific names are not always valid.

Hippocampus borboniensis   **Kenya**

Tigertail seahorse

Length: up to 15 cm.
Distribution: Andaman Sea to Philippines, Malaysia, Vietnam.
Depth: 1 - 20 m.
General: this seahorse species lives in habitats rich in soft corals, sponges, and *Caulerpa algae*. Its coloration is yellow to black: males are usually dark, females are often yellow (see pair in photo left). The tail usually shows contrasting bands of dark and yellow. The large photo from Richelieu Rock, Thailand, on the facing page shows a female of this species among soft corals.

Hippocampus comes   **Similan Islands, Thailand**

Common lionfish

Mauritius

Le: up to 40 cm. Di: entire area including Red Sea. De: 2 - 60 m. Ge: a widespread species, the most common lionfish encountered in our area. It is found singly or in groups in fringing coral reefs as well as in fields of algae. Juveniles have blackish transparent fins with large ocellated spots. Scorpionfishes are a complex family of about ten subfamilies. Lionfishes (Pteroinae) have a warning coloration of red and white, very long dorsal fin spines, and greatly enlarged pectoral fins, often reaching past the anal fin. **WARNING:** all species of the family possess venomous spines and a sting produces extreme pain, followed by numbness. If stung, the best thing to do is to apply heat to the wound as soon as possible, and as hot as the victim can bear it. Immersing the wound in very hot water is generally recommended, but hot air from a hair-dryer may be more practicable, can be just as effective, and can be controlled more precisely. Heat destroys the venom.

Pterois volitans   Ari Atoll, Maldives

Spotfin lionfish

Length: up to 20 cm. Distribution: East Africa to Sri Lanka. Depth: 5 -50 m. General: this common species inhabits coastal to offshore reefs from shallow reef flats to deep slopes, and lagoons. By day it often hangs under ledges, at night it feeds on small fishes, shrimps, and crabs. There are two forms which may represent different species: one lives deep and far from reefs, often on mud, another one is found on reefs. Body bands are of variable width and usually pale to dark brown, pectoral rays are white.

Pterois antennata   Felidhoo Atoll, Maldives

Clearfin lionfish

Length: up to 24 cm.
Distribution: entire area.
Depth: 3 - 30 m.
General: a common distinct
species with dark body colour
and white lines found in
lagoons and seaward reefs
from the reef flat downward.
Unusual in its preference for
habitats like rocky reefs with
limited coral growth. Corals
are probably sensitive to the
lionfish's poisonous stings, and
therefore it is rarely seen in
coral-rich areas. Hides under
ledges and in caves by day,
comes out at dusk to feed on
small crabs and shrimps.

Pterois radiata   Praslin, Seychelles

Ocellated dwarf lionfish

Length: up to 20 cm.
Distribution: entire area.
Depth: 3 - 50 m.
General: the only member of
the genus with a distinct pair
of ocelli on the soft-rayed dorsal fin, and long nostril barbels.
It inhabits exposed areas of
rich coral growth and clear
water. The species is secretive
and thus rarely seen during the
day, but commonly encoun-
tered on shallow coastal reef
flats and in caves at night, thus
mainly nocturnal. Usually seen
singly or as pairs during
courtship. The male can be
recognised by its grey ocelli.

Dendrochirus biocellatus   Pemba, Tanzania

Zebra dwarf lionfish

Le: up to 20 cm. Di: entire
area incl. Red Sea. De: 5 -
35 m. Ge: body with distinct
white bars like in species of
Pterois. Males are aggressive,
and maintain territories to
where they attract females.
Below: **Shortfin dwarf lionfish** *D. brachypterus,* 17 cm.

Dendrochirus zebra   Baa Atoll, Maldives

71

Stonefish

Length: up to 38 cm. Di: entire area. De: 5 - 45 m. Ge: in shallow waters of coral reefs, often among coral rubble, and also in tide pools during low tide. The voracious predator feeds on fishes and crustaceans. It is probably the world's most venomous fish: it has grooved fin spines with associated poison glands in most fins. An anti-toxin serum exists, but is expensive and has to be stored in a refrigerator. First aid is heating the wound respectively limb as has been described on page 72 for scorpionfish stings in general.

Synanceia verrucosa   Ari Atoll, Maldives

Bearded Scorpionfish

Length: 22 cm.
Distribution: entire area including Red Sea.
Depth: 3 - 30 m.
General: Inhabits coral reefs where it lies motionless, relying on its camouflage and poisonous defensive stinging weapons.
  The photo shows S. barbatus together with the larger S. verrucosa (see above).

Scorpaenopsis barbatus   Andaman Islands, India

Devil scorpionfish

Length: up to 22 cm.
Distribution: entire area including Red Sea.
Depth: 5 - 70 m.
General: a relatively uncommon inhabitant of rubble or weedy coralline-rock bottoms, reef flats, lagoons, and seaward reefs. This exceedingly ugly creature has a colourful surprise for those who disturb it: it flashes the underside of its pectoral fins that are brilliantly coloured in yellow, orange, and black. Presumably this is an effective warning.

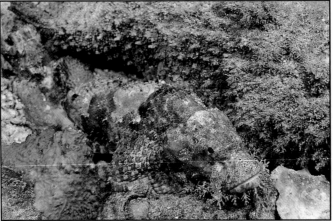

Scorpaenopsis diabola   Surin Island, Thailand

Leaf fish

Length: up to 12 cm.
Distribution: East Africa, Mascarenes, Maldives, Sri Lanka.
Depth: 8 - 134 m.
General: this unusual little fish resembles a leaf in structure as well as behaviour. Its body is laterally compressed and the Leaf fish has the habit of imitating a leaf or alga by swaying from side to side. The species is extremely variable in coloration, matching sponges and algae. Colours range from white, green, brown, and red to various spotted mixes (see photos for three colour variants). A common species in many areas, but so well-camouflaged that they are easily missed, even though specimens sitting high on corals can be obvious. It is found in coral reefs, usually on shallow reef crests and slopes with sparse vegetation or sponges. The Leaf fish has the peculiar habit of shedding its outer layer of skin from time to time. Juveniles settle at a length of about 20 mm; they are semi-transparent, and have a smooth skin. The bottom large photo shows *T. triacanthus* together with the **Indian waspfish** *Ablabys binotatus* of the family Tetrarogidae, the only species in our area (there are more in the West Pacific). It reaches up to 6 cm in length, lives in a depth of 10 - 25 m, and also rests on the substrate, waving its body and imitating the motion of seagrass or seaweeds in the water current. The bottom small photo (Mauritius) shows a 2-cm-juvenile of *T. triacanthus*.

Ari Atoll, Maldives

Taenianotus triacanthus   **North Male Atoll, Maldives**

73

Rhinopias frondosa   **Mauritius**

Weedy scorpionfish

Length: up to 24 cm.
Distribution: western Indian Ocean (East Africa, Madagascar, Mascarenes).
Depth: 13 - 90 m.
General: its body is laterally compressed and covered with weed-like tassles. When seen underwater, it resembles a lump of algae. It is perfectly adapted to a weedy habitat.

Rhinopias eschmeyeri   **Mauritius**

Mauritius scorpionfish

Length: up to 19 cm.
Distribution: western Indian Ocean, Sri Lanka to Mauritius.
Depth: 15 - 40 m.
General: this scorpionfish species inhabits rocky shores with weedy areas. Its deep body and its fins have no tassles and circular markings. Its coloration varies from light blue to yellow. This scorpionfish is a lurking ambusher and voracious predator of smaller fishes like all family members.

Inimicus filamentosus   **Madagascar**

Indian Ocean walkman

Le: up to 25 cm. Di: entire area. De: 10 - 55 m. Ge: uses its lower free pectoral rays as 'walking' legs even creating tracks in its sandy habitat. Dorsal spines extremely venomous. Often buried up to its eyes. Has deterrent pectoral and caudal fin coloration.

Coral grouper

Length: up to 40 cm.
Distribution: entire area
including Red Sea.
Depth: 2 - 100 m.
General: this grouper is typically found on well-developed
coral reefs in clear water,
often on exposed reefs with
areas of rich coral growth. The
coloration of adults is variable.
Small juveniles are uniformly
orange, they live secretively
amongst corals. The species
feeds on small fishes and crustaceans. See also photo from
the Andaman Sea on previous
page.

Cephalopholis miniata   **Baa Atoll, Maldives**

Golden grouper

Le: up to 60 cm. Di: East
Africa, Mascarenes. De: 40 -
250 m. Ge: this grouper is a
deep-water species, which is
generally found in depths of 50
to 200 m, it has also been
recorded from 300 m. Note
cleaner shrimp and wrasse.
   The Serranidae are a highly
diverse family with several
major groups, but classification
is continuously under review.
As presently defined, there are
nearly 50 genera and well over
400 species, distributed worldwide. The first subfamily presented here are the groupers
or Epinephelinae.

Cephalopholis aurantia   **Mauritius**

Saddle grouper

Length: up to 45 cm.
Distribution: entire area
including Red Sea.
Depth: 10 - 150 m and deeper.
General: this grouper is easily
recognised by six dorsal saddle
blotches. It is found in clear
water from coastal reefs to
outer reef drop-offs, often in
large caves with sponges, and
commonly seen swimming
upside down or positioned
vertically on a cave wall. It
feeds on the related fairy
basslets (subfamily Anthiinae,
see further below), cardinal
fishes (family Apogonidae, see
further below), and shrimps.

Cephalopholis sexmaculata   **Male Atoll, Maldives**

Tomato Grouper

Length: up to 65 cm.
Distribution: entire area.
Depth: 12 - 150 m.
General: the species is uncommon above 30 m, and usually found in deep lagoon reefs and on steep coastal outer reef slopes with rocky or coral outcrops on mixed rubble and mud bottoms. Adults usually live in the deeper part of the range. Very small juveniles are black with blue head and broad white margin on caudal fin; while growing they change to brown with orange spots, adults are bright red.

Cephalopholis sonnerati   **Réunion**

Blackfin grouper

Le: up to 30 cm. Di: East Africa to Sri Lanka. De: 1 - 40 m. Ge: common in shallow coastal seaward reefs, on crests with rich coral growth, mixed soft and stony corals. Adults have dusky pectorals; no white in caudal. Solitary, feeds on small fishes and crabs.

Cephalopholis nigripinna   **Mauritius**

Peacock grouper

Le: up to 40 cm. Di: entire area. De: 1 - 40 m. Ge: occurs on both lagoon and seaward reefs, particularly in areas of rich coral growth and clear water. Juveniles seem to prefer shallow, protected coral thickets. Adults may occur in pairs or in small groups.

Cephalopholis argus   **South Male Atoll, Maldives**

77

Blue-lined Grouper

Length: up to 34 cm. Distribution: West coast of India and Sri Lanka, Andaman Islands. Depth: 2 - 20 m. General: this grouper is a shallow-water species found in sheltered muddy, silty, or dead reefs, also in the vicinity of river mouths. Note cleaner wrasse near head.

Cephalopholis formosa   Andaman Islands

Slender grouper

Length: up to 52 cm. Distribution: entire area including Red Sea. Depth: 1 - 50 m. General: a secretive coral-reef species, more often found in protected than exposed reefs.

Except from the numerous species of the genera *Cephalopholis* and *Epinephelus* there are other very attractive groupers, which are shown in the following two pages. Below: **Lyretail grouper** *Variola albimarginata,* up to 60 cm, East Africa to Sri Lanka, 20 - 100 m, shy, deep-living, very uncommon, solitary species. Bottom: **Moon grouper** *Variola louti,* up to 80 cm, entire area including Red Sea, 1 - 150 m, common. The genus is easily recognised by its sickle-shaped caudal fin.

Anyperodon leucogrammicus   Mulaku, Maldives

GROUPERS

EPINEPHELINAE - SERRANIDAE

Coral grouper

Le: up to 110 cm. Di: entire area. De: 10 - 50 m. Ge: very common in coral reefs, also in sandy areas, seagrass beds, and ship wrecks. The huge predator has been observed attacking garden eels in their colony on a sandy slope with coral blocks. Colour variable.

Plectropomus pessuliferus Burma Banks, Thailand

Blacksaddle grouper

Le: up to 110 cm. Di: southern Indian Ocean to Maldives and Sri Lanka, not in Red Sea. De: 4 - 150 m. Ge: from silty reefs to clear outer reef drop-offs. Adult coloration variable. Juveniles (see small photo below, Aldabra) mimic the poisonous pufferfish *Canthigaster valentini*.

Plectropomus laevis Male Atoll, Maldives

African grouper

Le: up to 96 cm. Di: East Africa, Seychelles, Madagascar, Mascarenes, Chagos. De: 3 - 62 m. Ge: a solitary species that exclusively occurs on shallow coral and rocky reefs in the Indian Ocean. Tsmall photo below shows a juvenile 20 cm in length.

Plectropomus punctatus Beau Vallon, Seychelles

Plectropomus areolatus   Similan Islands, Thailand

Squaretail grouper

Length: up to 40 cm.
Distribution: entire area.
Depth: 6 - 200 m.
General: a common species in muddy habitats, mainly on coastal slopes with isolated rocky outcrops or terrestrial debris, often in small groups. The truncate caudal fin with its pale posterior margin readily distinguishes this species from other, similarly blotched groupers.

Being territorial, groupers are vulnerable to spear-fishing, which already caused a serious decline of some species in certain areas.

Dermatolepis striolatus   Des Roches, Seychelles

Smooth grouper

Le: up to 85 cm. Di: E-Africa, Seychelles. De: 5 - 70 m. Ge: in sheltered, rather turbid waters, also in clear and cloudy water. Below: **Red-mouth grouper** *Aethaloperca rogaa,* 60 cm, 5 - 40 m, shy, feeds on small fishes, prefers clear water of coral reefs, often found near or in caves.

Window grouper

Le: up to 45 cm. Di: southern Indian Ocean, Maldives, Sri Lanka. De: 6 - 150 m. Ge: inhabits steep outer reef slopes and drop-offs. Hovers a few meters above the bottom during the day, but is shy. Below (Aldabra): juveniles look like fairy basslets of the subfamily Anthiinae, see further below.

Gracila albomarginata   Astove, Seychelles

White-speckled grouper

Length: up to 35 cm.
Distribution: entire area.
Depth: 3 - 30 m.
General: the species is found in clear coastal bays and on mixed coral and rock substrates. It lives secretively along drop-offs, but is often seen at the entrance of a ledge or cave. Sometimes it rests on large sponges. This grouper can best be recognised by its somewhat darker head and densely spotted body and fins.

Epinephelus ongus　　　　　Male Atoll, Maldives

Long-spined grouper

Length: up to 55 cm.
Distribution: entire area.
Depth: 1 - 50 m.
General: this grouper prefers silty reef conditions, and is often found in sheltered muddy places with pieces of coral or other debris on open bottom. Juveniles are encountered on weed-covered rocks or dead coral from the intertidal zone down to a depth of more than 30 m. Widespread in Indian Ocean, ranging into West Pacific.

Epinephelus longispinis　　　　Trinco, Sri Lanka

Foursaddle grouper
35 cm, E-Africa, 1 - 25 m, in shallow clear rocky and coral reefs, shy. Below (Richelieu Rock): **Honeycomb grouper** *E. merra*, 28 cm, 1 - 50 m, with distinct lateral elongated spots.

Epinephelus spilotoceps　　　　South Africa, Maldives

GROUPERS
EPINEPHELINAE - SERRANIDAE

Epinephelus fuscoguttatus   Ari Atoll, Maldives

Brownmarbled grouper

Length: up to 90 cm. Distribution: entire area. Depth: 12 - 60 m. General: found in coral reefs and over rocky bottom. This is a wary species compared to most other groupers. It mainly feeds on fishes, crabs, and cephalopods. Small photo below from Aldabra.

Epinephelus tukula   Mozambique

Potato grouper

Length: up to 200 cm. Distribution: entire area. Depth: 3 - 80 m. General: although well-known in the Australian region as one of the least wary of all the groupers and often approaching divers closely, this is not true everywhere. The species is not common.

Giant grouper

Le: up to 250 cm. Di: entire area. De: 5 - 100 m. Ge: widespread, but rare. Up to at least 300 kg. Juveniles are often found in estuaries, while adults solitarily inhabit caves in coral reefs, wrecks, harbours, and deep estuaries. Feeds on spiny lobsters, crabs, teleosts, also on small sharks and skates.

Epinephelus lanceolatus   Sodwana Bay, South Africa

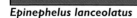

GROUPERS

EPINEPHELINAE - SERRANIDAE

Blue-and-yellow grouper

Le: up to 100 cm. Di: entire area. De: 10 - 150 m. Ge: juveniles in shallow water, adults prefer deeper reefs. Small adults are blue with yellow on caudal peduncle and fins. Large adults lose the blue and become black. Not shy.

Epinephelus flavocaeruleus   Mauritius

Blacktip grouper

Le: up to 40 cm. Di: entire area. De: 3 - 160 m. Ge: a common species of coral reefs and rocky bottoms that feeds on fishes and crustaceans. Easily identified by its bonnet-like dark patch on the head. The small photo below is from Kenya.

Epinephelus fasciatus   Lhaviyani Atoll, Maldives

Halfmoon grouper

Length: up to 40 cm. Distribution: western Indian Ocean (East Africa, South Africa, Madagascar to Mauritius), not recorded from Red Sea, Maldives, Seychelles. Depth: 1 - 150 m. General: this grouper is found in diverse habitats from coral reefs and rocky bottoms to algal flats and seagrass beds. Juveniles can also be found in mangrove areas. The species mainly feeds on small bony fishes, shrimps, and crabs.

Epinephelus rivulatus   Durban, South Africa

83

Jewel fairy basslet

Lenght: up to 15 cm. Di: entire area including Red Sea. De: 1 - 35 m. Ge: in huge schools in front of drop-offs, where they are the target of uw-photographers while feeding on plankton. Left: harem group of a male and many orange females. Below (Seychelles): a male.

Pseudanthias squamipinnis   **Durban, South Africa**

Cooper's fairy basslet

Length: up to 14 cm. Distribution: East Africa, Mascarenes, Maldives, not in the Red Sea. Depth: 5 - 60 m. General: occurs along current-swept drop-offs or on patch reefs with little coral growth. Photo shows the male, small photo below several females.

Pseudanthias cooperi   **Mauritius**

Yellowtail fairy basslet

Length: up to 10 cm. Distribution: East Africa, Mascarenes, Chagos, Maldives. Depth: 5 - 40 m. General: very common, but shy. During the day the species feeds on plankton in the water column over patch reefs. Photo shows the male, small photo below females.

Pseudanthias evansi   **Gaafu Atoll, Maldives**

Indian flame fairy basslet

Lenght: up to 6 cm. Di: Maldives, Sri Lanka. De: 10 - 30 m. Ge: in large aggregations on steep reef slopes around 30 m. Closely related to the West Pacific flame fairy basslet *P. dispar*. Photo shows a male.
Fairy basslets maintain harems of one male and a group of females. A harem may contain a few individuals that are on the way to transform into males, recognised by the changing coloration. After a male fell victim to a predator for example, the harem needs a new leader, which the strongest female will become.

Pseudanthias ignitus   Andaman Sea

Connell's fairy basslet

Length: up to 11 cm. Distribution: endemic to South Africa. Depth: found below 25 m. General: uncommon, mainly found on shipwrecks in the Durban and Aliwal Shoal areas. Feeds on zooplankton. The photos show a male (right) and a female (below).

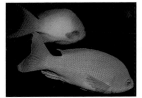

Pseudanthias connelli   South Africa

Redstripe fairy basslet

Lenght: up to 11 cm. Di: entire area including Red Sea. De: 50 - 60 m. Ge: males maintain harems and show courtship behaviour. The male (right) lacks the lateral red stripe of the female (below). Both photos are from South Africa, where the species is rare.

Pseudanthias fasciatus   South Africa

FAIRY BASSLETS

ANTHIINAE - SERRANIDAE

Threadfin fairy basslet
Le: up to 13 cm. Di: East
Africa, Seychelles, Maldives.
De: 4 - 30 m. Ge: in huge
schools over deep coral
columns. Maintains harems.
Protruding upper lip distinct.
Below: **Diadem fairy basslet**
P. parvirostris, to 9 cm, Maldives
(photo) to Mascarenes, 35 -
60 m, on outer reef slopes.

Nemanthias carberryi   **Amirantes, Seychelles**

SOAPFISHES

GRAMMISTINAE - SERRANIDAE

Arrowhead soapfish

Length: up to 15 cm.
Distribution: East Africa,
Comoros, Mascarenes to Maldives. Depth: 4 - 45 m.
General: a reef dweller, by day
found in caves, but nocturnally
active and moving out of its
shelter at dusk to feed.
   The Grammistinae or soapfishes have a slimy skin which
contains a toxin. It comprises
the most diverse group within
the Serranidae and several
genera will no doubt eventually
give rise to a subfamily or even
family status.

Belonoperca chabanaudi   **Surin Island, Thailand**

Double-striped soapfish

Length: up to 25 cm.
Distribution: Maldives, Sri Lanka.
Depth: 15 - 25 m.
General: a shy species, hidden
among corals or in crevices
during the day, moving to
more exposed places at night.
   The soapfishes are generally
more secretive than other ser-
ranids, living in caves or ledges,
remaining close to or hidden
in the substrate. Some species
can be found in loose groups
and are not shy towards
divers.

Diploprion bifasciatum   **Raa Atoll, Maldives**

Sixstriped soapfish

Length: up to 25 cm.
Distribution: entire area
including Red Sea.
Depth: 5 - 40 m.
General: inhabits coral reefs
and rocky bottoms with good
possibilities to seek shelter,
often in surprisingly shallow
water. Carnivorous. Its skin
produces a poisonous mucous.
The courtship behaviour has
been described (no external
sexual dimorphism): a pair's
more aggressive half seems to
be the male, which repeatedly
erects its dorsal fin, and bangs
its head into the side of its
partner.

Grammistes sexlineatus   **Burma Banks, Thailand**

Goldribbon soapfish

Length: up to 35 cm.
Distribution: entire area, but
records are rare and include
South Africa, Mauritius,
Réunion, and Thailand.
Depth: 12 - 48 m.
General: body deep blue with
a bright yellow band from
snout through eye and along
back. Carnivorous, mainly
feeds on benthic crustaceans
and small fishes.
   All soapfish species have a
skin with a thick coat of viscid
mucous containing the toxin
grammistin, which imparts a
bitter taste. The amount of
toxin increases under stress.

Aulacocephalus temmincki   **Durban, South Africa**

Snowflake soapfish

Length: up to 27 cm.
Distribution: Madagascar,
until Andaman Sea.
Depth: 10 - 35 m.
General: this species occurs in
areas of rich coral growth. It is
easily recognised by its chin-
barbel. Like other family members, the Snowflake soapfish
feeds on crustaceans and small
fishes and has a toxic skin
mucous, which makes it
impalatable. Sibling specien
P. punctata only west-pacific.

Pogonoperca ocellata   **Ari Atoll, Maldives**

87

Pseudochromis dutoiti   **Mozambique**

Rein dottyback

Length: up to 8.5 cm.
Distribution: African coast
from Kenya to South Africa.
Depth: 2 - 25 m.
General: after scientific revision this species proved to be
distinct from *P. aldabraensis*
occurring in the same area of
distribution, and thus a valid
species. The latter has the blue
stripe only running up to the
gill cover, and not around the
caudal fin as in this species.
  Dottybacks produce sticky,
demersal eggs, which sink to
the bottom where they adhere
to the substrate and to each
other to form clusters.

Pseudochromis andamanensis   **Mentawai, Sumatra**

Andaman dottyback

Le: up to 8.5 cm. Di: Andaman
Sea, Sumatra. De: 2 - 28 m.
General: recorded for the first
time from the coast of Sumatra, until now known only
from the Andaman Sea. Below:
Natal dottyback *Pseudochromis natalensis,* 9 cm, 1 - 25 m,
Kenya, S. Africa, Madagascar.

Chlidichthys johnvoelckeri   **Comoros**

Cerise dottyback

Length: up to 3 cm.
Distribution: Mozambique,
South Africa, Comoros.
Depth: 12 - 75 m.
General: in coral reefs, rare,
there are only a few records.
  Below (Sri Lanka): **Gold-
head dottyback** *Pseudo-
chromis dilectus,* 4.5 cm.

DOTTYBACKS   PSEUDOCHROMIDAE

Yellow dottyback

Length: up to 5 cm.
Distribution: Chagos Archipelago, Maldives, Sri Lanka.
Depth: 2 - 20 m.
General: the species was found
among dead coral and rock,
living in small holes and caves.
  Many dottybacks are
extremely colourful. Until now
there is no satisfactory explanation as to why some species
exhibit sexual dichromatism,
while others do not. Dottybacks are, however, invariably
hermaphroditic and can change
sex. The larger individual in a
pair of the same colour is
always the male.

Chlidichthys inornatus   Ari Atoll, Maldives

LONGFINS   PLESIOPIDAE

Comet longfin

Length: up to 16 cm.
Distribution: entire area.
Depth: 3 - 45 m.
General: the strikingly shaped
and patterned Comet longfin is
found living solitarily at hiding
places in coral reefs. The
species displays a threat behaviour: it is gaping its mouth that
is lined with white on the
inside. The number of white
spots distributed all over the
fish increases with age, while
the spots become smaller.

Calloplesiops altivelis   Trinco, Sri Lanka

FLAGTAILS   KUHLIIDAE

Barred flagtail

Length: up to 20 cm.
Distribution: entire area.
Depth: 0.5 - 20 m.
General: occurs in tightly
packed schools along coral
reefs and rocky shorelines.
Found from just beneath the
surfline to a depth of about
20 m. The fish are frequently
seen in the entrances of caves
along the waterline. Juveniles
are common in tide pools and
at the heads of surge channels.
The schools disperse at night
to feed on planktonic crustaceans.

Kuhlia mugil   Raa Atoll, Maldives

Mahe, Seychelles

Common bigeye

Length: up to 40 cm.
Distribution: entire area
including Red Sea.
Depth: 15 - 250 m.
General: the species is common on outer reef slopes and
deep lagoon pinnacles. It is
often encountered in large
aggregations (see also the
group on p.11). Unfortunately,
the Common bigeye is no
match for uw-spearfishermen:
it does not leave its daytime
hovering position when
approached.
　The body of bigeyes is laterally compressed. There is a
single dorsal fin with 10 spines
and up to 15 soft rays. Their
pectoral fins are much shorter
than the head. The rear margin
of the caudal fin is truncate,
convex or concave. A swim-
bladder is present in all species
of the family. The scales of
bigeyes are of the ctenoid
type. The lateral line is single,
complete, and is not continued
on the caudal fin. Head and
jaws are scaly. The upper jaw
is only slightly protrusible. All
teeth are small and conical,
there are no canines (large
fangs). The two nostrils are
closely set. Bigeyes are found
near the bottom in rocky
areas or reefs of tropical and
temperate regions in depths of
1 - 400 m. There are three
genera comprising about a
dozen species.

Priacanthus hamrur　　　North Male Atoll, Maldives

Bloch's bigeye

Length: up to 35 cm.
Distribution: Arabian Sea to
southern Indian Ocean, Maledives, Sri Lanka.
Depth: 15 - 30 m.
General: the solitary species
hides in caves during the day.
At night it moves out into the
water column and feeds on
larger zooplankton like
shrimps, crabs, and larval fishes. This bigeye can be distinguished from other family
members by its silvery rather
than plain red coloration.

Priacanthus blochii　　　South Male Atoll, Maldives

Goldbelly cardinalfish

Length: up to 10 cm.
Distribution: entire area, not in Red Sea.
Depth: 10 - 35 m.
General: seen singly or in pairs. The species lives hidden in caves and crevices in the shaded reef. The photo shows that the species may also be encountered in groups.

Cardinalfishes are small, carnivorous, and mainly live in shallow waters of all tropical and subtropical seas. They occupy a variety of habitats such as coral reefs, sandy and weedy bottom, turbid water, and mangrove areas.

Apogon apogonoides   Réunion

Indian tiger cardinalfish

Length: up to 25 cm.
Distribution: entire area.
Depth: 3 - 35 m.
General: a large, widespread species. The cardinal fish family comprises 3 subfamilies and 26 genera with an estimated 250 species. There are still many new species found, especially in tropical coral reefs, where they are most abundant. During the day, they occupy caves and crevices, at night they drift out into the open to feed on small planktonic invertebrates, a few species feed on fishes. Most have distinct patterns of stripes and dots.

Apogon lineatus   Ari Atoll, Maldives

Spiny-head cardinalfish

Le: up to 10 cm. Di: entire area including Red Sea. De: 2 - 45 m. Ge: this cardinalfish species lives solitary. At night it leaves the reef to feed on planktonic crustaceans. Below (Thailand): **Eight-spine cardinalfish** *Neamia octospina,* 5 cm, entire area including Red Sea.

Apogon urostigma   Praslin, Seychelles

CHAGOS

Right in the centre of the Indian Ocean, far south of the Maldives and over 1,500 km from the nearest major landmass lies a little known group of tiny coral islands: the Chagos Islands. This group comprises five atolls, and ten other reefs and submerged shoals. There are about 50 tiny islands, all very similar in general appearance to those of the Maldives. A marine biologist and photographer of all illustrations in this story presents some underwater specialities.

WELCOME TO BRITISH INDIAN OCEAN TERRITORY
1. IN ORDER TO PROTECT THE ENVIRONMENT, YOU ARE REMINDED:
   –COLLECTION OF LIVE SHELLS AND MOLUSKS IS FORBIDDEN.
   –KILLING AND EATING CRABS IS FORBIDDEN.
   –STORE ALUMINIUM TIN CANS AND BOTTLES IN BINS PROVIDED.
   BURN ANY OTHER RUBBISH IN INCINERATOR AREA.
   –COMMERCIAL FISHING WITHIN LAGOONS IS ILLEGAL. IF THIS IS SEEN PLEASE REPORT TO
   DIEGO GARCIA (FISHERY PROTECTION FREQUENCY) ON 5144 MG HZ OR 2.182.0 USB.
2. A CHARGE OF $55 (US) WILL BE LEVIED FOR CUSTOMS CLEARANCE FOR THE CHAGOS
   ISLANDS (ONCE PER VISIT). THIS WILL COMMENCE 1 JAN 1994.
                                                    BY ORDER
                                            BRITISH REPRESENTATIVE

ALL PHOTOS: CHARLES ANDERSON

A necessary welcome to visitors of Diego Garcia, one of the Chagos Islands that are British Indian Ocean Territory (BIOT).

The Chagos Islands belong to Britain and are known officially as the British Indian Ocean Territory (BIOT). Apart from Diego Garcia, the southernmost atoll of the Chagos group, the islands are uninhabited. It is a small, elongated atoll, roughly 20 km long and 8 km wide. The only entrances to the lagoon are at the northern end. Most of the rest of the atoll perimeter is occupied by a single sandy island, which stretches all the way along the atoll rim from one side of the entrance round the southern tip to the other side of the entrance. This V-shaped island is also called Diego Garcia and is roughly 60 km in total length, although it is nowhere more than a few hundred meters wide. Today the western arm of Diego Garcia island is home to a fully fledged US military facility, the ambiance of which is closer to that of the Florida Keys than that of the Maldives. Diego Garcia does not house a huge standing garrison, but is rather a strategic

The endemic Chagos anemonefish *Amphiprion chagosensis* with its host, the Magnificent sea anemone *Heteractis magnifica*, photographed at Petite Ile de la Passe.

staging post to be used in times of regional conflict. During the Gulf War against Iraq, and during the UN involvement in Somalia, Diego Garcia played an important role in supporting operations. Because of the military presence the whole archipelago is off-limits

The East African Zanzibar butterflyfish *Chaetodon zanzibariensis* at Ile Diamant.

to most would-be visitors. Some liveaboard dive boats have tried to visit, but they are invariably refused permission. So for the diver there are only three ways to get there: join the military; go on a private yacht; or go as part of an official scientific expedition. I was therefore delighted, when in late 1995 I was asked to join a British scientific diving expedition that would visit Chagos in February - March 1996. As a professional marine biologist special-

A 25-cm-long Blue-lined triggerfish *Xanthichthys caeruleolineatus*, photographed at Middle Brother.

ising in fishes, I was looking for and photographing fish species not recorded from the Chagos before. The Chagos archipelago may be isolated, but some scientific studies have been made there before. Previous work by visiting ichthyologists had resulted in a

Portrait of the Bearded moray *Gymnothorax breedeni*, photographed at Ile Manoel.

checklist of 703 species of fishes, published in 1989. My observations, together with those of other expedition members and museum specimen records published in the scientific literature since 1989, have added 100 new fishes to this list. There are

The endemic Chagos brain coral *Ctenella chagius*, photographed near the reef edge at Ile Diamant.

undoubtedly many more species to be uncovered in the Chagos, since 1,000 species of fishes are known from the Maldives, just to the north. In addition to just listing fish, an aim of this study was to provide information on the biogeography of the fishes of

A new species of flatworm, photographed at Ile du Coin.

Colonies of diverse species of ascidians settling on a fan coral, photographed at Ile Vache Marine.

Chagos. Preliminary results show, unsurprisingly, strong affinities with the fish fauna of the Maldives, particularly with that of the southern Maldives. There are several fish species found in both the Chagos and southern Maldives that have not been found in central and northern Maldives.

The diving in Chagos is very similar to that in Maldives. The reef forms are essentially the same, as are most of the corals and fishes. However, there are a few interesting differences. For one, the submerged 'offshore' reefs that are so common in the Chagos are absent from the Maldives. Also, Chagos is home to a few marine animals found nowhere else in the world. Such animals and plants that are only found in very restricted areas are known as endemic species.

One endemic is the Chagos brain coral, known scientifically as *Ctenella chagius*. Most corals have enormous distributions, so why this species, which is common in Chagos, should be restricted to such a small area, is a mystery. One possible explanation is that the larvae of *Ctenella chagius* have very short lifespans so the species cannot spread beyond the confines of the Chagos archipelago. However, the reproduction of *Ctenella chagius* has never been studied, so this is just an educated guess. Another unusual feature of *Ctenella chagius* is that it has no close relatives in the Indo-Pacific; the most closely related corals are to be found in the Caribbean. This suggests that the Chagos population is a relict, a left over from the time, when the Atlantic and Indo-Pacific Oceans were connected at tropical latitudes.

Another species found only in these islands is the Chagos anemonefish, *Amphiprion chagosensis*. Like all anemonefishes it lives exclusively in partnership with a giant sea anemone, but until 1996 the partner anemone of *Amphiprion chagosensis* was unknown. It is now known to live only in the Magnificent sea anemone *Heteractis magnifica*. This is the same anemone that

A sea star of the genus *Mithrodia*, photographed at Middle Brother.

the Maldive anemonefish, *Amphiprion nigripes,* lives in. In fact, at home in their anemones the two species look very similar. The only obvious difference is the second white band on *Amphiprion chagosensis* and, less obviously, its slightly less dark underparts.

A number of other species that appear to be endemic in the Chagos have not yet been scientifically described. These include a stunning, purple-coloured flatworm, a razorfish, and a sanddiver.

Grey reef sharks *Carcharhinus amblyrhynchos* at the Great Chagos Bank.

Rhabdosargus thorpei   **South Africa**

Bigeye stumpnose

Le: up to 45 cm. Di: South Africa. De: 4 - 18 m. Ge: eyes large, broad yellow band on the underside. Often found in schools in shallow coastal waters, usually over sandy bottoms. Feeds on benthic crustaceans and molluscs.

The photo on the previous page (Sodwana Bay, South Africa) shows the **Zebra seabream** *Diplodus cervinus,* 50 cm, entire area, 5 - 40 m. It is found singly or in pairs on inshore rocky reefs and enters mangrove areas to spawn. The species feeds on fishes, molluscs, crustaceans, and worms.

Chrysoblephus anglicus   **South Africa**

Englishman
Le: up to 80 cm. Di: endemic to Mozambique and Natal coast of South Africa. De: 15 - 100 m. Ge: lives in reefs, singly or in small groups. Pink bands may be faint or dark. Blows crustaceans from sand. Not easily approached. Below: the **German** *Polyamblyodon germanum,* 45 cm, 12 - 30 m, common.

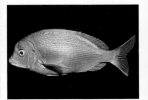

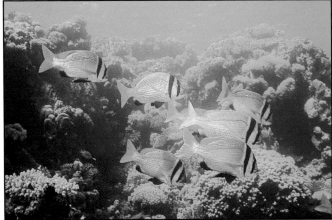

Acanthopagrus bifasciatus   **Shimoni, Kenya**

Twobar seabream

Le: up to 50 cm. Di: entire area. De: 2 - 25 m. Ge: single or in loose groups. Inhabits the sheltered waters of bays, estuaries, and shallow coral reef areas. It is easily distinguished from other seabreams by the two vertical black bars on the head.

Oriental sweetlips

Length: up to 50 cm.
Distribution: East Africa, Mascarenes, Chagos, Maldives,
Arabian Sea.
Depth: 2 - 40 m.
General: adults occur in
schools in clear water on outer lagoon and reef slopes.
Adults are not shy towards
divers, but juveniles (small
photo below) hide among
coral branches. The species
was formerly known as *P. orientalis*, which became a junior
synonym according to a recent
Japanese revision.
    The family comprises the
subfamilies Plectorhinchinae,
sweetlips (genera *Plectorhinchus*
and *Diagramma)*, and Haemuli-
nae, estuarine grunts (genus
Pomadasys). The large family
includes about 120 species.
Their taxonomy has been difficult because juveniles look
very different from adults;
some were only recently
linked to the corresponding
species.
    Sweetlips are mostly reef
dwellers, sheltering in caves
and shipwrecks during the day,
and feed mainly at night, when
venturing over sand and rubble
in search of benthic invertebrates. They occur singly or in
groups, depending on the
species or area, and are pelagic
spawners. Their postlarvae
settle at a very small size,
often less than 10 mm in
length. Small juveniles live
singly and have a different
colour pattern (see above).
Most swim close to the substrate in an unusual way by
waving the tail in an exaggerated manner. Apart from colour
pattern, adults differ from
juveniles in having a relatively
smaller mouth with enormously thick lips. In South Africa
they are also called rubberlips.

Aldabra, seychelles

Plectorhinchus vittatus   Richelieu Rock, Thailand

Plectorhinchus sp.   Negombo, Sri Lanka

Sweetlips species

Intensive research showed this species (length: 35 cm) to be new to science. Below: **Giant sweetlips**. Length: up to 100 cm. Distribution: entire area. Depth: 8 - 50 m. General: in loose aggregations over reef flats and rubble slopes. Distinct by a silvery grey body with most fins dark in colour.

P. obscurus

African sweetlips

Length: up to 45 cm. Distribution: East Africa, Seychelles, Mascarenes. Depth: 12 - 25 m. General: found in shallow inshore waters. Single individuals mix with other sweetlips or snappers (see small photo below from Aldabra). Rare.

Plectorhinchus paulayi   Amirantes, Seychelles

Yellowmouth sweetlips

Le: up to to 90 cm. Di: African coast from Socotra southward, Seychelles to Madagascar. De: 2 - 25 m. Ge: seen in small groups, prefers lagoons and mangrove areas. The yellow lips are excellent for identification in murky waters. Photo below from the Comoros.

Plectorhinchus plagiodesmus   Cosmoledo, Seychelles

Blackspotted sweetlips

Length: up to 45 cm.
Distribution: entire area
including Red Sea (where most
common species of sweetlips).
Depth: 5 - 55 m.
General: hides in groups under
coral ledges during the day.
The juvenile colour pattern
comprises three double-
stripes, which change to black
spots in the adult.
   Huge schools of sweetlips
gather in a convenient place
for spawning. They mill
around, swim in circles, and
finally rise in waves to the surface to synchronously release
eggs and sperm.

Plectorhinchus gaterinus   Amirantes, Seychelles

Harlequin sweetlips

Length: up to 60 cm. Distribution: Maldives, Sri Lanka.
Depth: 8 - 35 m. General:
common in clear lagoons and
seaward reefs rich in corals.
Usually seen hovering under
ledges or table corals. Feeds
primarily at night on crustaceans, molluscs, and fishes.

Plectorhinchus chaetodontoides   Male Atoll, Maldives

Silver sweetlips

Length: up to 90 cm. Distribution: entire area, including Red
Sea. Depth: 3 - 30 m. General:
common, seen singly or in
small groups in lagoons and
inner reefs. Sweetlips show no
external sexual dimorphism.
Small photo below is also from
Mahe, Seychelles.

Diagramma punctatum   Mahe, Seychelles

Slate sweetlips

Le: up to 100 cm. Di: entire area including Red Sea. De: 1 - 30 m. Ge: coastal inner reefs. Adults in small groups, often mistaken for *D. pictum*. Taxonomic revision in progress. Juveniles singly, subadults (see small photo below from Trinco, Sri Lanka) change pattern.

Diagramma cinerascens   Baa Atoll, Maldives

Smallspotted grunt

Le: up to 80 cm. Di: western Indian Ocean. De: 1 - 15 m. Ge: inhabits coastal waters, mangrove areas, sheltered estuaries, and tidal creeks. Feeds on crustaceans and fishes, blowing them from mud or sand. Below: **Striped grunt** *P. striatum*, to 22 cm, 1 - 40 m.

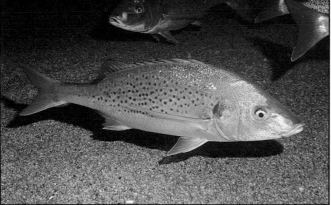

Pomadasys commersonni   Durban, South Africa

Grey grunt

Le: up to 50 cm. Di: South Africa, Madagascar. De: 1 - 15 m. Ge: sandy areas near rocks. In juveniles the bands are bifurcated anteriorly, in adults the bands are double lines. Below: **Javelin grunt** *P. kaakan*, to 45 cm, 1 - 75 m, enters estuaries and freshwater.

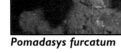

Pomadasys furcatum   KwaZulu-Natal

Bigeye snapper

Length: up to 30 cm.
Distribution: entire area
including Red Sea.
Depth: 2 - 90 m.
General: found on exposed
reefs of the continental
shelves, but absent from
oceanic islands. There are similar species in the family, all of
which have deeper bodies and
smaller eyes. Often seen in
schools together with other
snapper species: on the previous page it is shown with the
most common snapper of our
area, the **Bluestriped snapper** L. kasmira (most specimens in lower part of school).

Lutjanus lutjanus   Negombo, Sri Lanka

Bengal snapper

Length: up to 35 cm.
Distribution: Arabian Sea to
Sri Lanka, Mascarenes.
Depth: 15 - 30 m. General:
mainly solitary, but also in
groups. Distinct from similar
blue-striped snapper species by
continuous grey belly coloration. Below: juvenile.

Lutjanus bengalensis   Flic en Flac, Mauritius

Five-line snapper

Length: up to 38 cm.
Distribution: entire area.
Depth: 2 - 40 m.
General: found in coastal reefs,
lagoons, and on outer reef
slopes. In small aggregations or
large schools. Juveniles live in
estuaries and feed in sandy
areas. They look similar to the
adults, but are less yellow and
always show a distinct dark
spot. Adults can 'turn off' the
spot and are easily confused
with *Lutjanus kasmira* (see previous page), but have five
instead of four stripes.

Lutjanus quinquelineatus   Hikkaduwa, Sri Lanka

Twinspot snapper

Le: up to 80 cm. Di: entire area. De: 10 - 55 m. Ge: adults inhabit caves on outer reef slopes. Solitary or in huge schools (large photo) over reefs or sandy areas with patch reefs. Often single individuals are separated from the school and eaten by sharks (small photo immediately below). The popular name relates to the coloration of the juvenile (second small photo).

Lutjanus bohar   Felidhoo Atoll, Maldives

Humpback snapper

Length: up to 50 cm.
Distribution: entire area, not in Red Sea.
Depth: 2 - 35 m.
General: adults in schools, moving along reef flats and drop-offs. Clearly distinct from other snapper species by the hump on its back. Rather common around the oceanic islands. Juveniles usually in intertidal mangrove areas or seagrass beds. Single very large individuals are often seen in shipwrecks. The coloration is greatly variable, adults are often red, juveniles are similar. The small photo below shows a large adult with the typical hump.

Lutjanus gibbus   Ari Atoll, Maldives

Lutjanus argentimaculatus   **Similan Islands, Thailand**

Mangrove snapper

Length: up to 100 cm, probably to 120 cm.
Distribution: entire area including Red Sea.
Depth: 1 - 120 m.
General: juveniles are found in mangrove areas and in the lower reaches of freshwater systems. Larger juveniles school on coastal reefs and eventually move out to deeper water.

Lutjanus fulviflamma   **Beau Vallon, Seychelles**

Dory snapper

Length: up to 35 cm.
Distribution: entire area including Red Sea.
Depth: 1 - 35 m.
General: found in small groups in the turbid waters of inner reefs or mangrove areas, often also over rocky bottoms. Juveniles enter brackish habitats. The prominent oblong black spot on the lateral line below the anterior soft portion of the dorsal fin unfortunately is not a specific character for this species alone, as other family members also show a very similar spot in the same place.

Lutjanus fulvus   **Negombo, Sri Lanka**

Blacktail snapper

Length: up to 40 cm.
Distribution: entire area.
Depth: 1 - 40 m.
General: adults are usually encountered singly deep in lagoons and on coastal to outer reef slopes. Juveniles are usually found in the intertidal zone and in freshwater run-offs, where they may form loose groups; they differ from the adults by lacking the black on the tail.

Ehrenberg's snapper

Length: up to 35 cm,
but rarely over 25 cm.
Distribution: entire area
including Red Sea.
Depth: 5 - 20 m.
General: a coastal species, usually schooling over shallow
reefs near mangroves (large
photo), also encountered in
lagoons, sometimes congregating in large numbers near river
mouths. Juveniles mainly live in
brackish mangrove and estuarine areas. Small juveniles have
broader and fewer orange
lines. The small photo below
shows an adult over coral rubble.

Lutjanus ehrenbergii   Richelieu Rock, Thailand

One-spot snapper

Length: up to 60 cm.
Distribution: entire area
including Red Sea.
Depth: 5 - 30 m.
General: adults occur in sheltered reefs with caves and are
often found near shipwrecks.
Mainly solitary or in small
loose groups (large photo)
that start swimming in attractive formations whenever they
notice an uw-photographer
approach. Juveniles are not yet
known and perhaps over-
looked because they are very
similar to juveniles of other
snapper species. A nocturnally
active snapper, predominantly
feeding on fishes.

Lutjanus monostigma   Ari Atoll, Maldives

Emperor snapper

Le: up to 80 cm. Di: entire area, not in Red Sea. De: 2 - 100 m. Ge: adults singly or in small groups (large photo), red and white coloration distinct. Preferably in coral-rich lagoons. Small photo below: *L. malabaricus.*

Lutjanus sebae   Similan Islands, Thailand

Black-and-white snapper
Le: up to 60 cm. Di: entire area incl. south. RS. De: 5 - 20 m. Ge: adults occur in groups along steep slopes of lagoons, channels, and seaward reefs. They probably disperse to feed at night. The popular name results from the juvenile colour pattern shown in the small photo below.

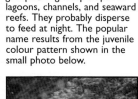

Macolor niger   Praslin, Seychelles

Yellowhead snapper
Le: up to 55 cm. Di: Maldives, Sri Lanka. De: 5 - 50 m. Ge: adults usually singly or in small groups along steep slopes of lagoons, channels, and seaward reefs. Often confused with the less colourful *M. niger.* Postlarvae associated with crinoids. Solitary juveniles with distinct colour pattern (photo below).

Macolor macularis   Kilifi, Kenya

Big jobfish

Le: up to 100 cm. Di: entire area incl. RS. De: 10 - 100 m. Ge: a voracious piscivore that darts into the reefs to hunt octopus, cuttlefish, and diverse reef fishes. Large individuals may be ciguatoxic. Very shy towards divers. Below: **Small jobfish** Aphareus furca, 40 cm.

Aprion virescens   Mary Anne Island, Seychelles

Sailfin snapper

Length: up to 60 cm.
Distribution: eastern Indian Ocean, Pacific.
Depth: 5 - 60 m.
General: adults and juveniles are both found in similar habitats: sandy flats with coral bommies between reefs, or in deep lagoons. Large adults (photo right) develop an almost vertical head profile. Subadult shown in bottom large photo, juvenile in small photo below.

This unusual snapper species is one of the most attractive members of the family because of its distinct coloration and the shape of its body and fins. The elongated soft fin rays of the juvenile's dorsal and anal fin become increasingly shorter during the development to the adult. Also the bottom-oriented habits of the juveniles change to a life in the open water above the reef. Both developments as well as the changing overall coloration are nicely documented in the photos shown here.

Mentawai Islands, Sumatra

Symphorichthys spilurus   Mentawai Islands, Sumatra

Bigeye emperor

Length: up to 60 cm,
common to 40 cm.
Distribution: entire area
including Red Sea.
Depth: 5 - 50 m.
General: relatively common
over sandy bottom. Adults
form loose aggregations during
the day, often seen in large
numbers. At night they move
out to feed on the substrate in
deep water. The juvenile (small
photo below) shows broad
brown bars on a lighter background, which fade to an overall silvery coloration in adults.
Small juveniles found singly on
rubble or sand patches in shallow lagoons or on reef crests
from clear coastal to outer
reef habitats.

Monotaxis grandoculis   Raa Atoll, Maldives

Yellowspot emperor

Length: up to 30 cm.
Distribution: entire area,
not in Red Sea.
Depth: 2 - 30 m.
General: a common species
found in shallow coral reef
areas. Often seen in small
groups directly on the reef,
rarely in huge schools with
hundreds of individuals as in
the large photo. Single specimens prefer to hide in caves of
drop-offs. The yellow blotch
below the soft part of the dorsal fin usually remains prominent in all colour variations.
The species feeds mainly on
the bottom of lagoon reefs and
at deep drop-offs. Small photo
below shows a large juvenile.

Gnathodentex aureolineatus   Grande Baie, Mauritius

Yellowfin emperor

Le: up to 60 cm. Di: East
Africa to the Maldives, not in
Red Sea. De: 10 - 120 m. Ge:
solitary, often hiding in the
reef. Feeds on molluscs and
echinoderms. May be ciguatoxic in some areas. The photos
were taken in front of a deep
cave at a depth of only 12 m.

Lethrinus erythracanthus   Ari Atoll, Maldives

Longnosed emperor

Le: up to 100 cm. Di: entire
area incl. RS. De: 1 - 185 m.
Ge: without conspicuous body
markings, but with the longest
snout of all genus members.
Swift swimmer, in lagoons and
coral reefs. Feeds primarily on
bottom-dwelling fishes, less on
invertebrates.

Lethrinus olivaceus   Male Atoll, Maldives

Yellowlips emperor

Length: up to 70 cm.
Distribution: entire area
including Red Sea.
Depth: 5 - 50 m.
General: this emperor species
is an aggressive hunter that is
mainly found living on coral
heads and fringe reefs. The
swift swimmer is usually
encountered singly. It is easily
recognised by its yellow upper
lip. Both, scientific and popular
name relate to this excellent
characteristic for identification.
   As postlarvae many emperor
species settle in seagrass beds,
are camouflaged green, and
can change colour quickly.

Lethrinus xanthochilus   Male Atoll, Maledives

Lethrinus crocineus — KwaZulu-Natal

Yellowfin emperor

Length: up to 60 cm.
Distribution: western Indian Ocean, south to Natal.
Depth: 10 - 150 m.
General: fins always yellow, cheeks sometimes with spots. Body of young specimens may show indistinct crossing bars. Adults usually have a darker head, lighter body, and a dark spot at the base of each scale.
The Emperor family comprises five genera and about 40 species, distributed all over the Indo-Pacific. Most juveniles look very different from adults and some species even have intermediate colour phases.

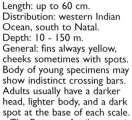

Lethrinus harak — South Male Atoll, Maldives

Blackpatch emperor

Length: up to 60 cm.
Distribution: entire area including Red Sea.
Depth: 5 - 20 m.
General: a solitary living shallow-water species found over sand, rubble, or seagrass bottoms of inner reefs and coastal lagoons. It is sometimes also seen in mangrove areas. The emperor's diet comprises a wide variety of benthic invertebrates like polychaetes, crustaceans, molluscs, and echinoderms, as well as small fishes. Easily recognised by the dark patch on the side, which does not fade even after preservation.

Lethrinus obsoletus — Beau Vallon, Seychelles

Goldenstriped emperor

Length: up to 40 cm.
Distribution: entire area including Red Sea.
Depth: 10 - 30 m.
General: a solitary species, only occasionally seen in small aggregations. This emperor is found near patch reefs in sandy areas. The conspicuous yellow stripe is distinct.
Emperors are carnivorous bottom dwellers, feeding on a variety of invertebrates and small fishes. Some species feed only at night and rest on the reef by day, others feed during both periods and alternate between open sand and reef.

Bluescale emperor

Length: up to 80 cm.
Distribution: entire area
including Red Sea.
Depth: 2 - 50 m.
General: a common species,
often encountered in small
groups over coral reefs, seagrass beds, rubble, and sandy
areas, rarely seen in large
schools as shown in the top
large photo. The Bluescale
emperor has been observed
swimming up seagrass-covered
slopes to ambush cuttlefish
hidden among the plants.
   The eggs of emperors are
pelagic, less than 1 mm in
diameter, and produced in vast
numbers. The larvae hatch at
less than 2 mm and postlarvae
are about 30 mm long.
   Emperors are regarded as
first-rate food fishes, but some
of the family members may
contain a lot of iodine, which
causes cooking problems. In
addition in some areas these
fishes can be affected by ciguatoxic poisoning.

Nosy Be, Madagascar

Lethrinus nebulosus   Mauritius

Smalltooth emperor

Le: up to 65 cm. Di: western
Indian Ocean incl. RS. De: 10 -
30 m. Ge: singly over sand and
seagrass on coastal slopes with
low patch reefs, adjacent to
deep water. Feeds on crabs,
molluscs, and small fishes.
Assumes a mottled pattern
when stopping to feed (below).

Lethrinus microdon   Praslin, Seychelles

Twoline threadfin bream

Length: up to 20 cm.
Distribution: entire area, not
in Red Sea.
Depth: 5 - 25 m.
General: a shy species, usually
encountered singly. It is nocturnally active and feeds on
benthic invertebrates like
worms, shrimps, and poly-
chaetes.
   The threadfin bream family
comprises five genera (65
species), two of which are primarily deepwater dwellers.
While diving, one will most
probably encounter one of the
almost 20 species of Scolopsis.

Scolopsis bilineatus   **Mulaku Atoll, Maldives**

Pearly spinecheek
Le: 18 cm. Di: east. Ind. Oc.. De:
3 - 40 m. Ge: singly or in small
groups along slopes and drop-
offs of coastal and inner reefs.
Juv. with broad black lateral line
and a thinner one higher on
back; yellow above. Below:
Arabian threadfin bream
S. ghanam, up to 20 cm, entire
area, 3 - 20 m, very common.

Scolopsis margaritifer   **Mentawai Islands, Sumatra**

Lattice spinecheek

Length: up to 30 cm.
Distribution: Andaman Sea to
Northwest Australia.
Depth: 3 - 50 m.
General: the species is
encountered solitarily on sand
flats in lagoons and on coastal
reef slopes. Juveniles are found
in shallow estuaries and harbours. Adults are usually seen
in depths of 15 m or more and
are very shy, always staying at a
distance away from divers.
   The family members included
here are benthic feeders and
mainly active during the day. At
night they rest on the substrate among rocks and corals.

Scolopsis monogramma   **Similan Islands, Thailand**

Bridled threadfin bream

Length: up to 26 cm.
Distribution: East Africa to
Seychelles and Chagos, southward to Madagascar and Mauritius.
Depth: 5 - 30 m.
General: adults in large groups,
juveniles and subadults solitarily over sand and coral rubble.
  The top large photo shows a
group of adults in their coral
reef habitat. The centre large
photo shows the more colourful pattern of the juvenile. The
small photo below is a close-
up of an adult.
  Most family members presented here feed on small
crustaceans, worms, some also
on small fishes, which are
located by the Theadfin
breams' excellent sense of
vision; a few other species in
the family are planktivores.
Mouths full of sand are taken
up by the benthic feeders to
sift out invertebrate prey. Most
species occur in small, but
loose aggregations. While
feeding, they swim just above
the substrate, stopping suddenly to study their surroundings.

Beau Vallon, Seychelles

Scolopsis frenatus   Chagos Islands

Whitecheek threadfin bream

Length: up to 25 cm.
Distribution: western Indian
Ocean to Sri Lanka, including
Red Sea, not around the
oceanic islands.
Depth: 5 - 45 m.
General: inhabits inner reefs
and lagoons, also found in the
murky water of river mouths.
Seen solitary or in pairs digging for bottom-dwelling invertebrates.
  Juvenile Threadfin breams
usually have distinct longitudinal stripe patterns, which
change to completely different
colour patterns in adults.

Scolopsis torquata   Hikkaduwa, Sri Lanka

Robust fusilier

Length: up to 40 cm.
Distribution: entire area.
Depth: 3 - 40 m.
General: this fusilier species is encountered in coastal reefs and lagoons and usually seen in large schools. There are several similar species, but this one is conspicuously less slender than most family members. It has a stripe below the eye and the lower half of the body is reddish in colour. It is also one of the larger fusiliers.

Caesio erythrogaster   Surin Island, Thailand

Lunar fusilier

Length: up to 28 cm.
Distribution: entire area including Red Sea.
Depth: 2 - 20 m.
General: mainly encountered hovering in groups over reef flats and fringe reefs, where the species feeds on plankton in the open water. Adults of this species often occur in deep clear water somewhat further off the reef than other family members.

Caesio lunaris   Male Atoll, Maldives

Gold-striped fusilier

Le: up to 24 cm. Di: entire area incl. RS. De: 3 - 18 m.
Ge: schooling, in groups of up to 50 specimens (see large photo). Distinct by the lateral golden stripe continuing onto the upper lobe of the caudal fin (see small photo below).

Caesio caerulaurea   Beau Vallon, Seychelles

Manylined fusilier

Length: up to 22 cm.
Distribution: western Indian
Ocean including Red Sea, to
Sri Lanka and Seychelles.
Depth: 3 - 25 m.
General: the species has been
described only recently. It is
encountered in huge schools
(see large photo) over rocks
and coral reefs, and often mixes with other fusilier species
like the Gold-striped fusilier.
The small photo below is a
close-up of individuals at the
edge of the school.

Caesio varilineata   Lhaviyani Atoll, Maldives

Neon fusilier

Length: up to 25 cm.
Distribution: East Africa, Seychelles, Madagascar, Mas-
carenes, Chagos, Maldives, Sri
Lanka, not in Red Sea.
Depth: 2 - 20 m.
General: the species is easily
identified by a broad blue band
along the entire body (very
bright in ambient light) and the
lack of black caudal fin tips. At
night the lower half of the
body turns bright red. Occurs
in large, often densely packed
schools along outer reef
slopes, in clear atoll lagoons,
and along steep drop-offs. In
the Maldives at night one can
observe this species resting
underneath every second coral
head.

Pterocaesio tile   Hikkaduwa, Sri Lanka

Yellowback fusilier

Le: up to 30 cm. Di: East
Africa to Maldives and
Andaman Sea. De: 2 - 50 m.
Ge: close to outer reefs along
slopes and drop-offs. Also seen
in the brackish water of river
mouths. Similar to *C. teres*, but
yellow colour extends to dorsal fin, sometimes over head.

Caesio xanthonota   Praslin, Seychelles

Blue-and-gold fusilier

Length: up to 30 cm.
Distribution: East Africa and
Mauritius to Sri Lanka.
Depth: 10 - 35 m.
General: a shy species, which
stays hidden in caves during
the day. The yellow area on
the back extends to the nape
only in juveniles, and retreats
to the tail and its base during
growth. The species schools in
midwater in deep lagoons and
along outer reefs. Schools
spawn immense numbers of
eggs near the surface in the
entrances of deep channels
during outgoing tides on a
lunar cycle.

Caesio teres   Flic en Flac, Mauritius

Yellow-band fusilier

Length: up to 30 cm.
Distribution: entire area.
Depth: 3 - 25 m.
General: the coloration of
juveniles is slightly different
from that of adults: the yellow
band becomes increasingly
broader with age. Usually
found in small groups on coral-
rich reef slopes, from coastal
to outer reefs and lagoons.
  A very similar species,
P. lativittata, occurs in our area
(Chagos eastward); it is yellow
above and below along most of
the lateral line.

Pterocaesio chrysozona   Mahe, Seychelles

Twinstripe fusilier

Le: up to 32 cm. Di: southern
Indian Ocean from East Africa
eastward, Seychelles, Mauritius. De: 5 - 35 m. Ge: seen in
huge aggregations over deep
rocky and coral reefs. The
lower yellow stripe lies over
the lateral line for most of its
length (see small photo below).

Pterocaesio marri   Beau Vallon, Seychelles

Southern fusilier

Length: up to 17 cm.
Distribution: Mozambique,
Kenya, Comoros, Seychelles.
Depth: 2 - 23 m.
General: this fusilier has been
described only a few decades
ago from the coast of Mozambique. It is a relatively rare
species that is encountered
singly or in schools (see photo) around coral reefs.
   Members of the genus *Pterocaesio* are variable in shape
from slender to moderately
deep bodied. Usually species of
Caesio have deeper bodies and
are more robust, while *Gymno-
casio* spp. are most slender.

Pterocaesio capricornis   Punto d'Oro, Mozambique

Naked fusilier

Length: up to 13 cm.
Distribution: East Africa, Maldives, also Red Sea; more
abundant eastward of our area.
Depth: 2 - 25 m.
General: this fusilier species
lives in schools like other family members and swims along
coral reefs in order to feed on
zooplankton organisms in the
open water column. Its popular name refers to the scaleless unpaired (or median) fins.

Gymnocaesio gymnoptera   Ari Atoll, Maldives

117

ST. BRANDON

When one started diving in the 1960s, 'further' meant 'better'. It meant getting away from crowds and cities. And surely there would be more fishes and corals. But it did not always stay this way. The demand for fish swept many reefs, especially in the Indian Ocean area, empty. They look like they have been cleaned out with a vacuum cleaner. But, fortunately, not all is grim. Mauritius is a country, whose government saw its coastal fisheries collapsing and decided not to make the same mistakes in one of its remote areas, the archipelago of St. Brandon. The photographer recalls his visit there.

ALL PHOTOS: JAN CORNELIS POST

At the left a Bull shark, at the right last night's meal, a Tiger shark, parts of which were found in the Bull's stomach.

A few years ago the government of Mauritius asked the World Bank in Washington to help prepare a management plan for the St. Brandon area to preserve its outstanding natural beauty and wealth. Then one Mauritius fishing company held a permanent lease to 13 of the islands and has held a renewable lease to 15 more. This renewable lease has now expired and there are many other companies interested in fishing there. They have overfished their own areas and are seeking to exploit others. The government of Mauritius wants objective advice as to what to do.

So, heading an official team of seven to investigate this area, about which very little is known, off I went to St. Brandon on the only live-aboard, which goes there from Mauritius, the *Umbrina II*. St. Brandon, also known as the Cargados Carajos Islands, lies about 370 km north of Mauritius. Is consists of a crescent-shaped reef oriented north-south with 55 small islands and sand banks. The reef is some 60 km long and 20 km wide. The outer side of the crescent faces east, from which prevailing currents and winds come, winds and currents so strong that the eastern side of the reef has not even been charted. In fact, the sea chart that we had reads: "This eastern coast was sketched by Lieutenant Mudge in 1825 by means of boats, which penetrated from the western side among the reefs as no vessel could venture to approach its seaward face." It is a rough place, hard hit by hurricanes and

Drying fishes at Raphael Island.

trade winds and lacking any permanent habitation except for two fishing stations run by a fishing company.

When we finally arrived at St. Brandon after a rough crossing in high seas, we first brought some supplies to the fishing station. There we had a first taste of what awaited us. Two sharks had just been caught. A line with some baited hooks set that night had first hooked a Tiger shark, which was partly eaten by a larger Bull shark. The Bull shark had later taken the second bait. When we cut it open, we found large chunks of the Tiger shark and razor-sharp pieces of metal, including a bag made out of chicken mesh. Those bags are used by fishermen to put bait in for their fish traps. Apparently the Bull shark had first raided the fish trap and devoured a part of the trap in the process before being hooked itself. It is unbelievable how sharks can survive with razor-sharp pieces of metal in their stomachs.

After seeing this, it was with a little apprehension that we jumped into the water for our first dive. We had our backs covered by Daniel, an aquarium fish exporter from Mauritius, who had a three-metre-long Hawaiian sling with an explosive tip to fend off possible shark attacks. But the excitement of the first dive did not come from sharks. The real excitement came from the sighting of a small fish, Daniel had never seen before and which did not appear in any of the books we brought with us. Could

The endemic sabretooth blenny *Meiacanthus fraseri.*

it be that we had discovered a new species? It is a nice-looking fish, but one with a nasty character. It was clearly a *Meiacanthus*, a small blenny with long poisonous fangs in the lower jaw, with which it can inflict a painful bite.

A pair of Koran angelfishes on a St. Brandon reef.

We finally caught five of them and sent them to the Smith Institute of Ichthyology in South Africa for identification. It appeared to be *Meiacanthus fraseri,* found in St. Brandon in 1970, and is an endemic (found nowhere else). Our team split up into three teams to make an inventory of the area: a land team for the islands; a shallow water team for the lagoon; and a deep water team which, as one of its tasks, was going to see, if there would be interesting dive sites for the development of diving tourism. The first thing striking us under water was the abundance of larger reef fishes - groupers, snappers, emperors, and jacks. Here was a reef, where the fish fauna was still in great shape! Strangely enough though, we did not see very big ones such as the Potato grouper *Epinephelus tukula,* a fish I hoped to encounter after having seen it in Madagascar and Seychelles waters.

St. Brandon forms part of the Shoals of Capricorn or Mascarene Ridge, an arch of shallow banks in the Indian Ocean running from Mauritius to the Seychelles. This means that there are no steep drop-offs. The bottom largely consists of sand with patch reefs and the underwater scenery is fairly uniform. The best diving areas are around the islands in the lee of the reef, where the bottom slopes down to some 30 metres. Being some sort of lagoon environment, the water in the leeward side of St. Brandon is not very clear and visibility is only about 20 metres.

On a calm day we made a dive on the

Fairy and Roseated terns at St. Brandon.

This St. Brandon Yellowfin grouper is also known from Mauritius.

western, windward side and found to our surprise the bottom in 15 m covered with the seagrass *Thalassodendron* and the calcareous alga *Halimeda*. However, we saw none of the big sharks we had anticipated. Back on board the boat we discovered the possible reason. The wind was carrying a foul smell, and sailing along the reef we saw a huge dead whale washed onto the shore. I decided to have a closer look, and was dropped by a dinghy. I started to wade through the knee-deep water towards the whale. All of a sudden, I heard screaming and shouting from the others. They were calling to me to turn back. I was soon to learn why. The shallow water around the whale was infested with sharks, some of which came almost half out of the water to grab a bite of the whale meat.

Sailing among the 55 islands and sand cays of St. Brandon we spotted enormous colonies of seabirds on those covered with vegetation. Fairy terns lay their eggs on a bare branch without making a nest. Unfortunately, rats, introduced on some of the islands, eat eggs and chicks wreaking havoc with bird populations and one of the management activities will be a rat eradication campaign. Exploring the islands, we found a lot of tracks of Green and Hawksbill turtles on the beaches. Both species are still very common in St. Brandon. They dig their nests where the vegetation starts as this is a sign that the sea does not reach here at high tide. We counted the turtle tracks to get an idea of the population size and watched at night, when the large females came ashore to lay their eggs. Scores of Ghost crabs emerge from their burrows at night, waiting to prey upon the hatchlings. The hatchlings dash to the sea in a mad rush to avoid the crabs only to fall victim to groupers and sharks waiting on the reef. I am amazed that any survive their childhood in places like this, where there are predators wherever you turn your head.

A Green turtle off Raphael Island.

We saw another example of the fact that sea creatures must have an acute sense of navigation. The *Umbrina II* had attracted dozens of remoras, which stayed with us throughout our survey of St. Brandon. As soon as we anchored they swarmed around the ship to pick up any scraps thrown overboard, attaching themselves again to the hull as soon as we moved. Strangely enough, on our way back to Mauritius they all of a sudden left as soon as we rounded Shark Point, the southern edge of St. Brandon. It was as if they knew exactly when we left St. Brandon waters.

Places like St. Brandon are getting rare and the mere experience of being out in the middle of nowhere, in a place, which is still practically pristine, is worth a rough sea ride and the expense. After spending ten days in St. Brandon, we all agreed on one thing: the place is one of the few reef areas, which is ecologically still intact and should stay that way.

Experience all over the world has shown that fisheries based on a quota system have not worked. It appears to be impossible to determine, who can fish how much and where. And as long as the mentality is "if I do not catch this fish today, my competitor will do so tomorrow" stocks will be overfished. So more and more there is a change to systems, where a single operator or cooperative is responsible for the management of an area, so that they have a long-term interest in the sustainable exploitation. This is what we are going to propose to the Mauritian government. To be able to give this system a legal basis, St. Brandon has to be declared a Marine Protected Area and managed on the basis of a multiple use zoning plan according to the model provided by the Great Barrier Reef Marine Park in Australia. We have good hopes that our plan will be implemented and set an example for the Western Indian Ocean, where small island states like Seychelles and Mauritius have become conservation-oriented. St. Brandon will not travel the same road as the Dodo.

Fairy tern guarding its egg.

Platax teira   **Beau Vallon, Seychelles**

Longfin batfish

Length: up to 50 cm.
Distribution: entire area, RS.
Depth: 1 - 35 m.
General: pairs of adults are living close to the bottom. The species feeds on zooplankton and jellyfish. It is not shy at all, and also found at wrecks. The popular name is based on the long fins of the juveniles. See also the impressive photo on the preceding page of *P. teira* schooling in front of a wreck at the Maldives. This batfish has recently been observed swimming and staying together with marine turtles.

Platax batavianus   **Mentawai Islands, Sumatra**

Hump-headed batfish

Length: up to 50 cm.
Distribution: eastern Indian Ocean, West Pacific.
Depth: 1 - 45 m.
General: the species is usually found over sandy and muddy bottoms, but also ventures into coral reef areas. Furthermore it is encountered in the murky water of estuaries. It is absent from oceanic islands. Juveniles have vertical white lines in areas between bars, they live in inshore waters. Adults grow elongate with a hump on the head (see photo) and move to deeper waters.

Tripterodon orbis   **Negombo, Sri Lanka**

Sri Lanka spadefish

Length: up to 25 cm.
Distribution: East Africa and Arabian Sea eastward.
Depth: 10 - 30 m.
General: a solitary species, which prefers the murky waters of river mouths and estuaries, also found in shallow inshore areas over silty bottoms near reefs.

Circular batfish

Le: up to 50 cm. Di: entire area, RS. De: 5 - 35 m. Ge: head rounded, lacks the black pectoral spot of *P. teira*. Ventral and anal fins with black edges. Adults in pairs or small groups near coral reefs. Juveniles inshore, in brackish water, or mangrove areas, lying on their side resembling drifting brown leaves. Feeds on algae, invertebrates, and small fishes.

Platax orbicularis　　　　Aldabra, Seychelles

Shaded batfish

Length: up to 35 cm. Distribution: Andaman Sea into West Pacific. Depth: 2 - 50 m. General: adults sometimes singly, in small groups, or in large schools from shallow coastal to deep outer reefs, also often seen in shipwrecks. Postlarvae settle on coastal protected reefs or in mangroves. Juveniles (small photo below) found under jetties, but they also move to deep water, where they inhabit caves.

Platax pinnatus　　　　Surin Island, Thailand

SILVER BATFISHES   MONODACTYLIDAE

Beau Vallon, Seychelles

Silver batfish

Length: up to 23 cm.
Distribution: entire area
including Red Sea.
Depth: 0.5 - 8 m.
General: a schooling species
that is common not only in
marine habitats, but also in
pure freshwater, brackish estuaries, and harbours. While diving, it may be encountered
over silty coastal reefs. The
species feeds by day and night
in the open water on planktonic organisms, and even on
insects drifting on the water
surface. Its coloration is dark
in juveniles and silver in adults.
Juveniles live in brackish water,
but also move into freshwater.
  Monodactylidae are a small
family with three genera and
five species, with only the
genus *Monodactylus* found in
our area. Juveniles have tiny
ventral fins, which become
rudimentary or even absent in
adults. The spines of dorsal
and anal fins are reduced and
covered by skin and scales at
the front margin of these fins.
Both jaws with numerous tiny
teeth. The upper jaw is slightly
protrusible.

Monodactylus argenteus   Mary Anne Island, Seychelles

RUDDERFISHES   KYPHOSIDAE

Snubnose rudderfish

Le: up to 45 cm. Di: entire
area. De: 1 - 15 m. Ge: occurs
over hard bottoms of exposed
outer reef flats. Omnivorous.
Below: **Brassy rudderfish**
Kyphosus vaigiensis, to 60 cm.
Feeds primarily on algae.

Kyphosus cinerascens   Ari Atoll, Maldives

Yellowsaddle goatfish

Length: up to 50 cm.
Distribution: entire area including Red Sea.
Depth: 5 - 35 m.
General: the species prefers coral, rock, or rubble bottoms. Unlike most goatfish species which feed on benthic invertebrates, it feeds primarily (up to 70%) on small fishes. There are two markedly different colour phases: yellowish grey with blue markings on each scale and a yellow saddle-like spot on the caudal peduncle (large photos); all yellow with an even brighter yellow spot on the caudal peduncle. The small photo below of the yellow colour phase shows the extended barbels. All goatfishes are benthic feeders and use their strong barbels to find prey in or on the substrate.

The top large photo shows a remora (see p.128) attached to the back of the goatfish. Visible is the underside of the remora, as it is attached with its dorsal fin, which is modified into a sucking disc. Remoras do not care, if the are transported upside down or else.

Similan Islands, Thailand

Parupeneus cyclostomus   Nosy Be, Madagascar

Round-spot goatfish

Length: up to 30 cm.
Distribution: entire area.
Depth: 10 - 40 m.
General: found in the clear water of coral reefs, in lagoons, and on slopes. Usually encountered singly or in small groups. Juveniles are entirely coastal and often seen in small aggregations. They are similar in coloration to adults, but typically much more slender. The large black spot directly followed by the white area readily identifies adults of this species.

Parupeneus pleurostigma   Ari Atoll, Maldives

Parupeneus rubescens   Richelieu Rock, Thailand

Redstriped goatfish

Length: up to 30 cm.
Distribution: entire area
including Red Sea.
Depth: 5 - 35 m.
General: often seen over
coastal rocks and rubble. The
photo nicely shows the typical
saddle-like blotch on the back
of the caudal peduncle.
   Goatfishes are easily identified by the presence of a pair
of barbels on the chin. The
family comprises six genera
and about 35 species with a
global distribution in tropical
and sub-tropical seas. They
typically have elongated bodies
with large scales.

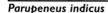

Parupeneus indicus   Negombo, Sri Lanka

Yellow-spot goatfish

Length: up to 40 cm.
Distribution: entire area.
Depth: 5 - 25 m.
General: occurs in coastal
waters and inner reef lagoons,
usually in small agregations of
less than 10 individuals, sometimes singly. Juveniles are similar
to adults, but more slender. The
species is distinct by the lateral
orange-yellow blotch.
   In goatfishes all fins are pointed
or angular, there are two separate dorsal fins, and a forked tail.
Except for coloration many
species of the same genus are
difficult to separate on morphological features alone.

Parupeneus bifasciatus   Lhaviyani Atoll, Maldives

Doublebar goatfish

Length: up to 35 cm.
Distribution: entire area, not
in Red Sea.
Depth: 1 - 80 m.
General: a coral reef dweller,
inhabiting mainly pure coral
reef areas with only few sand
patches. Usually encountered
singly, often seen resting on
corals. There is some geo-
graphical variation in coloration, but all juveniles have
two distinct dark bars, which
may be reduced in adults to
short saddles or an indistinct
barring (not so in the photo).

Longbarbel goatfish

Le: up to 32 cm. Di: entire area, RS. De: 2 - 25 m. Ge: similar to *P. rubescens,* but blotch on caudal peduncle smaller, not saddle-like, lateral in position. Stripe may be faint in either species. Below: **Dash-and-dot goatfish** *P. barberinus,* 40 cm, entire area, not in RS.

Parupeneus macronema   Ari Atoll, Maldives

Yellowfin goatfish

Le: up to 38 cm. Di: entire area including Red Sea. De: 2 -25 m. Ge: the only goatfish regularly seen in schools of up to 200 speci-mens in open water. The species often mixes with differ-ent kinds of sweetlips and snappers (see large photo).

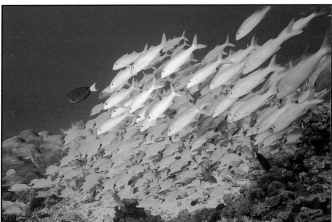

Mulloides vanicolensis   Cosmoledo, Seychelles

Yellowstripe goatfish

Length: up to 40 cm. Distribution: entire area including Red Sea. Depth: 5 - 20 m. General: this species is clearly distinct from the Yellowfin goatfish (see above) by its black blotch, which is always present on the yellow stripe.

Mulloides flavolineatus   Ari Atoll, Maldives

Striped remora

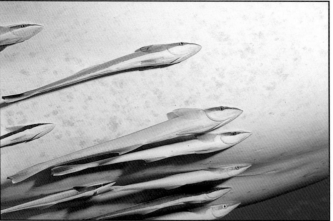

Le: up to 80 cm. Di: entire area, RS. De: dependend on host. Ge: most abundant family member. First dorsal fin modified into a sucking disc that is used to attach to sharks, rays, large bony fish, and sea turtles. The group in the photo are attached to a Whale shark and oriented in a normal position (see also p.125 top). The family comprises 4 genera and 8 species. Some are host-specific, others attach to anything that moves, e.g. ships and divers. Food and transportation are provided by the host, which is searched for parasites.

Echeneis naucrates   **Richelieu Rock, Thailand**

COBIAS   RACHYCENTRIDAE

Cobia

Richelieu Rock, Thailand

Length: up to 200 cm, common to 110 cm. Distribution: entire area including Red Sea. Depth: 2 - 60 m. General: a primarily pelagic species, but it is also found over shallow coral reefs and off rocky shores, occasionally even in estuaries. Cobias almost always accompany sharks, rays, and other large marine vertebrates over long distances and participate in the meals of their hosts. The juveniles (see bottom photo) have white lateral stripes and are easily confused with remoras, but this stripe pattern fades to a uniform brownish in adults. Juveniles are usually seen singly, adults live in small groups of several individuals.

The family Rachycentridae is monotypic, which means it contains only a single species. The Cobia is wide-ranging in all warm oceans. When suddenly coming into sight under water, this impressive and fast swiming fish has the appearance of a shark, which may scare unexperienced divers or snorkellers. The species is curious and often approaches quickly, coming into close range.

Rachycentron canadum   **Similan Islands, Thailand**

Blue dwarf-angelfish

Length: up to 9 cm.
Distribution: known only from
Mauritius, Réunion, and since
Nov. 1998 also from Aldabra.
Depth: 15 - 90 m.
General: this angelfish species
is found in deep water, where
it occurs along algae-covered
vertical drop-offs. It is apparently rare; only a single specimen was observed during each
of two dive-trips to Mauritius.
The photo to the left, taken
off Aldabra, Seyschelles, in a
depth only 20 extend its range
considerably. See also photo
on previous page.

Centropyge debelius   **Aldabra, Seychelles**

Brown dwarf-angelfish

Le: up to 10 cm. Di: East
Africa to Thailand. De: 1 -
30 m. Ge: the most abundant
and common dwarf-angelfish
of our area. It occurs over
rubble bottom in coral reef
areas. There are different
colour morphs. It feeds almost
exclusively on algae and detritus.

Centropyge multispinis   **Male Atoll, Maldives**

Moonbeam
dwarf-angelfish

Le: up to 10 cm. Di: Sri Lanka
and Maldives to Andaman Sea.
De: 3 - 20 m. Ge: over rubble
bottom with sparse coral
growth. The species is similar
to *C. multispinis*, but can easily
be distinguished by its yellow
pectorals. Usually seen singly.

Centropyge flavipectoralis   **Similan Islands, Thailand**

ANGELFISHES

POMACANTHIDAE

Lemonpeel dwarf-angelfish

Length: up to 14 cm, usually to 11 cm. Distribution: Christmas and Cocos-Keeling Islands (eastern Indian Ocean); another population in Micronesia (Pacific), where the species is common. Depth: 1 - 10 m. General: a shallow water species with an interesting disjunct distribution and slightly different colour morphs: the Indian Ocean form has no blue ring around the eye as can be seen in the photo.

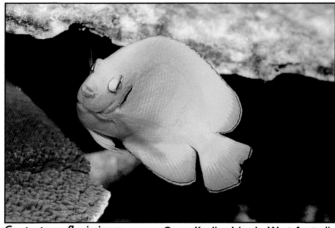

Centropyge flavissimus　　　Cocos Keeling Islands, West Australia

Cocos dwarf-angelfish

Le: up to 9 cm. Di: known only from Christmas (small photo) and Cocos-Keeling Is. De: 8 - 70 m. Ge: on steep outer slopes and drop-offs.

Centropyge joculator　　　Cocos Keeling Islands, West Australia

Eibl's dwarf-angelfish

Le: up to 10 cm. Di: eastern Indian Ocean: India and Sri Lanka to Thailand and Northwest Australia. De: 3 - 25 m. Ge: sibling species of the Indo-West Pacific *C. vroliki*, hybrids between both species are not uncommon. Found on reefs with rich coral growth. Serves as model for the juveniles only of the Indian Ocean mimic surgeonfish *Acanthurus tristis*. The significance of this nearly faultless imitation (mimicry) is poorly understood; it probably serves in predator avoidance.

Centropyge eibli　　　Richelieu Rock, Thailand

Centropyge bispinosus   Kilifi, Kenya

Coral beauty

Length: up to 10 cm.
Distribution: entire area
except Northwest Indian
Ocean.
Depth: 3 - 60 m.
General: a common deep
water species, but also found
in clear water lagoons among
rich and dense coral growth or
fields of algae (see photo).
Highly variable from totally
blue to red and very pale with
thin vertical lines, coloration
usually related to depth and
habitat. Usually blue with reddish sides. In pairs or loose
aggregations.

Centropyge acanthops   KwaZulu-Natal

African dwarf-angelfish

Le: up to 8 cm. Di: East Africa
to Maldives and Oman. De: 10
- 40 m. Ge: an untiring swimmer in coral-rich areas, also on
algae-covered substrates. With
the looks and movements of a
damselfish, but the spine on its
operculum proofs it to be a
true angelfish.

Whitetail
dwarf-angelfish

Length: up to 8 cm.
Distribution: East Africa, Mascarenes to Maldives, Sri Lanka,
and Thailand.
Depth: 10 - 60 m.
General: the species occurs on
rubble bottoms of reef channels or outer reef slopes with
sparse coral growth. It is usually common, but very shy. Its
coloration and shape closely
resemble that of a damselfish,
for which it is often mistaken.

Centropyge flavicauda   Trinco, Sri Lanka

Tiger angelfish

Length: up to 20 cm.
Distribution: only known from
Kosi Bay to Aliwal Shoal in the
Durban area, South Africa.
Depth: 10 - 30 m.
General: this angelfish species
is easily recognised by its tiger-
like colour pattern. It was dis-
covered only recently (1984),
named after its discoverer
Dennis King from South
Africa, and seems to be more
abundant than previously
thought.

Apolemichthys kingi   Sodwana Bay, South Africa

Threespot angelfish

Length: up to 20 cm.
Distribution: entire area.
Depth: 3 - 40 m.
General: found on outer reef
slopes and clear lagoon reefs.
Prefers areas of high vertical
relief. Feeds mainly on sponges
and tunicates. Adults form
small aggregations where common. Small photo below: a
courting pair; at bottom: juvenile with extra black spot.

Apolemichthys trimaculatus   Beau Vallon, Seychelles

Indian smoke-angelfish

Le: up to 15 cm. Di: Mauritius,
Maldives, Sri Lanka, East coast
of India. De: 10 - 25 m. Ge:
prefers coral-rich areas, but
also in rocky areas, e.g. at the
West coast of Sri Lanka. Seen
swimming upside down in
caves. Lives singly or in pairs.
Small photo below: juvenile.

Apolemichthys xanthurus   Ari Atoll, Maldives

Vermiculate angelfish

Length: up to 18 cm.
Distribution: a West Pacific
species, in our area only
known from the Indian Ocean
coast of Sumatra.
Depth: 6 - 30 m.
General: inhabits coastal reefs
and lagoons, encountered in
areas of rich coral growth.
Adults almost always live in
pairs, swimming close together.
Small juveniles live singly and
secretively among corals.

Chaetodontoplus mesoleucus   Mentawai Islands, Sumatra

Lyretail angelfish

Length: up to 20 cm.
Distribution: South Africa to
Maldives, also in Red Sea.
Depth: 15 - 70 m. General: the
species occurs on coral-rich
fringe reefs as well as on steep
drop-offs, where it feeds on
zooplankton. Large photo:
male; small photo: female.

Genicanthus caudovittatus   KwaZulu-Natal

Emperor angelfish

Le: up to 40 cm. Di: entire area incl. RS. De: 3 - 70 m. Ge: adults near ledges and caves in areas of rich coral growth in clear lagoons, channels, and seaward reefs; singly or in pairs. The juvenile (below) has a very different colour pattern and lives singly and secretively.

Pomacanthus imperator   **Ari Atoll, Maldives**

Trapeze angelfish

Length: up to 46 cm.
Distribution: South Africa to Mozambique. Any literature record from north of this area is incorrect.
Depth: 5 - 30 m.
General: this species is a unique member of the genus regarding its appearance (drab coloration, deep body) and behaviour: adults (photo right) occur on rocky shores and coral reefs, and often congregate in loose groups above the reef or even near the surface to feed on plankton in open water (bottom large photo). Juveniles (small photo below) and are found solitarily in intertidal rock pools. They have a totally different colour pattern with dark background and slightly curved vertical, pale blue and white bars on the sides; they are very similar to the juveniles of *Pomacanthus annularis* (see p.137), which does not occur at the African coast.

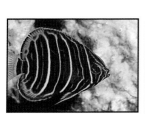

Pomacanthus rhomboides   **all photos: KwaZulu-Natal**

Pomacanthus chrysurus   KwaZulu-Natal

African angelfish

Length: up to 33 cm.
Distribution: East Africa, Seychelles, Comoros, Madagascar.
Depth: 1 - 25 m.
General: this uncommon
species occurs in shallow reefs
with rich coral growth. The
top large photo shows the
adult, the second small photo
the juvenile. The centre large
photo shows a hybrid between
P. chrysurus and the **Arabian
angelfish** *Pomacanthus maculosus;* an adult of the latter
species, which is distributed
from all around the Arabian
Peninsula to Kenya, is shown in
the small photo immediately
below. Hybridisation occurs, if
a solitary, rare species mates
with a related species because
it cannot find a partner of its
own species. This is often the
case at distribution boundaries.

Pomacanthus hybrid   Kilifi, Kenya

Koran angelfish

Le: up to 40 cm. Di: entire
area, common at Seychelles.
De: 3 - 30 m. Ge: adults occur
in coastal reefs with a rich
coral growth. Generally solitary. Feeds on sponges, tunicates, and seaweeds. The small
photo below from the Sey-
chelles shows a juvenile.

Pomacanthus semicirculatus   Beau Vallon, Seychelles

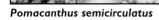

Blue-faced angelfish

Le: up to 40 cm. Di: Maldives, India, Sri Lanka eastward. De: 5 - 45 m. Ge: in areas of rich coral growth in lagoons, channels, and on outer reef slopes, also in caves. Adults solitary or in pairs, juveniles on shallow reefs. Below: an unusual specimen lacking the dorsal fin spot.

Pomacanthus xanthometopon   Lhaviyani Atoll, Maldives

Ring angelfish

Le: up to 45 cm. Di: India, Sri Lanka to Thailand. Records from Africa are erroneous. De: 5 - 35 m. Ge: prefers murky habitats. Feeds on zooplankton, sponges, tunicates. Adults in pairs in depths of 20 m or more. Small photo below: the author's first underwater photo with a lent camera (1974).

Pomacanthus annularis   Dickwella, Sri Lanka

Royal angelfish

Le: up to 25 cm. Di: entire area. De: 1 - 48 m. Ge: an unmistakeable species found singly, in pairs, or uncommonly in small groups in areas of rich coral growth on seaward reefs, also in the vicinity of caves. Small photo: juvenile with distinctive white-edged ocellus.

Pygoplites diacanthus   Pemba, Tanzania

137

Longfin bannerfish

Length: up to 25 cm.
Distribution: entire area.
Depth: 2 - 75 m, usually
below 10 m.
General: this species is
encountered in lagoons and on
outer reef slopes. In protected
areas it also inhabits shallower
water. The elongated fourth
dorsal fin spine is characteristic for most genus members,
but is especially long in this
species. Adults occur singly, in
pairs or rarely in small groups.
They almost always swim close
to the reef. The species' main
diet is plankton, but benthic
invertebrates are also taken as
food. Juveniles are solitary and
have been observed removing
ectoparasites from other fishes, hence they have to be
added to the list of cleaner fish
species. In contrast to *H.
diphreutes*, *H. acuminatus* has a
rounded anal fin.

Heniochus acuminatus   **Similan Islands, Thailand**

Schooling bannerfish

Length: up to 18 cm.
Distribution: entire area
including Red Sea, but absent
from the more remote oceanic
islands.
Depth: 1 - 210 m, usually
below 15 m.
General: the species is found
in sometimes large aggregations in the water column high
above the reef tops, feeding on
zooplankton. Juveniles live
much more bottom-oriented
in the vicinity of reef patches,
while adults spend all of the
day in open water, where they
are protected by swimming in
a school. Territorial schools of
up to 1,000 specimens have
been observed.
    The photo on the facing page
from the Similan Islands, Thailand, shows a small group
swimming between whip corals
in a depth of 25 metres, where
the bannerfishes display their
own "whips."

Heniochus diphreutes   **Male Atoll, Maldives**

BUTTERFLYFISHES

CHAETODONTIDAE

Heniochus monoceros Ari Atoll, Maldives

Masked bannerfish

Le: up to 23 cm. Di: entire area. De: 2 - 25 m. Ge: encountered in pairs or small schools in lagoons and seaward reefs with rich coral growth. Occasionally found in dead areas of the reef. Juveniles are solitary. Paired adults are often found under table corals.

Heniochus pleurotaenia Lhaviyani Atoll, Maldives

Phantom bannerfish

Le: up to 19 cm. Di: Maldives, Sri Lanka eastward. De: 1 - 25 m. Ge: in pairs or groups of up to 25 individuals. Two horn-like bony projections above eyes, hump on nape (see below). Aggressive behaviour: push each other out of a territory forehead against forehead.

Hemitaurichthys zoster Ari Atoll, Maldives

Black pyramid butterflyfish

Le: up to 16 cm. Di: entire area, absent from Southeast Indian Ocean. De: 1 - 35 m. Ge: in large aggregations above edges of current-swept outer reef slopes. Feeds on plankton. The black and white pattern is clearly visible under water.

Big long-nose butterflyfish

Le: up to 22 cm. Di: East Africa to Thailand. De: 2 - 60 m. Ge: adults singly or in pairs on outer reefs with rich coral-growth. Picks prey from corals with its snout. Below: **Long-nose butterflyfish** *F. flavissimus,* 22 cm, most widely distributed family member.

Forcipiger longirostris   Male Atoll, Maldives

Saddleback butterflyfish

Le: up to 20 cm. Di: East Africa to Mascarenes, Chagos to Maldives, Sri Lanka, and Andaman Islands. De: 3 - 15 m. Ge: in pairs, but also in small aggregations of up to 20 individuals. Easily approached by snorkellers, as they hardly care about human intruders.

Chaetodon falcula   Comoros

Madagascar butterflyfish

Le: up to 14 cm. Di: southern Indian Ocean to Sri Lanka. De: 5 - 25 m. Ge: rocky and coral reefs, especially common on steep outer edges, also on man-made marine structures like piers, breakwaters, harbour wharfs. Feeds mainly on small crustaceans, also on algae.

Chaetodon madagaskariensis   Ari Atoll, Maldives

Chaetodon ornatissimus   Praslin, Seychelles

Ornate butterflyfish

Length: up to 20 cm. Distribution: Andaman Sea and tropical West Pacific. Depth: 1 - 40 m. General: almost always in pairs swimming over reef crests near drop-offs. Feeds on corals, nibbling at the polyps. Similar to *C. meyeri* (see opposite).

Yellowhead butterflyfish

Le: up to 20 cm. Di: East Africa to Chagos, Maldives, and Sri Lanka. De: 5 - 25 m. Ge: a true Indian Ocean species, seen singly or in pairs. Moves long distances over shallow lagoon reefs, uses channels and openings as shelter. Photo below: juvenile.

Chaetodon xanthocephalus   Gaafu Atoll, Maldives

Indian butterflyfish

Le: up to 14 cm. Di: mainly at the islands from East Africa to Cocos and Christmas Is. De: 22 - 78 m. Ge: thought to be a deep-dwelling species, but found by author in a cave at a depth of 22 m. The large photo is the first Maldives record (1979).

Chaetodon mitratus   Male Atoll, Maldives

Meyer's butterflyfish

Le: up to 18 cm. Di: entire area, not in Red Sea. De: 3 - 25 m. Ge: in areas of rich coral growth of clear lagoons and seaward reefs. Adults in pairs, more rarely in schools (right). Juveniles (below) use branching corals as shelter. Feeds exclusively on coral polyps.

Chaetodon meyeri   Des Roches, Seychelles

Red-tailed butterflyfish

Le: up to 16 cm. Di: Maldives to Thailand. De: 1 - 20 m. Ge: inhabits outer reef slopes and rocky shores, also found in coral-rich areas. Feeds mainly on coral polyps and polychaete worms. In pairs, also often in schools of up to 25 individuals (large photo). Not shy.

Chaetodon collare   Lhaviyani Atoll, Maldives

Raccoon butterflyfish

Le: up to 20 cm. Di: entire area. De: 1 - 25 m. Ge: juveniles live secretively in shallow areas on coastal reefs and in harbours, usually in 1 - 2 m depth. Adults are found in various habitats from coastal to outer reefs. They usually pair, but also school (large photo).

Chaetodon lunula   Trinco, Sri Lanka

143

Threadfin butterflyfish

Le: up to 18 cm. Di: entire area including Red Sea. De: 5 - 40 m. Ge: mainly singly or in pairs, rarely in small groups like shown here (Aldabra lagoon, left). Most common in areas of mixed sand, rubble, and coral on shallow reef flats and in lagoons.

Chaetodon auriga   **Aldabra, Seychelles**

Teardrop butterflyfish

Le: up to 23 cm. Di: eastern Indian Ocean to central Pacific. De: 5 - 25 m. Ge: in pairs or small groups (left) in shallow reef areas. Feeds on small crustaceans. Similar to *C. interruptus* (see below), but lacks most of the yellow on body. Large adults with bulbous snout.

Chaetodon unimaculatus   **Cocos Keeling Islands, West Australia**

Indian teardrop butterflyfish

Le: up to 20 cm. Di: East Africa to Andaman Sea; recently found off Similan Is., Thailand. De: 10 - 40 m. Ge: singly or in groups in lagoon and outer reefs, mainly in areas rich in soft and hard corals. Compare to sp. above.

Chaetodon interruptus   **Male Atoll, Maldives**

Zanzibar butterflyfish

Le: up to 14 cm. Di: East
Africa, Madagascar, Seychelles,
Mauritius, Chagos; numerous
off Tanzania. De: 3 - 40 m. Ge:
a small group was observed at
Aldabra eating sperm and eggs
of spawning stony corals. They
followed the rising spawn, and
continued to feed on it.

Chaetodon zanzibariensis   Comoros

Eclipse butterflyfish

Le: up to 18 cm. Di: entire
area. De: 5 - 30 m. Ge: singly
or in pairs in lagoons and outer reefs with rich coral
growth. Not common. Feeds
almost exclusively on coral
polyps. Juveniles often in shallower water among the
branches of stony corals.

Chaetodon bennetti   Beau Vallon, Seychelles

Butterflyfish species

Le: up to 15 cm. Di: Maldives,
Sri Lanka, Andaman Sea. De: 2
- 25 m. Ge: new for Indian
Ocean. Similar to **Blue-spot
butterflyfish** C. plebeius
(below, Abrolhos Is., WA), up
to 15 cm, Northwest Australia
to West Pacific, to at least
10 m in shallow reefs.

Chaetodon sp.   Similan Islands, Thailand

145

Spotted butterflyfish

Le: up to 12 cm. Di: entire area. De: 2 - 25 m. Ge: singly, in pairs or small groups on lagoon and slope reefs. Below: **Speckled butterflyfish** *C. citrinellus*, 13 cm, entire area, 1 - 36 m, on exposed reef flats, usually in pairs, feeds on coral polyps and filamentous algae.

Chaetodon guttatissimus   Negombo, Sri Lanka

Klein's butterflyfish

Le: up to 14 cm. Di: entire area, RS. De: 2 - 60 m. Ge: in coral and rocky reefs. Singly, in pairs or groups of up to 30 individuals. Prefers zooplankton, but feeds also on benthic invertebrates. Below: **Triangular butterflyfish** *C. triangulum*, 15 cm, Mad. to Andaman Sea.

Chaetodon kleini   Nosy Be, Madagascar

Rip butterflyfish

Le: up to 15 cm. Di: East Africa to Mascarenes, Chagos to Sri Lanka and Andaman Sea, not RS. De: 3 - 20 m. Ge: in coral-rich areas of lagoons and semi-protected seaward reefs. Adults usually in pairs, feed almost exclusively on coral polyps. Below: juvenile.

Chaetodon trifasciatus   Lhaviyani Atoll, Maldives

Pig-face butterflyfish

Le: up to 30 cm. Di: Chagos, India, Sri Lanka to Andaman Sea. De: 10 - 40 m. Ge: coastal and outer reef slopes with rich coral growth. Usually encountered in pairs. Feeds mainly on coral polyps and anemones. Similar to the largest of the butterflyfishes, *C. lineolatus* (see below). The distributional ranges of both species overlap and they are sometimes seen together on the same reef.

The large photo at the right nicely demonstrates that one can see a lot of reef fish species while snorkelling and not necessarily has to SCUBA-dive in order to study or simply enjoy the wealth of tropical coral reefs.

Chaetodon oxycephalus   Ari Atoll, Maldives

Lined butterflyfish

Length: up to 30 cm. Distribution: entire area including Red Sea. Depth: 5 - 35 m. General: this is the largest species of the genus. It inhabits lagoons and seaward reefs, and is mainly found in areas of rich coral-growth. Although it feeds primarily on coral polyps and small anemones, it also takes algae. Usually seen in pairs, also in groups of up to 15 individuals. Below: **Vagabond butterflyfish** *C. vagabundus*, up to 18 cm, entire area, not RS, 1 - 30 m, coastal inner and outer reefs, lagoons, coral-rich slopes. Usually swimming in pairs close to the substrate, grazing on small invertebrates and algae.

Chaetodon lineolatus   Surin Island, Thailand

147

Marley's butterflyfish

Length: up to 17 cm. Distribution: East to South Africa (from Delagoa Bay to around the Cape). Depth: 2 - 120 m. General: juveniles have two dorsal fin spots. A subtropical species and the only butterflyfish that occurs in both the Indian and Atlantic Oceans.

Chaetodon marleyi   **Sodwana Bay, South Africa**

Shadow butterflyfish

Le: up to 13 cm. Di: Kenya to South Africa, Madagascar, Mascarenes. De: 15 - 55 m. Ge: singly or in pairs near edges of shallow rocky reefs. Feeds on amphipods, worms, plankton. Below: **Somali butterflyfish** *C. leucopleura*, 18 cm, RS to Zanzibar, Aldabra, Sey., 7 - 75 m.

Chaetodon blackburni   **KwaZulu-Natal**

African butterflyfish

Le: up to 14 cm. Di: along the East African coast from Somalia to Natal, South Africa; also Mauritius and probably Madagascar. De: 40 - 200 m. Ge: regarded as deep water species. Small photo: juvenile photographed in a depth of 8 m (West coast of Mauritus).

Chaetodon dolosus   **Mauritius**

The Cocos-Keeling Islands are located 12° 12' South and 96° 56' East, along an imaginary line running across the Indian Ocean from West Australia to Sri Lanka. To the south there is an atoll comprising 25 small islands (South Keeling), of which only a few are inhabited. Thirty kilometres to the north lies the solitary, large island of North Keeling. In 1914 a German warship, the *Emden*, found its final resting place beneath the waves that still crash against this island's southern shore. The present author describes his memorable experience 75 years later, as the first German to dive down to the wreck of the *Emden*.

The small German cruiser *Emden*, Gentleman of War, was active in the Indian Ocean during September to November 1914.

There are not many islands in the Indian Ocean as isolated as the Cocos-Keeling group. One has to take a very close look at the map in order to spot these tiny dots in the midst of a watery expanse. Following its discovery by Captain William Keeling in 1609 and the turbulent and fluctuating history it went through thereafter, the Cocos-Keeling atoll now belongs to Australia, even though Perth is no less than 2,768 km away.

The small German cruiser *Emden* achieved some notoriety as a knightly privateer at the beginning of World War I, when it single-handedly challenged the British hegemony in the Indian Ocean. In November 1914, however, the *Emden* was drawn into a one-sided duel with the allied cruiser Sydney just off the shore of Cocos-Keeling. The superiorly armed Australian ship severely disabled the *Emden*, whereupon Commander Karl von Müller decided to run the burning ship aground on the reef before North Keeling. When a naval historian I got to know informed me that my great uncle, **Wilhelm Debelius**, had been one of the survivors of the *Emden*, my next diving destination was a decided matter: the Cocos-Keeling Islands.

The problem of getting there was quickly solved. In 1989, exactly 75 years after the *Emden*'s last sea battle, the Western Australian Museum (WAM) in Perth made plans to conduct some research in the area around Cocos-Keeling. Thanks to a friend of mine who is a respected ichthyologist, I received an invitation to come along. WAM had already chartered

Aerial view of Home Island, South Keeling, with a village of the Cocos-Malay-People.

KETIKA DARWIN MELAWAT DI PULU COCOS
WHEN DARWIN VISITED COCOS

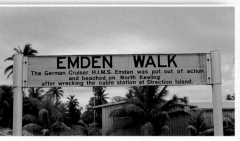

EMDEN WALK
The German Cruiser H.I.M.S. Emden was put out of action
and beached on North Keeling
after wrecking the cable station at Direction Island.

Famous visitors to Cocos-Keeling are honoured in the museum and with street names.

a ship months before the planned departure from Perth in order to have scientific and diving equipment transported to South Keeling ahead of time. On our approach to West Island the visibility was hazy, but one could still make out the horseshoe shape of South Keeling and its shallow lagoon. North Keeling was still too far off to make a decent areal photograph of the *Emden's* final resting place. A warm tropical wind greeted us after the landing. As always happens whenever an airplane lands, the entire island population was on its feet to catch a glimpse of the new arrivals.

The Cocos-Malay-People have established an autonomous administration, the Cocos Islands Cooperative Society Ltd. Even though there had not been much tourism in the area until then, there were still a few simple bungalows available for guests. A well-stocked supermarket and regular meals on West Island made it easier for the scientists to concentrate on their work. After all, we were moving on historically momentous ground. Charles Darwin, on his way back to England on board the H.M.S. Beagle, stopped over here from April 1 to16, 1836. His classical theory concerning the formation of atolls matured right here and was subsequently published in 1842 in

his The Structure and Distribution of Coral Reefs. Here is an excerpt taken from Darwin's journal describing his impressions of the South Keeling Atoll: "The ocean throwing its waters over the broad reef appears an invincible, all-powerful enemy: yet we see it resisted, and even conquered, by means which at first seem most weak and inefficient."

Little had changed in all these years. Even though it rained almost every night, I was quite content helping the scientists of WAM collect materials from South Keeling's lagoon and outer reefs. But as the president of the Cocos Dive Club heard about my plans concerning the *Emden,* he dampened my spirits somewhat. Seven attempts had

The speedboats of the Cocos Diving Club on their way to North Keeling.

been made to dive the *Emden* since 1986, and all of them ended in failure. The main problem was the location of the wreck: in order to get to it from the inhabited South Keeling Atoll, one has to traverse 30 km of open water. An impossible endeavor if the weather conditions are not absolutely ideal for the small motorboats available. In addition, the wreck of the *Emden* lies precisely where the strongest breakers crash against North Keeling. This makes diving there a dangerous business. Not enough, one also has to obtain an official permit because the wreck of the *Emden* is classified as a historical memorial. Indeed, the sea battle between the Sydney and the *Emden* 75 years ago does mean a great deal to Australians. After all, it was the young nation's very first victory at sea! I was reminded of it daily, as my accommodation was located on the intersection of Sydney Highway and Emden Walk. There is also a small Malay museum on Home Island that dedicates an entire corner to the *Emden.*

The members of the WAM expedition to Cocos-Keeling had wisely chosen to undertake the journey in February of 1898 as the cyclone period from January until March usually guarantees the calmest waters for the entire year. We had been having fairly rough conditions as we worked along the reef, causing us to fall into bed in complete exhaustion each evening. All of us felt much better when the weather improved, especially after a colleague at the weather station predicted even better conditions for the weekend. After all, my purpose for being here was to photograph the wreck of the *Emden* and its finny occupants with the assistance of the local diving club.

Almost every member of the Cocos Diving Club was present on Friday evening. The president prepared a list of functional speedboats, checked the communications system and diving gear, and went over the following day's schedule with the active partici- pants. As our convoy of eight boats departed from West Island on Saturday morning the weather really couldn't have been any bet- ter. The boats gliding over the perfectly smooth surface of the South Keeling lagoon made an impressive sight. Out on the open sea, however, we soon lost con- tact with each other. It was com- forting to know that we still had radio contact. I quickly became aware of the fact that we were heading 30 km out into the open sea as waves continually crashed against the bow in spite of the fair weather and no land appeared in sight. The appropriate authorities in Canberra had finally radioed us

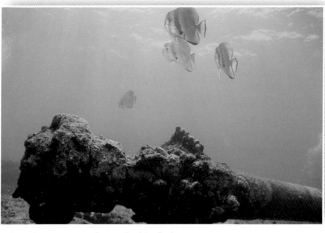

Batfishes lead the way to the wreck of the *Emden.*

permission to dive the wreck of the *Emden,* but the outcome of our project still depended entirely upon the surge. Karl von Müller had grounded the cruiser precisely where the strong winds permanently drive huge breakers towards North Keeling's southernmost beach. A number of sailors had drowned in the attempt to reach the safe- ty of the land just beyond the breakers. Even now, the surge was much too rough for safe diving. After all of the boats had arrived we held a quick parley. It was decided to wait and see what the noon tide would bring. We headed back out to the open sea and killed the time by throwing out a few lines. I was utterly amazed at the great number of wahoos, barracudas, or yellowtail tunas that seemingly leaped voluntarily into our boats after just a

few minutes. I continued to watch in fascination as the anglers pulled in more of these rare denizens of the deep and looked forward to meeting them underwater later. North Keeling rises several thou- sand metres from the bottom of the Indian Ocean, which entices myriads of pelagic deep-sea predators and even porpoises to chase after the smaller fishes and squids swimming along the shallower reefs.

There is not much left of the *Emden* to see on the surface anymore. Just one year after running aground, its main mast and gutted stern disappeared beneath the waves. But the bow managed to with- stand the storms and was gradually despoiled of all its precious metals by the British colonial rulers. Finally, in 1954, a cyclone dragged the last remains of the *Emden* under water.

Noon at last! With the president of the club as my buddy, my first destination is the ship's screw pro- pellers lying at a depth of 9 m. We encounter a strong surge along the smooth rocky bottom. When it pushes us out towards the deep, we hold fast; when it turns back towards the shore, we quickly paddle forward. The visibility is fairly clear. A group of batfishes lead us directly to the wreck. I can make out one of the two screw propellers and the large stern-post. There is still much more left of the *Emden* than I had hoped to find. A huge wheel, later identified as a capacitor from the auxiliary engine- room, makes a grand motif standing out against the surface. I wave my buddy over in order to get a con- trast in size. A little further off is a bulky high-pres- sure cylinder from the triple-expansion steam engine. A group of triggerfishes hover above it, oblivious to the powerful surge. My initial excite- ment has abated somewhat and I concentrate on

One of the two propellers of the *Emden.*

151

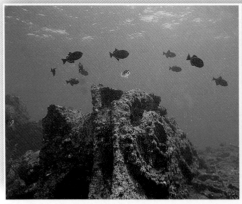

Trigger-, Bat-, Butterfly-, and Damselfishes in their new home, the artificial reef *Emden.*

the task of catching it all on film. My depth gauge shows a mere 4 m as the first breakers crash over our heads. I can hardly see my buddy through the churning bubbles, but then am able to make him out again as he proudly holds out the empty casing of a 10.5 cm shell he has just found. I take a picture. The next breaker hits us and I hang on to my camera as I get tumbled along the ground. As soon as the cloud of bubbles disperses and the visibility returns to normal, my buddy and I retreat from this inferno, away from the scraps of rusting metal that are still much tougher than any human body.

Back at the *Emden*'s propellers it is almost peaceful again. Close-ups are out of the question, however, as the continuous surge makes it impossible to focus. But I can still get a few interesting shots with the wide-angle lens: one of the cruiser's 10.5 cm cannons points towards the open sea, flanked by a solitary stone coral block. The lower blades of the ship's screw propellers were bent as it ran aground, but otherwise they seem to be in fairly good shape considering that they have not been serviced in 75 years. A duplex steam pump and a high-pressure cylinder are still clearly identifiable as well. As I catch my breath again, I even discover a pair of Abudefduf damsels that have just deposited their eggs on the artificial reef created by the *Emden* and are now frantically trying to protect the egg-carpet from hungry predators. There are not very many coral fishes around here, but quite a few goat-, trigger-, and surgeonfishes. Moorish idols and butterflyfishes also seem to feel quite at home in the protective environment provided by the remains of the *Emden*. A number of them are picking away at algae, while a group of batfish are busy ingesting plankton in the open water. The wreck of the *Emden* has become their home turf.

Other divers have joined us in the brief tidal lull and are now weathering the surge by hanging on to the screw propellers. Fortunately I have taken all the pictures that I needed, as my air supply is getting low. I have to swim the final 100 metres to the boat in open water because the bottom suddenly drops out from under me. Before I finish taking my first deep breath back on board, my buddy hands me an Australian beer with a big grin and then proceeds to congratulate me with the following words: "Now you are the first Teuton to visit the *Emden* after 75 years. Too bad we didn't meet up with your uncle down there." Australian humor....

The underwater photos have been taken exactly 75 years after the sea battle off Cocos-Keeling. Hence the age of sessile invertebrates settling on the wreck, like this *Pocillopora* coral, is easily determined.

Parapriacanthus ransonneti   Praslin, Seychelles

Yellow sweeper

Length: up to 10 cm.
Distribution: entire area including Red Sea.
Depth: 10 - 50 m.
General: a nocturnal species, forming huge dense schools that frequently fill large caves along drop-offs. The schools disperse at night into the open water to feed on zooplankton. There are light organs associated with the gut. The large photo on the previous page is from the Comoros. Specimens from the Red Sea and western Indian Ocean were formerly known as *P. guentheri*, which now is a junior synonym.

Pempheris oualensis   Beau Vallon, Seychelles

Copper sweeper

Length: up to 16 cm.
Distribution: entire area including Red Sea.
Depth: 1 - 36 m.
General: during the day found in clear coastal to outer reefs along drop-offs and slopes in small caves or under ledges. The species has a straight lateral line with a long curve at the origin. It is very similar to *P. vanicolensis* (see below) and found in the same habitats, but can be easily distinguished by a black spot at the base of the pectoral fin. Seen in the photo together with soldierfishes.

Pempheris vanicolensis   Mozambique

Cave sweeper

Length: up to 18 cm.
Distribution: entire area including Red Sea.
Depth: 3 - 40 m.
General: during the day schools of this species hover below ledges or in caves, more rarely small groups venture over patches of sand with scattered coral heads. At night the schools disperse on the reef in search for food. This species lacks the black spot on the pectoral fin base of the otherwise very similar *P. oualensis* (see above).

Stocky sand tilefish

Le: up to 12 cm. Di: Maldives
to Thailand. De: 30 - 70 m.
Ge: one of the mound-building
family members.
  Tilefishes are a small family
of 2 genera and 9 species, represented worldwide in tropical
waters. The majority of
species belongs to the genus
Hoplolatilus, which is confined
to tropical coral reefs. The
slender fishes are found on
sandy reef flats, either singly or
in pairs, swimming just above
the bottom and dashing over
short distances for a quick
stop to study the surroundings.

Hoplolatilus fronticinctus   Hin Daeng, Thailand

Pale tilefish

Length: up to 11 cm.
Distribution: South Africa,
Mascarenes eastward.
Depth: 30 - 115 m.
General: inhabits mud or rubble areas of outer reef slopes
at considerable depths. Some
individuals build a large mound
of rubble with a burrow, into
which they disappear in a dash
when threatened. Burrows are
made under rocks on sand or
rubble. Adults may build large
nesting sites, shifting enormous
quantities of substrate. The
species feeds on small zooplankton organisms.

Hoplolatilus cuniculus   Grande Baie, Mauritius

Flagtail blanquillo

Le: up to 30 cm. Di: entire
area, RS. De: 20 - 80 m. Ge:
benthic, in pairs in burrows,
often beneath ledges. Two
black stripes on caudal distinct
(juv. and adults). Below: **Blue
blanquillo** M. *latovittatus*,
45 cm, 10 - 70 m, feeds on
plankton high above ground.

Malacanthus brevirostris   Aldabra, Seychelles

Jawfish species 1

Length: up to 12 cm.
Distribution: known only from Similan Islands, Thailand.
Depth: about 25 m.
General: several specimens recorded, one with a *Palaemonella* shrimp.

Jawfishes are a family of small species, many of which are undescribed, comprising 3 genera and about 70 species. All live in tropical waters and have large eyes, placed high and forward on the head. The large mouth is used to incubate their eggs. The fishes build burrows, usually vertically in the sand, reinforced with small rocks or coral bits. Often they are found with just the head peeking out, watching for zooplankton food drifting by. Retreat to a burrow is tail-first. Some species live in colonies with burrows evenly distributed over a suitable area, usually rubble surrounded by coral reef. Stealing of building material is not uncommon. Centre large photo: pair at burrow. Small photo below: mouth-brooding jawfish, eggs visible inside mouth.

Opistognathus sp.   **all photos: Similan Islands, Thailand**

Jawfish species 2

Length: up to 16 cm.
Distribution: known only from the Maldives.
Depth: 12 m.
General: the photographer was lucky to get these superb shots after the male returned from visiting the female in a neighbouring burrow.

Opistognathus sp.   **Ari Atoll, Maldives**

Spotted hawkfish

Length: up to 10 cm.
Distribution: entire area
including Red Sea.
Depth: 1 - 40 m.
General: inhabits areas of rich
coral growth and the clear
water of lagoons, channels, or
seaward reefs from below the
surge zone to depths of at
least 40 m. It rests on, in, or
beneath hard or soft corals or
other reef growth as can be
seen in the photos.

Hawkfishes are a tropical
family, at present comprising 9
genera and 35 species, most of
which are distributed in the
Indo-Pacific region. Usually
they are perched on the thickened lower pectoral fin rays,
but often change position.

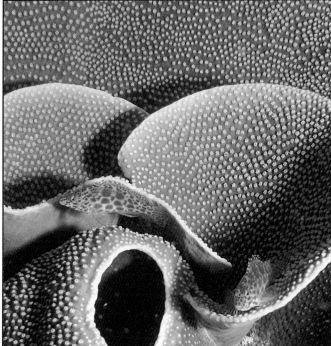

Cirrhitichthys oxycephalus   **Baa Atoll, Maldives**

Longnose hawkfish

Length: up to 13 cm.
Distribution: entire area
including Red Sea.
Depth: 5 - 70 m.
General: primarily a deep
water dweller on outer slopes,
mainly seen below 30 m, but in
some areas as shallow as 5 m,
where sponges or gorgonians
grow, which they seem to
associate with and use as lookout (see photos). The species
feeds on small benthic and
planktonic crustaceans. Its eggs
are demersal, which means
they sink to the bottom.

Oxycirrhites typus   **Gaafu Atoll, Maldives**

157

Cirrhitichthys falco   Male Atoll, Maldives

Dwarf hawkfish

Length: up to 7 cm.
Distribution: Maldives,
Sri Lanka and eastward.
Depth: 2 - 46 m.
General: inhabits coral-rich
seaward reefs. It typically rests
at the bases of coral heads on
hard bottoms rather than in or
on them.

Paracirrhites arcatus   Praslin, Seychelles

Monocle hawkfish

Le: up to 14 cm.
Di: East Africa to Maldives
and Sri Lanka. De: 1 - 33 m.
Ge: inhabits heads of small
branching corals; it usually
perches on the outermost
branches of diverse stony
corals. Feeds on crustaceans.
Coloration variable (photos).

Forster's hawkfish

Le: up to 22 cm. Di: entire
area including Red Sea. De: 1 -
40 m. Ge: feeds on small fishes
that are caught darting off a
branched coral watch post
(see photos).

Paracirrhites forsteri   Beau Vallon, Seychelles

Blackspotted hawkfish

Length: up to 29 cm.
Distribution: Cocos and
Christmas Islands eastward.
Depth: 1 - 18 m.
General: the uncommon
species is found reched on
corals or rocks in exposed
seaward reefs. It is absent
from most large continental
islands in its range of distribution. There are two colour
morphs: one is shown in the
photo, the other has an overall
dark background retaining the
black spots of the shown form,
but the white lateral stripe is
reduced to a spot below the
posterior part of spiny dorsal.

Paracirrhites hemistictus   Christmas Island

Stocky hawkfish

Length: up to 28 cm.
Distribution: entire area
including Red Sea.
Depth: 0.3 - 3 m.
General: the species is found
on rocky shorelines and reef
fronts exposed to surge. It primarily feeds on crabs, but also
takes small fishes, shrimps, sea
urchins, and brittle stars.

Cirrhitus pinnulatus   Similan Islands, Thailand

Swallowtail hawkfish

Length: up to 15 cm.
Distribution: entire area, not
in Red Sea.
Depth: 10 - 132 m.
General: this is the only
species of the family that does
not perch on hard substrates,
but hovers in the open water
column to feed on zooplankton, including crustaceans and
fish larvae. It is easily distinguished from other family
members by its elongated caudal fin tips.

Cyprinocirrhites polyactis   Mauritius

Skunk anemonefish

Beau Vallon, Seychelles

Length: up to 11 cm.
Distribution: East Africa,
Madagascar, Seychelles, to
India and Andaman Sea.
Depth: 1 - 25 m.
General: inhabits outer reef
slopes. Associated with the
anemone *Heteractis magnifica*
(see photos). With a relatively
narrow white stripe from the
top of the head to the beginning of the dorsal fin, and continuing along the base of the
fin along its entire length.

Damselfishes are a very large
family, with many species and
individuals particularly in tropical coral reef habitats. Some
species occur in such great
numbers that they are probably the most numerous fishes
in those areas. An estimated
300 species are distributed
worldwide in tropical and subtropical waters. The species
included here belong to three
subfamilies: Amphiprioninae,
the anemonefishes; Chromini-
nae, the pullers; and Pomacentrinae, the demoiselles. Most
genera are distinct in shape
and other characters, but
within a genus many species
are similar and show geograph-
ical variations. Juveniles are
often very different from the
adults, while differences
between sexes are small and
colour changes commonly
occur only during the spawning
period.

Amphiprion akallopisos   Praslin, Seychelles

Maldives anemonefish

Length: up to 11 cm.
Distribution: Maldives to
Sri Lanka.
Depth: 2 - 25 m.
General: lives in pairs or family
groups (see photos left and on
facing page) exclusively in the
anemone *Heteractis magnifica*.
Found in lagoon and outer
reefs.

Amphiprion nigripes   Male Atoll, Maldives

AMPHIPRIONINAE - POMACENTRIDAE

Amphiprion allardi   Pemba, Tanzania

Allard's anemonefish

Length: up to 12 cm.
Distribution: East African coast from Durban to Kenya (where common).
Depth: 1 - 30 m.
General: occurs in lagoon reefs and on outer reef slopes. Associated with the anemones *Entacmaea quadricolor, Heteractis aurora,* and *Stichodactyla mertensii.*

Clark's anemonefish

Length: up to 10 cm.
Distribution: Maldives, Chagos, Sri Lanka, Thailand.
Depth: 1 - 55 m.
General: usually black with variable amount of orange on head, ventral parts, and fins (compare photos); three white bars on head, body and base of caudal fin, but widely distributed with different colour morphs. Not host-specific: associated with at least 10 anemone species, e.g. *Cryptodendrum adhesivum, Entacmaea quadricolor, Heteractis aurora, H. crispa, Stichodactyla gigantea, S. haddoni,* and *S. mertensii.*

    The small photo below from the Maldives shows a parent animal guarding the eggs, which are glued to hard substrate in the immediate vicinity of the host anemone. They are visible as oval, transparent, reddish bulbs to the left of the fish.

Amphiprion clarkii   all photos: Ari Atoll, Maldives

Seychelles anemonefish

Length: up to 11 cm.
Distribution: Seychelles including Aldabra.
Depth: 5 - 30 m.
General: this anemonefish species is encountered in lagoon and outer reefs, particularly in patch reefs. It is associated exclusively with the anemone *Stichodactyla mertensii*. Occasionally it is found living together with *A. akallopisos* in the same anemone.

Amphiprion fuscocaudatus   Praslin, Seychelles

Mauritius anemonefish

Length: up to 12 cm.
Distribution: Mauritus, Réunion.
Depth: 5 - 40 m.
General: associated with the anemones *Heteractis aurora, Stichodactylus haddoni,* and *S. mertensii,* also with *Macrodactyla doreensis*.

Amphiprion chrysogaster   Grande Baie, Mauritius

Northern Indian anemonefish

Length: up to 12 cm.
Distribution: Maldives, India to Andaman Sea.
Depth: 2 - 25 m.
General: an uncommon species of anemonefish, which occurs in pairs in lagoons and coastal reef areas. It is associated with only one species of anemone, *Stichodactyla haddoni*, as far as is known at present.

Amphiprion sebae   **Negombo, Sri Lanka**

Chagos anemonefish

Length: up to 11 cm.
Distribution: known only from the Chagos Islands.
Depth: 10 - 25 m.
General: this anemonefish species is encountered mainly on outer reef slopes, but sometimes it is also found on lagoon reefs and reef tops. The species of host anemone is not yet known.

Amphiprion chagosensis   **Chagos Islands**

Anemonefish species

Length: up to 10 cm.
Distribution: only known from Chagos Islands.
Depth: 5 - 20 m.
General: similar to *A. bicinctus* from the Red Sea in body shape and coloration, but this species is much more brightly yellow than its well-known relative. Further specimens and records are needed to correctly define the status of this species.

Amphiprion sp.   **Chagos Islands**

164

ANEMONEFISHES

Tomato anemonefish

Le: up to 12 cm. Di: Andaman Sea. De: 3 - 15 m. Ge: associated with the anemones *Entacmaea quadricolor* and *Heteractis crispa*. Juveniles have a white head band. Usually in pairs, but a single individual was observed moving over a wide area between unoccupied anemones.

Amphiprion ephippium   Similan Islands, Thailand

Western clownfish

Length: up to 8 cm. Distribution: eastern Indian Ocean: Andaman Sea to Northwest Australia and eastward. Depth: 1 - 15 m. General: a common species in its area of distribution, usually found in pairs or small groups in protected coastal and lagoon reefs. Associates with the host anemones *Heteractis magnifica, Stichodactyla gigantea,* and *S. mertensii*. Melanistic (entirely black) populations are known.

Amphiprion ocellaris   Richelieu Rock, Thailand

Indian Ocean spinecheek

Le: up to 14 cm. Di: only Indian Ocean coast of Sumatra and Java. De: 3 - 15 m. Ge: only with *E. quadricolor*. Large photo male. Distinct spine crosses head band (see female below).

Premnas epigrammata   Mentawai Islands, Sumatra

165

Humbug damsel

Le: up to 8 cm. Di: entire area including Red Sea. De: 1 - 20 m. Ge: the most abundant fish of shallow lagoons and subtidal reef flats. The species occurs in large aggregations above *Acropora* corals, or in smaller groups on isolated coral heads.

First small photo below: **Three-spot damsel** *D. trimaculatus,* up to 8 cm, entire area incl. RS, 1 - 50 m. Juvs. often in large numbers associated with anemones, sometimes sharing them with anemonefishes. Found from shallow reef tops to remote coral heads on wide empty sand flats.

Second small photo below: **Two-bar damsel** *D. carneus,* 6 cm, East Africa to Andaman Sea, 5 - 35 m, on corals. Damsels feed on zooplankton and benthic invertebrates.

Dascyllus aruanus   **Lhaviyani Atoll, Maldives**

Vanderbilt's puller

Length: up to 6 cm.
Distribution: entire area.
Depth: 2 - 20 m.
General: the species is usually encountered in small aggregations above prominent coral heads in exposed outer reefs.

Chromis vanderbilti   **Male Atoll, Maldives**

DAMSELFISHES

Bluegreen puller

Length: up to 9 cm.
Distribution: entire area
including Red Sea. Widespread
in the Indian Ocean.
Depth: 1 - 12 m.
General: this abundant species
often occurs in huge aggregations above thickets of branching corals in sheltered reef
areas. Schools of juveniles are
closely tied to smaller isolated
coral heads, in which they find
shelter.

Chromis viridis   Ari Atoll, Maldives

Ternate puller

Length: up to 10 cm.
Distribution: entire area.
Depth: 2 - 36 m.
General: the species is
encountered in aggregations
above branching corals at the
upper margins of clear lagoon
and outer reefs.

Chromis ternatensis   Beau Vallon, Seychelles

Bicolor puller

Length: up to 9 cm.
Distribution: entire area
including Red Sea.
Depth: 1 - 36 m. General: a
very common species. Inhabits
coastal and off-shore coral
reefs. Often seen in large
schools over reef flats. It feeds
primarily on zooplankton.

Chromis dimidiata   Beau Vallon, Seychelles

167

Abudefduf sexfasciatus   Praslin, Seychelles

Scissortail sergeant

Length: up to 14 cm.
Distribution: entire area
including Red Sea.
Depth: 1 - 15 m.
General: often encountered in
schools in the coral rich areas
of shallow reefs, from rocky lagoons to outer reefs. The
widespread and common
species often aggregates high
in the water column to feed
on zooplankton; to a lesser
amount it also feeds on benthic algae.

Abudefduf vaigensis   Mahe, Seychelles

Sergeant major

Le: up to 17 cm. Di: entire
area, RS. De: 1 - 12 m. Ge: like
other, similar species often
seen in schools in the coral
rich areas of reefs. Below:
Pearl sergeant A. *margariteus*,
up to 16 cm, Mascarenes, 2 -
10 m, feeds on zooplankton,
algae, and small invertebrates.

Abudefduf notatus   Beau Vallon, Seychelles

Yellow-tail sergeant

Length: up to 17 cm.
Distribution: East Africa, Seychelles, Maldives, Sri Lanka.
Depth: 1 - 12 m.
General: the widely distributed
species occurs in small groups
or pairs in various shallow
coastal habitats from quiet
areas near freshwater run-offs
to fast current channels; it is
also schooling in deep water
and feeds on zooplankton and
benthic algae. The species
changes its coloration to pale
grey, when swimming away
from the substrate.

DAMSELFISHES

POMACENTRINAE - POMACENTRIDAE

Blue-yellow damsel

Le: up to 7 cm. Di: East Africa, Seychelles, Mascarenes, Chagos, Maldives. De: 1 - 10 m. Ge: the species occurs singly or in small groups over coral reefs and rubble patches at outer reef slopes. It feeds primarily on zooplankton and to a lesser extent on algae.

Pomacentrus caeruleus Astove, Seychelles

Blue-green damsel

Le: up to 11 cm. Di: entire area. De: 1 - 16 m. Ge: colour variable (pale green in Andaman Sea), male may have yellow pectorals. Below: **Lemon damsel** *P. sulfureus,* up to 9 cm, East Africa to Mauritius, 1 - 8 m, found in coastal fringing reefs, also in turbid areas.

Pomacentrus pavo Ari Atoll, Maldives

Dick's damsel

Le: up to 9 cm. Di: entire area. De: 1 - 12 m. Ge: in loose groups in coral-rich surge areas of clear lagoons and seaward reefs. Feeds on algae, small benthic invertebrates, and small fishes. Below: **Jewel damsel** *P. lacrymatus,* 8 cm, entire area incl. RS, 2 - 12 m.

Plectroglyphidodon dickii Beau Vallon, Seychelles

ALDABRA

The Aldabra Atoll is situated along the western extremes of the Seychelles Islands. There is no soil, no fresh water, no anchorage for larger ships to be found anywhere around here. Aldabra is not very hospitable, lacking as it does in just about all of the basic necessities of life. For centuries, its unproductiveness rendered it commercially valueless for seamen, fishermen, or settlers. No other island in the Indian Ocean has withstood human intervention as long as Aldabra. And this is exactly what makes Aldabra so unique. The author gives us his account of a living museum.

ALL PHOTOS: HELMUT DEBELIUS

Not very attractive for the Aldabra expedition: the dismal island Grande Terre, part of the Aldabra atoll ring, in the background.

My quest was a compliacted matter: how do I get to Aldabra within a limited time span? I found out that it is only possible to get there from Mahé because of diverse regulations and requirements. No less than 1,000 km of Indian Ocean separate Mahé from Aldabra, so that a voyage from the eastern coast of Africa would actually be much shorter. Connoisseurs of the Seychelles informed me about the availability of irregular charter trips, but also warned me about irresponsible skippers and unacceptable boats. Finally, in 1992, I located a dependable liveaboard, the *Fantasea II*.

The crossing from Mahé took us three days, just as we had calculated. As soon as we cast anchor just off the 40-km-long island of Grand Terre, the most extensive island of the Aldabra Atoll, the dinghy was cleared for a transfer to the beach. Sand dunes with a sparse covering of grass, jagged coral rocks, thorny bushes, and screw pines compose the wild scenery. Only a handful of coconut palms, otherwise so common in these latitudes, rise above the brush. This is sufficient for its present-day inhabitants. Besides the ten Seychellois who administrate the island, the island is populated by approximately 150,000 giant tortoises. This is a great deal more than can be found on the Galapagos Islands. At one time, these terrestrial animals that can weigh up to over 300 kg and live as long as humans also inhabited other islands in the Indian Ocean. But since they served seafarers as a welcome supply of fresh meat - the upturned tortoises were stacked in rows down in the hold - they soon disappeared in those parts. The same tenacity which had kept them alive for thou-

sands of years as they made the perilous journey across the ocean from Madagascar, eventually proved to be their pitfall. They could float over the waves in their carapaces like a nutshell, stretching out their long necks to catch a breath of fresh air. Undoubtedly many of them never reached land again. But a few managed to establish themselves on the coral islands of the Seychelles.

Aldabra and the surrounding islands are of volcanic origin. The name that reminds one of "A Thousand and One Nights" was

Western Indian Ocean fish pond (!).

bestowed by Arabic seafarers more than a thousand years ago. The Portugese arrived in the 16th century, followed by the French and British. Various attempts were made to settle Aldabra, the last one as recently as 1955. A new threat came in 1966, as Aldabra still belonged to the British Indian Ocean Territory. Plans to build a landing strip for British and American military forces were thwarted by worldwide protest. Particularly vehement opposition came from the British Royal Society and the American

Giant tortoises at the scientific station on the island Picard.

Smithsonian Institution, who immediately set up research stations there. In 1982 UNESCO classified the atoll as a world heritage site. Since then nothing may be modified in Aldabra, and the number of visitors allowed is strictly limited. Following the independence of the Seychelles in 1976, the Seychelles Island Foundation has taken over the responsibility for the maintenance of this unique ecological niche in 1979.

The giant tortoises at the scientific station on Picard are unusually large specimens as the station crew's leftovers provide them with an abundant source of nourishment. Here they can easily weigh up to 100 kg, while the skimpiest specimens at Grand Terre still average 22 kg. Other than 22 species of grass, they devour practically everything that gets tossed out of the barracks. They eliminate about half of what they consume undigested. But that too serves a purpose as land crabs, particularly the coconut crab *Birgus latro,* are constantly on the lookout for food on the barren coraline surface. Periodically, up to 150,000 giant tortoises *Dipsochelis gigantea* have lived in Aldabra. But the

The Potato groupers of the atoll can be aggressive.

islands could not provide them with a permanent source of nourishment. Shady bushes were also scarce. Wild goats imported by the settlers browsed too many of the bushes under which the giant tortoises were accustomed to seek shelter side-by-side from the burning noonday sun. They can easily perish from overheating. Large numbers of empty carapaces lying about are sad reminders of those who didn't make it. As carefully conducted studies have shown, this species of tortoise has adapted admirably to the scarcity of water in Aldabra: it can take up water through its nostrils as well as its mouth. This is especially effective, as it can insert its snout into shallow depressions on the ground to get at the moisture!

Aldabra rail, a flightless, endemic species of the atoll.

In the meantime, we divers had also learned to appreciate our ship. On the way over we were already deeply impressed by the effectivity of the satellite navigation system, which enabled the skipper to cast his anchor precisely over the remote shallow he had been steering towards. What a first dive in an unknown site! I had hardly dropped down to the bottom at 15 m, when a huge Potato grouper *E. tukula* of about 1.5 m in length shot at me with his mouth wide open as if I were an intruder into his realm. It really scared me for a moment because normally this species tends to be quite shy. I was to encounter this solitary predator, that is hardly found in the Maldives, for instance, on several occasions during my upcoming dives.

Between the islands of Picard and Polymnie there is a passage deep enough for the *Fantasea* to enter the Aldabra Lagoon. We anchor for the night and look for new diving sites on the outer reef the following morning. Skipper Eran is an experienced diver and shares our surprise as almost every dive turns out to be a winner. In other words, the masses of fish (sweetlips, snappers) and the numerous unknown species (dottybacks, fairy basslets,

Fixed on smallest fishes, one easily overlooks the hammerhead shark.

mackerels) found here leave us in perfect bliss.

Our bird watchers on board are just as happy. The maze of mangroves and coral heads provide sufficient well-protected nesting places, and unnatural enemies such as cats and rats are missing here altogether. Various species of terns and flamingos are found here. Whereas many of these birds can also be seen on other islands of the Indian Ocean, a few species can only be encountered here: the Dimorphic egret, the Madagascar ibis, and the Aldabra rail. My favorite is the nimble Aldabra fody, which frequents the cisterns in the ruins close to the station. A former church is still standing here, as well

Majestically an African angelfish swims through the Aldabra reef.

as few scattered boats belonging to the former inhabitants. But everything is rotting away in the tropical climate, for no one will ever settle here again. Animals have the priority.

Mula, a member of the crew, is a passionate angler and spends the entire day along the railing with hook and line in hand. I can hardly believe what he manages to pull out of the ocean with this primitive method. Groupers, jobfishes, mackerel, and small tunas are just part of his daily booty. Each catch is anounced beforehand as Mula proudly lets us know its name long before the angled fish is pulled to the surface.

My birthday is coming up. The skipper leaked out the information and in the morning of that memorable day Mula asks me what kind of fish I would like to have for my special

A sailfish is an adequate birthday present.

birthday menu. Jokingly, I tell him I would love to have some marlin. He then proceeds to attach something to his nylon line that I have not seen him use before and which looks suspiciously like the dummy of a squid. We anchor about one hundred metres off the shore. It is raining cats and dogs. I just don't feel like diving today and choose to watch a video in the saloon instead. Suddenly Mula calls out my name excitedly. His hands hurt because there must be an uncommonly strong fish on the other end of the line. I hold on to the nylon line as he wraps a towel around his fingers. What happens then has us hopping up and down the deck in glee: a sailfish shoots out of the water and tries to break free of the line. Mula is doing his thing now. With infinite patience he lets the line go, pulls it in again, and finally hoists the sailfish on board with his bare hands. Breathless, he stares at his catch and lets us know that this is the first time in 25 years that he has caught such a rare deep-sea fish, the little brother of the marlin. One question plagued me throughout that night. Why did the sailfish have to choose this very day to jump aboard? Can you answer me that?

The Aldabra lagoon at sunset. At the right a katamaran diving vessel.

Cheilinus fasciatus   Felidhoo Atoll, Maldives

Red-breasted splendour wrasse

Length: up to 38 cm.
Distribution: entire area including Red Sea.
Depth: 4 - 40 m.
General: this wrasse is common in lagoons and seaward reefs with mixed coral and rubble, where it feeds on benthic invertebrates.
The Labridae are a large family of at least 60 genera and about 500 species. They are divided into several subfamilies. The subfamily, to which the species on one page belong, is denoted in the family name bar on top of each page.

Cheilinus chlorourus   Male Atoll, Maldives

Floral splendour wrasse

Length: up to 45 cm.
Distribution: East Africa, Mascarenes, Chagos, Maldives (where common), Sri Lanka.
Depth: 2 - 30 m.
General: the species has a wide range of distribution in the entire area, it also ranges into the Pacific Ocean. This wrasse is common in areas of mixed sand, rubble and corals of lagoon reefs. It feeds on benthic invertebrates including molluscs, crustaceans, polychaetes, and sea urchins. Can be observed moving coral and rock fragments in search for its invertebrate prey.

Cheeklined splendour wrasse

Le: up to 30 cm. Di: entire are including Red Sea. Moderately common in the Maldives. De: 3 - 120 m. Ge: this wrasse is encountered solitarily in coral-rich areas of lagoons and seaward reefs. Large photo: male; small photo: female.

Oxycheilinus digrammus   Beau Vallon, Seychelles

Napoleonfish

Length: up to 200 cm.
Distribution: entire area
including Red Sea.
Depth: 0.5 - 60 m.
General: as shown in the large
photos this wrasse is the diver's favourite. Adults can be
recognised by the their large
size and the hump on the forehead (see top large photo;
length 120 cm). Juveniles can
be distinguished by a pair of
dark diagonal stripes crossing
the eye (large bottom photo;
length 30 cm). The napoleon-
fish is the largest and heaviest
(up to 150 kg) of all wrasses.
The species feeds mainly on
molluscs, which are crushed
with molariform teeth located
in the back of the mouth cavity. While large individuals easily get acquainted with divers
and even snorkellers, juveniles
below a length of 20 cm are
very secretive and hard to
photograph at all.
   Unfortunately, live Napoleon-
fish have been top ranking in
Asian seafood restaurants
(small photo immediately
below shows a suffering specimen at the Hong Kong fish
market). Today it has become
a rare, expensive (US $ 200
per kilo) speciality due to
overfishing. A dish made from
its thick lips (an aphrodisiac in
China!) is sold for even US $
300. The catching method
using sodium cyanide is grue-
some. When the dazzled fish
seeks shelter in the reef, its
catchers break all the corals
around it in order to get it
alive. A rope is strung through
mouth and gill openings and
the fish is dragged to the boat.

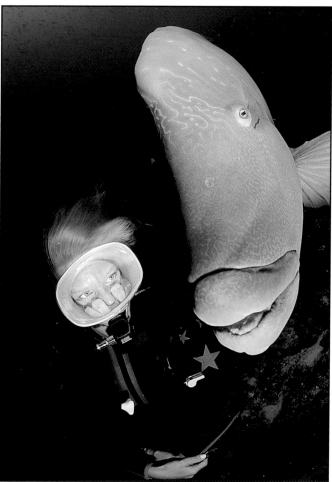

Ari Atoll, Maldives

Cheilinus undulatus   South Male Atoll, Maldives

175

Epibulus insidiator   Beau Vallon, Seychelles

Sling-jaw wrasse

Length: up to 38 cm.
Distribution: entire area
including Red Sea. Common in
the Maldives.
Depth: 4 - 40 m.
General: this wrasse species
lives solitarily in coral-rich
areas of lagoons and seaward
reefs. It can extend its mouth
to form a long tubular probe,
which serves to suck in coral-
dwelling shrimps, crabs, and
fishes. The photo is quite
unique, because it shows a
male (at the left) and a female
(at the right) together.

Xyrichtys pavo   Mauritius

Blue razor wrasse

Le: up to 40 cm. Di: entire
area incl. RS. De: 3 - 100 m.
Ge: over large expanses of fine
to coarse sand in lagoons and
seaward reefs. Very wary, dis-
appears extremely fast into the
sand. Large photo: juv. with
greatly elongated first dorsal
fin spine; small photo: adult.

Xyrichtys aneitensis   Ari Atoll, Maldives

White-blotch razor wrasse

Le: up to 20 cm. Di: entire
area. De: 2 - 40 m. Ge: common on sand flats and slopes,
often in groups, each specimen
with its own sand patch, where
it can hide by burying in the
substrate. Large photo: juvenile; small photo below: adult.

Rockmover wrasse

Le: up to 27 cm. Di: entire
area incl. RS. De: 2 - 40 m. Ge:
solitary on semi-exposed reef
flats. Relatively common in
areas of mixed sand and rubble. Feeds on benthic invertebrates, turns over rocks in
search of prey. Large photo:
juvenile; small photo: adult.

Novaculichthys taeniourus   Mulaku Atoll, Maldives

McCosker's dwarf wrasse

Length: up to 7 cm.
Distribution: entire area, an
Indian Ocean species. Pacific
siblings are markedly different
in coloration.
Depth: 25 - 50 m.
General: encountered in
groups over sandy areas covered with weed or rubble. Rises only a short distance from
the substrate, when feeding on
plankton. Males are haremic
with up to 10 females. The
photo shows one male with
several females of its harem.
Apart from coloration males
are readily identified by their
extended dorsal fin rays.

Paracheilinus mccoskeri   Male Atoll, Maldives

Eightline dwarf wrasse

Length: up to 12 cm.
Distribution: East Africa,
Mascarenes, Chagos, Maldives,
Sri Lanka.
Depth: 2 - 50 m.
General: this small wrasse
species lives secretively on
coral rubble bottoms and
among the branches of living
corals in clear outer reef habitats. In the Indian Ocean area
the species often has orange
spots. Like its congeners, it is
mainly feeding on small benthic
invertebrates.

Pseudocheilinus octotaenia   Astove, Seychelles

177

Saddleback hogfish

Le: up to 55 cm. Di: entire area, rare in the Maldives (probably deep). De: 8 - 108 m. Ge: mainly in outer reef habitats like offshore reefs and drop-offs. By day foraging in the reef, at night often hiding in a cave or crevice. Large photo: juvenile; small photo: adult.

Bodianus bilunulatus   **Mauritius**

Lyretail hogfish

Length: up to 21 cm. Distribution: entire area including Red Sea. Depth: 6 - 60 m. General: usually found below 25 m along steep outer reef slopes. Solitary, common. Small juveniles in black coral bushes (see large photo) and sponges. Small photo: adult.

Bodianus anthioides   **La Digue, Seychelles**

Diana's hogfish

Le: up to 25 cm. Di: entire area. Replaced by a sibling species from Bali eastward into Pacific. De: 6 - 30 m. Ge: in rocky and coral reef areas from the surf zone downward. Solitary, by day searching the reef for food. Large photo: juvenile; small photo: adult.

Bodianus diana   **Ari Atoll, Maldives**

Indian sand wrasse

Length: up to 50 cm.
Distribution: western Indian
Ocean including southern Red
Sea. Common in the Maldives
and Seychelles.
Depth: 2 - 30 m.
General: this wrasse occurs at
moderate depths, adults down
to about 30 m, in weedy or
rocky coral reef areas, often in
sand channels between reefs
with rubble-covered bottom.
The species feeds on diverse
benthic invertebrates that are
often caught after turning over
pieces of rubble, which are lift-
ed with the help of the snout.
Juveniles (top large photo;
4 cm) are found in shallow
rocky tide pools and on patches of sand. They are distinct
from very similar juveniles of
other wrasses (see next
species below) by a black spot
on the dorsal fin and the third
white saddle bar running all
the way down the side. The
female (centre large photo;
18 cm) lives solitary or in
small groups. The male (small
photo below; 35 cm) defends a
large territory against neighbouring males.

Aldabra, Seychelles

Coris frerei   Comoros

African sand wrasse

Le: up to 30 cm. Di: entire
area; range overlaps that of
Pacific sibling *C. gaimard* at
Christmas Is. De: 5 - 50 m.
Ge: juv. (large photo; 4 cm)
common in tide pools, adults
(photo below; 20 cm) shy and
solitary. The species has previously been called *Coris africana*.

Coris cuvieri   Shimoni, Kenya

179

Clown sand wrasse

Le: up to 60 cm. Di: entire area, RS. De: 5 - 40 m. Ge: on weedy rubble and sand areas adjacent to coral reefs. The adult male (small photo) develops a hump on the forehead and a ragged hind margin of the caudal fin. Juveniles (large photo) with distinct pattern.

Coris aygula   **Raa Atoll, Maldives**

Spottail sand wrasse

Le: up to 20 cm. Di: entire area, RS. De: 2 - 25 m. Ge: commonly found on protected lagoon reefs in areas of mixed sand, rubble, rocks and corals. Feeds primarily on hard-shelled benthic invertebrates. Large photo: juvenile; small photo: adult.

Coris caudimacula   **Grande Baie, Mauritius**

Twist's wrasse

Le: up to 18 cm. Di: entire area, RS, not common. Depth: 2 - 20 m. Ge: a wide-ranging species that is found in coral reefs. Feeds on benthic invertebrates. Photo: male. Below: **Lined wrasse** A. *lineatus*, 13 cm, 10 - 45 m, entire area, singly or in small groups.

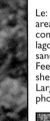

Anampses twistii   **Praslin, Seychelles**

Yellowtail wrasse

Length: up to 22 cm.
Distribution: entire area
including Red Sea.
Depth: 4 - 60 m.
General: it is a special delight
for the uw-photographer,
when the females of this
species gather in small, loose
groups in coral-rich areas, as
can be seen in the large photo
at the right. The yellow-tailed
females are constantly on the
move and stop only to take up
invertebrate prey from the
bottom. The dark coloured
male (small photo below) is
much rarer; it is mainly
encountered singly, but sometimes joins a group of females
and then its coloration bright-
ens in courtship display.

Anampses meleagrides   Beau Vallon, Seychelles

Six-barred wrasse

Le: up to 20 cm. Di: entire
area, not in Red Sea. De: I -
25 m. Ge: adults are encountered mainly singly as can be
seen in the large photo, which
was a lucky shot while practic-
ing split-image photography.
This wrasse tested the focus
of the camera, being only 5 cm
in front of the lens(!) The
species occurs in coastal reef
habitats as well as along outer
reefs near drop-offs and
lagoons, in shallow water,
sometimes intertidal. Juveniles
live secretively in habitats with
algae and seagrass, forming
small aggregations. Prior to
mating, adults are found in
moderate-sized loose aggregations, often with several males.

Thalassoma hardwicke   Ari Atoll, Maldives

Moon wrasse

Le: up to 25 cm. Di: entire area, RS. De: 1 - 25 m. Ge: often in harem groups over reefs. One of the most abundant labrids. Can be very inquisitive towards divers. Feeds on invertebrates, also on small fishes. Large photo: male; photo below: female.

Thalassoma lunare   **Hikkaduwa, Sri Lanka**

Two-tone wrasse

Le: up to 16 cm. Di: entire area. De: 0.5 - 15 m. Ge: inhabits shallow lagoon and seaward reefs. Feeds on plankton and benthic invertebrates. In the Maldives it has specialised in cleaning huge Manta rays. Large photo: male; small photo below: juvenile.

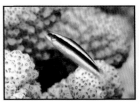

Thalassoma amblycephalum   **Ari Atoll, Maldives**

Blueback wrasse

Length: up to 20 cm.
Distribution: Mascarenes to South Africa.
Depth: 5 - 25 m.
General: this wrasse is found in groups on patch reefs. It is a swift swimmer like all its congeners. Large photo: male; small photo below: female.

Thalassoma genivittatum   **Mauritius**

Christmas wrasse

Length: up to 30 cm.
Distribution: entire area.
Depth: 2 - 25 m.
General: this colourful wrasse is mainly encountered in the surge zone of rocky and coral reefs. It is very shy and thus hard to photograph. Often misidentified as *T. purpureum,* females of both species are similar in coloration, but the head of male *T. trilobatum* has no stripes as can be seen in the photo. This species also lives deeper than its ever-moving sibling. Both are often mistaken for parrotfishes.

Thalassoma trilobatum   Sodwana Bay, South Africa

Goldbar wrasse

Length: up to 25 cm, common to 21 cm.
Distribution: East Africa to South Africa and Maldives.
Depth: 1 - 30 m.
General: the common species inhabits rocky and coral reefs, also shallow tide pools. It feeds primarily on hard-shelled benthic invertebrates and is not shy, often circling around divers. The photo depicts a male, females are lacking the prominent yellow bar.

Thalassoma hebraicum   Beau Vallon, Seychelles

Bird wrasse

Le: up to 30 cm. Di: entire area, RS. De: 2 - 30 m. Ge: mainly in coral-rich or rocky reef areas. Distinct by undulate way of swimming and elongated snout, which is used to probe branched corals for small crustaceans. Large photo: male; small photo: female.

Gomphosus caeruleus   Flic en Flac, Mauritius

![Halichoeres cosmetus](Lhaviyani Atoll, Maldives)

Halichoeres cosmetus   Lhaviyani Atoll, Maldives

Adorned wrasse

Le: up to 13 cm. Di: East Africa to Chagos and Maldives. De: 2 - 30 m. Ge: on coral and rocky reefs. Sleeps buried in the sand at night. Photo: male. Small photo below: **Vrolik's wrasse** *H. vrolikii,* 12 cm, Seychelles to Andaman Sea, 1 - 20 m, in small loose groups.

Halichoeres leucoxanthus   Male Atoll, Maldives

Indian canary wrasse

Le: up to 12 cm. Di: Maldives, Sri Lanka. De: 10 - 60 m. Ge: on seaward reefs, usually below 20 m. Coloration distinct. Follows goatfishes to pick up prey stirred up by them. Below: **Checkerboard wrasse** *H. hortulanus,* 27 cm, entire area, 1 - 30 m.

Halichoeres scapularis   Beau Vallon, Seychelles

Zigzag wrasse

Le: up to 20 cm. Di: entire area, RS. De: 1 - 50 m. Ge: usually in loose groups with a single large colourful male in lagoons near reefs or rocks. Follows goatfishes and emperors for food. Below: male of **Dusky wrasse** *H. marginatus,* 17 cm, entire area, 1 - 30 m.

Barred thicklip wrasse

Length: up to 50 cm.
Distribution: entire area
including Red Sea.
Depth: 1 - 18 m.
General: adults of this distinct
wrasse are found in loose
groups on shallow coral reef
crests, slopes, and in rubble
areas. Its coloration is variable
from green to black, always
with lighter vertical bars (at
least one as shown in the photo). During courtship the male
changes the coloration of its
head and then shows a horse
shoe-shaped mark on the
cheek. Juveniles secretive, small
ones among sea urchin spines.

Hemigymnus fasciatus   Beau Vallon, Seychelles

Vermiculate wrasse

Length: up to 13 cm.
Distribution: western Indian
Ocean including Red Sea, eastward to the Maldives and Mauritius.
Depth: 1 - 30 m.
General: this common but
beautifully coloured wrasse
inhabits lagoons with mixed
coral, rubble, and sand bottom, also semi-protected reefs
rich in invertebrates. It has
two pairs of large canine teeth
in the upper jaw. All phases
can be readily identified by
their distinct colorations:
males (bottom large photo)
maintain harems of females
(top large photo). Juveniles
(small photo below shows a
single small one) often feed
with females in groups.

Wrasses change sex during
their life. Most of them are
protogynous hermaphrodites,
which means that males initially develop as females. But
there also are "primary"
males, which were born thus,
in contrast to the "secondary"
males, which started life as
females and changed into
males later on.

Macropharyngodon bipartitus   all photos: Beau Vallon, Seychelles

185

Bicolor cleaner wrasse

Le: up to 14 cm. Di: entire area. De: 2 - 20 m. Ge: juveniles and subadults at cleaning stations along ledges. Adults well above the reef, they are the nomads among the cleaners, cover a large area actively "pursuing" customers. Left: adult; below: in a moray's gill.

Labroides bicolor   South Male Atoll, Maldives

Blackspot cleaner wrasse

Length: up to 8 cm.
Distribution: in our area found only at Christmas Island, eastern Indian Ocean. Otherwise distributed further eastward in the Pacific.
Depth: 2 - 28 m.
General: this small cleaner wrasse species is usually encountered in pairs in the clear water of outer reefs and in lagoons with a rich coral growth. It can be readily distinguished from other species of the genus by its coloration. There is a black spot at the base of the pectoral (name).

Labroides pectoralis   Christmas Island

Common cleaner wrasse

Le: up to 11 cm. Di: entire area incl. RS. De: 0.5 - 40 m. Ge: most abundant cleaner fish. A pattern of longitudinal stripes clearly identifies cleaner wrasses to host fishes. Small photo below shows it cleaning a *Paracanthurus hepatus*.

Labroides dimidiatus   Negombo, Sri Lanka

Humphead parrotfish

Le: up to 120 cm. Di: entire
area including RS. De: 1 -
30 m. Ge: the widespread parrotfish species inhabits singly
or in small groups reef flats
and drop-offs of fringing and
outer reefs. The largest of all
parrotfishes is shy, but easily
recognised by its large size and
the hump on the forehead
developing during growth. The
large photo nicely shows a distinct characteristic of many
parrotfishes: the front teeth of
both jaws are fused into dental
plates, which are used to
break coral (the plates resemble a parrot's beak, hence the
name). The pieces of coral are
ground to very fine material by
flat molariform teeth in the
mouth cavity. The breaking and
grinding of the hard stony
corals can clearly be heard
underwater. While passing the
gut, most organic material
(algae, coral tissue) is digested.
What leaves the fish at the
rear end is new coral sand.
Parrotfishes produce much of
the sand in reef areas. They
are sex (and colour) changers
like the related wrasses.

Bolbometopon muricatum   Praslin, Seychelles

Ragged-tail parrotfish

Le: up to 44 cm. Di: Sri Lanka.
De: 5 - 20 m. Ge: this bump-
headed parrotfish belongs to a
group of three very similar
species, and has been described
only very recently from Sri
Lanka. This species has not yet
been reported from other
locations. It is found on coastal
rocky and coral reefs, especially on deep rocky reefs. The
shy species lives solitarily and
feeds on algae, which are
scraped off the hard substrate.
It is very similar to *C. cyanescens* (see next page), but lacks
the yellow-green saddle on the
posterior half of the body.

Chlorurus rhakoura   Dickwella, Sri Lanka

Blue humphead parrotfish

Le: up to 50 cm. Di: Zanzibar to Natal, Mauritius, Madagascar. De: 8 - 30 m. Ge: not rare, range restricted. Below: **Rusty parrotfish** *Scarus ferrugineus*, 40 cm, entire area, 1 - 60 m, on coral slopes. Dental plates bluish-green. Juveniles are similar to females.

Chlorurus cyanescens   KwaZulu-Natal

Bullethead parrotfish

Length: up to 40 cm.
Distribution: entire area including Red Sea.
Depth: 1 - 25 m.
General: the common species inhabits open rubble areas on reef flats and reef slopes. Large photo: male; small photo below: female.

Scarus sordidus   Mauritius

Indian Parrotfish

Le: up to 70 cm. Di: East Africa, Mascarenes, Seychelles, Maldives, Chagos. De: 2 - 35 m. Ge: singly or in pairs in lagoons and on outer reefs, rarely in schools. Male (left) with yellow patch on cheek, head pattern variable. Small photo below shows female.

Scarus strongylocephalus   Ari Atoll, Maldives

Ember Parrotfish

Length: up to 66 cm.
Distribution: entire area.
Depth: 1 - 30 m.
General: this parrotfish species
inhabits lagoons and seaward
reefs. It is encountered singly,
in pairs, or in harem groups.
Juveniles have two somewhat
indistinct dark spots on the
outer posterior scales of the
caudal fin and a pale area in
front of the dorsal fin. They
live singly on shallow to deep
reef crests. Adults sometimes
mix with other parrotfish
species to feed in schools. The
splendid top large photo
depicts a group of females with
their male harem master. The
bottom large photo is a portrait of a male resting at the
entrance of a crevice behind a
soft coral. The small photo
below shows a large school of
females moving over a reef
slope.
   Like the related wrasses, parrotfishes are protogynous
hermaphrodites. After the in
many species distinctly
coloured juvenile phase they
develop into females (initial
phase), later into males (terminal phase) with a completely
different colour pattern, usually a mixture of brilliant contrasting colours, though blue
or green are often dominating.
Identification of the more drab
coloured females is sometimes
only possible by observing the
interaction with males.
   The parrotfish family comprises 9 genera, and an estimated 80 species, the majority
of which feed by scraping algae
off hard substrates. As these
fishes are abundant on coral
reefs, often feeding in densely
packed large schools, they are
an important component of
the reef community.

Similan Islands, Thailand

Scarus rubroviolaceus   Richelieu Rock, Thailand

Bluebarred parrotfish

Le: up to 75 cm. Di: entire area, RS. De: 1 - 70 m. Ge: common in various habitats, also deep, penetrating silty environments more readily than other parrotfishes. Dental plates pale pink. Photo: male. Below: *S. frenatus,* 47 cm, entire area, 2 - 25 m, alga eater.

Scarus ghobban   Similan Islands, Thailand

Bicolour parrotfish

Length: up to 90 cm.
Distribution: entire area including Red Sea.
Depth: 1 - 30 m.
General: a large species found in coral reefs and often seen in pairs. Territorial males maintain harems, but the females of a harem are usually widely distributed over the reef territory. This species is a nice example for a species of parrotfish exhibiting clearly defined phases each with a different and distinct coloration: the centre large photo shows a male, the bottom large photo two juveniles, the small photo below depicts the female.

Ari Atoll, Maldives

Spawning of parrotfishes usually occurs during dusk and most species group together in strategic places for the pelagic eggs to drift away with the currents to the open sea. Pelagic eggs mean wide distribution. After they have developed, the larvae hatch to join the zooplankton. The postlarvae settle in the reef habitat when about 12 - 15 mm long to become juveniles.

Cetoscarus bicolor   Beau Vallon, Seychelles

Pickhandle barracuda

Length: up to 140 cm.
Distribution: entire area
including Red Sea.
Depth: 1 - 33 m.
General: as can be seen in the
photos, this barracuda species
has a yellow caudal fin like
S. *flavicauda* (see next page),
but more pronounced vertical
dark bars. The shy diurnal
(active by day) species is seen
singly or in small schools.
   The larger barracuda species
may be quite curious and may
approach a diver closely, but in
clear water conditions and
unprovoked they are not dangerous at all, in spite of all the
tales of horror about the
impressive teeth of these
predatory fishes.

Sphyraena jello   Male Atoll, Maldives

Forster's barracuda

Length: up to 65 cm.
Distribution: entire area,
not Red Sea.
Depth: 2 - 300 m.
General: the species is mainly
encountered in schools at outer reefs and in lagoons. Large
adults are solitary. A dark base
of the pectoral fin is distinct.
Forster's barracuda also lacks
the vertical bars, which are so
typical for most other family
members. There are about 20
species in the family with a
worldwide distribution in tropical and warm seas. Little is
known of their reproduction,
but they seem to gather in
large migratory schools to
spawn at full moon.

Sphyraena forsteri   Gaafu Atoll, Maldives

Blackfin barracuda

Le: up to 130 cm. Di: entire area including RS. De: 10 - 90 m. Ge: one of the common barracudas in our area. Nocturnal, in large dense schools, distinct by approximately 20 vertical dark bands and the black margin of the caudal fin. Below: juvenile (15 cm).

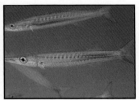

Sphyraena qenie   **Mauritius**

Great barracuda

Le: up to 190 cm. Di: entire area, RS. De: 3 - 100 m. Ge: juveniles occur in groups in mangrove and sheltered shallow inner reef areas. Solitary adults are distinct by the characteristic dark blotches on their arrow-shaped body. Small photo below: juvenile (30 cm).

Sphyraena barracuda   **Lhaviyani Atoll, Maldives**

Yellowtail barracuda

Length: up to 45 cm.
Distribution: entire area including Red Sea.
Depth: 5 - 70 m.
General: the relatively small Yellowtail barracuda occurs in schools over lagoons and seaward reefs. It can be identified by the overall yellowish colour, which is especially prominent on the caudal peduncle and the caudal fin (compare this photo to those of the also yellowish S. jello on the previous page).

Sphyraena flavicauda   **Cosmoledo, Seychelles**

Fringelip mullet

Le: up to 60 cm. Di: entire area, RS. De: 0.5 - 10 m. Ge: in schools of up to 100 individuals in shallow water. Feeds like all family members on detritus and algae scraped from the substrate with thick lips; while eating, sand gushes from the gill openings (below).

Crenimugil crenilabis   Praslin, Seychelles

Spotted sandperch

Le: up to 13 cm. Di: East Africa to Seychelles and Mauritius. De: 2 - 21 m. Ge: yellow-edged black spot on first dorsal. Below: **Belt sandperch** *P. signata,* up to 11 cm, Maldives, 12 - 35 m, has large ventral orange spots.

Parapercis punctulata   Mary Anne Island, Seychelles

Black-dotted sandperch

Le: up to 18 cm. Di: Maldives eastward into Pacific. De: 3 - 50 m. Ge: white spots on caudal and ventral. All family members lie motionless to ambush prey, which is sucked into the big mouth. Below: **Speckled sandperch** *P. hexophthalma,* 26 cm, entire area, RS, 2 - 22 m.

Parapercis millepunctata   Beau Vallon, Seychelles

SEX ON THE REEF

In the game of life there is one ultimate goal: to reproduce. To ensure reproduction we are equipped with a powerful urge for sex. This applies to every generation, and to every living creature. Sex is just as important to sea snails and sea squirts as it is to us. However, the creatures of the reef enjoy a diversity of sexual practices that put even the most enthusiastic human sexual activist in the shade. Among the common and seemingly innocent inhabitants of Indian Ocean reefs are hermaphrodites, transsexuals, monogamists, polygamists, orgiasts, harem masters and dominatrices. Anything goes, as long as it works!

FRED BAVENDAM

A staghorn coral colony, *Acropora* sp., releasing its eggs and sperm bundles during the annual mass spawning.

Fishes provide examples of many sexual possibilities. Among the parrotfishes, wrasses and groupers it is normal for young fish to develop first as females, and to change into males as they grow larger. In contrast, among the anemonefishes (Amphiprion) young fish develop first as males. The largest individual in an anemone will be a dominant female. Her presence inhibits the smaller males, and only after she dies is one of the males able to change into a female and grab the top spot.

Fish are able to move around relatively easily, so finding a mate is not normally a problem for them. However, for small and slow-moving invertebrates such as sea slugs and flatworms simply locating a prospective partner on the vastness of a coral reef can be a major headache. How they do so remains a mystery in many cases. In others it may be a case of finding a good dinner as a pre-

Also this large sponge releases its sex products into the water synchronously with others of its kind.

lude to sex. Many sea slugs have very specific diets, for example some feed only on particular types of sea squirt, others only on certain varieties of sponge. If a sea slug can find its food (in which a highly developed sense of 'smell' may play a role) then there is a

HELMUT DEBELIUS

After the female of the Maldives anemonefish *Amphiprion nigripes* has placed its eggs on hard substrate right next to their host anemone, the smaller male immediately fertilises them.

good chance that another member of its species will turn up as well. However, if two animals of the same gender turn up for the same meal, sex is a non-starter. To get around this problem, sea slugs are hermaphrodites, that is they have both male and female sexual organs. So whenever two sea slugs meet they are able to mate.

While sea slugs and the like have their problems, completely sessile organisms such as corals and sponges have even greater difficulties. They are stuck firmly in place, so they have absolutely no chance of cosying up to a prospective partner. For them the only option is to release their eggs or sperm into the water and hope that fertilisation will take place. To maximise the chance of this happening, all members of the same

A pair of Potato groupers *Epinephelus tukula* display intimate courtship behaviour.

species will spawn at the same time. This synchronous spawning is achieved by having a sophisticated internal calendar, which is set by natural cues. For example, on Ningaloo Reef in Western Australia, many species of hard corals spawn together in March each year. The corals are able to synchronise their spawning by developing their eggs and sperm as day light and sea temperature both decrease in the autumn. Spawning actually occurs at night, one week after the full moon. An exception to the general pattern of

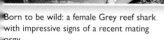

Born to be wild: a female Grey reef shark with impressive signs of a recent mating orgy.

broadcast spawning among sessile animals is found in the barnacles. These highly modified crustaceans carry out internal fertilisation. They usually live in dense aggregations, so it is not difficult for one barnacle to fertilise its neighbour, providing that its penis is long enough. Indeed, in terms of length relative to body size, the humble barnacle has the longest penis in the known universe!

The nudibranch sea slug *Nembrotha megalocera* has no problems finding a partner: whenever one of these hermaphrodites meets another, e.g. at a food source, they can mate.

HELMUT DEBELIUS

The female octopus retreats from the coral shelter, where it has been approached by the male. He follows her without hesitating...

Mating of octopus - the widespread species *Octopus cyanea* in this case - always is a complicated matter. At first, the uniform coloration of the female indicates that it is not interested in a partner at all. The male can be seen behind the female displaying its intentions by a warty and white-spotted skin surface.

Soon the pair find themselves together again near another coral umbrella. The male's prospects obviously have changed now: while the female holds still, the male extends one of its eight arms to thoroughly caress the beloved one. It is this arm that is modified into an intromittant organ to transfer a spermatophore into the female's body cavity. The specialised arm is called hectocotylus, and a feature of all cephalopod males.

HELMUT DEBELIUS

Finally the female responds to the courting of the male. Sexually aroused - indicated by colour and skin surface structure changes - it waits for the male to insert its magic arm.

Mission successful. "Let's go back into the shade of our octopusses' garden..."

Ecsenius midas   **Mentawai Islands, Sumatra**

Midas blenny

Le: up to 13 cm. Di: entire area, RS. De: 2 - 30 m. Ge: has colour variations, yellow to blue. Feeds on zooplankton, often together with Fairy basslets. See also previous page.
  Blennies are a large and complex family of mainly small species, comprising more than 50 genera and well over 300 species, most of which are distributed in tropical waters. Skin scaleless, slimy; dentition comb-like arrangement of tiny teeth in each jaw, with greatly enlarged canines in certain species. Various subfamilies, each with diverse tribes.

Ecsenius bicolor   **Lhaviyani Atoll, Maldives**

Two-colour blenny

Le: up to 11 cm. Di: Maldives eastward. De: 1 - 25 m. Ge: on rock or coral in clear water of outer reef crests and also in lagoons. Colour variation (not sex-related): dark top, white belly. Territories are defended with mocking fights.

Ecsenius lineatus   **Male Atoll, Maldives**

Lined blenny

Le: up to 10 cm. Di: Maldives eastward. De: 1 - 30 m. Ge: found in sheltered deep lagoons with isolated coral heads, always perching on top of corals or rocks. Coloration variable from very dark band-ed to the band broken up into a series of spots (see photos).

Eyespot blenny

Le: up to 5 cm. Di: Andaman Sea eastward. De: 1 - 5 m. Ge: on algae-covered rocks and rubble. Ocelli on back distinct. Most blennies are territorial and live in small holes in rocks or empty worm tubes and shells. Males attract gravid females to their home by dancing and displaying gayly coloured fins. Eggs are deposited inside, inseminated, and guarded by the male. A few weeks later the tiny transparent larvae (about 2 mm long) hatch, ascend to the surface, and are taken out to sea by the currents. Hatching is timed by the tides.

Ecsenius paroculus　　　　　Richelieu Rock, Thailand

Collar blenny

Le: up to 5 cm. Di: only known from the Maldives. De: 5 - 25 m. Ge: the shy endemic species is found on rubble or dead corals. It is identified by series of pale spots along the brownish body and a dark line on the gill cover (operculum). Eye often with star-like pattern.

Ecsenius minutus　　　　　South Male Atoll, Maldives

Earspot blenny

Length: up to 9 cm. Distribution: entire area, not in Red Sea. Depth: 1 - 20 m, often below 10 m. General: this blenny inhabits shallow outer reefs and perches on coral heads (seen in the photo on a *Millepora* fire coral). It defends a territory against conspecifics. Easily identified by a yellow-edged dark blue "earspot." The characteristic cirri above the eyes of blennies are forked (comblike, "eyelashes") in the species of *Cirripectes*.

Cirripectes auritus　　　　　Mozambique

Aspidontus taeniatus   **Flic en Flac, Mauritius**

Mimic sabretooth blenny

Le: up to 11 cm. Di: entire area, RS. Ge: some blennies mimic other fish species, including other blennies. The best known is this species that copies the cleaner wrasse *Labroides dimidiatus*. Sabretooth and fangblennies attack other fishes well above the substrate, where they feed on their prey's external parts (scales, fins, pieces of skin, mucus), approaching them by mimicking harmless species. Distinct from model by mouth not terminal, but subterminal. Rare photo of a group together.

Plagiotremus tapeinosoma   **Beau Vallon, Seychelles**

Scale-eating sabretooth blenny

Length: up to 14 cm. Di: entire area, Red Sea. De: 1 - 20 m. Ge: seen singly or in small numbers, often together with similar planktivores to attack larger fishes that swim by. Takes bites from fins, scales or mucus in "hit and run" fashion, and quickly retreats into the coral thicket, when chased by an angry victim. Attacks on divers and snorkellers have been reported. In this rare photo seen together with the **Bluestriped sabretooth blenny,** *P. rhinorhynchos,* up to 12 cm, entire area, 1 - 40 m.

Plagiotremus phenax   **Ari Atoll, Maldives**

Imposter sabretooth blenny

Le: up to 5 cm. Di: Maldives eastward. De: 5 - 25 m. Ge: in sheltered coral reefs. Closely resembles the venomous *Meiacanthus smithi* (next species), thus easily overlooked underwater. Best distinguished by lack of stripe starting on eye.

Smith's fangblenny

Length: up to 8 cm.
Distribution: Maldives
eastward.
Depth: 1 - 35 m.
General: in sheltered clear
water reef habitats with coarse
rubble and mixed algae and
coral growth. Also on soft
bottom with a rich growth of
sponges and other invertebrate fauna, and in caves and
crevices of coralline drop-offs.
This venomous species is mim-
icked by the non-venomous,
but scale- and fin-eating
Plagiotremus phenax (previous
species). Distinct by black
stripe that camouflages the eye.

Meiacanthus smithi   Nosy Be, Madagascar

Mozambique fangblenny

Length: up to 10 cm Distribution: East Africa to Madagascar.
Depth: 1 - 8 m. General:
inhabits rubble bottoms of
coral reefs. The species of
Meiacanthus are unique among
fishes by possessing a pair of
large grooved fangs in the lower jaw with associated venom
glands.
    See also photo of **Fraser's
fangblenny** *M. fraseri* on page
119, a relatively rare endemic
species of up to 11 cm in
length and found only in the
islands of St. Brandon that
belong to Mauritius.

Meiacanthus mossambicus   Mozambique

Blooddrop rockskipper

Le: up to 13 cm. Di: Maldives
eastward. De: 0.5 - 6 m. Ge:
this colourful blenny lives in
empty worm tubes on reef
flats and outer reef crests
exposed to surf, where it can
hide among stony corals. Feeds
on algae and tiny invertebrates.
Red dots and stripes distinct.

Istiblennnius chrysospilos   Raa Atoll, Maldives

201

Starry dragonet

Le: up to 6 cm. Di: entire area. De: 10 - 40 m. Ge: commonest species of the genus in our area. Its starry pattern is variable. Top large photo shows a male, centre photo a differently coloured female, the small photo below (Similan Islands, Thailand), shows another specimen, probably of this species.

Callionymidae are a large family comprising at least 9 genera and about 125 species, many small ones are living in tropical waters, some species are undescribed. All have broad spiny heads, a tough slimy skin without scales, which has a bad taste and a strong odour ("stinkfish"). The mouth is greatly protrusible, extending downward. All species are benthic, many are buried in sand most of the time, others are reef dwellers hugging the substrate and skipping over it with their fins. During spawning the pair rise slowly from the substrate, with ventral fins touching. Eggs and larvae are planktonic. Adults range from very shallow water to 400 m, depending on species.

Ari Atoll, Maldives

Synchiropus stellatus   Flic en Flac, Mauritius

Sawspine dragonet

Length: up to 12 cm.
Distribution: East Africa, Madagascar, Mascarenes, also southern Red Sea.
Depth: 1 - 10 m.
General: this dragonet inhabits tide pools and algae-covered rocks in shallow lagoon reefs. Its colour pattern is a good camouflage in the surrounding habitat. The first dorsal spine of males is prolonged like in all other dragonet species.

Diplogrammus infulatus   Grande Baie, Mauritius

Blotched partner goby

De: 10 - 20 m. Di: entire area, RS. Le: up to 11 cm. Ge: usually seen singly, also in pairs on coral rubble in reefs. Found living together with a pair of the White-saddle snapping shrimp *Alpheus ochrostriatus* in their burrow, but also seen with other grey or brown species. There are many such species pairs of partner gobies and shrimps. It is always the goby that selects a certain species of shrimp. It also takes over the part of the guardian as the goby's eyes are looking much farther over the sand as those of its almost blind partner.

Amblyeleotris periophthalmus   Hikkaduwa, Sri Lanka

Burgundy partner goby

De: 10 - 40 m. Di: entire area. Le: to 10 cm. Ge: photo shows the shrimp keeping contact to the goby via its antenna. Below: goby at end of large burrow.

Amblyeleotris wheeleri   Comoros

Pinkbar partner goby

Le: up to 11 cm. Di: entire area. De: 10 - 35 m. Ge: inhabits mixed sand and rubble bottoms. Always associated with the red-banded shrimp *Alpheus randalli*. Below: **Sidespot partner goby** *Cryptocentrus strigiliceps*, 10 cm, entire area, to about 10 m, with grey shrimps.

Amblyeleotris aurora   Similan Islands, Thailand

203

Cryptocentrus fasciatus   Myanmar

Black partner goby

Le: up to 10 cm. Di: entire
area. De: 10 - 30 m. Ge: on
open sand flats and slopes near
reefs, often in pairs together
with the Cute snapping shrimp
Alpheus bellulus. Left: yellow
form; below (Maldives): the
more common variant: dark
with white saddle blotches.

Luther's partner goby

Le: up to 11 cm. Di: East Africa,
RS. De: 10 - 28 m. Ge: with
Alpheus djiboutensis. The shrimp
continuously works in the burrow, using the front legs as
shovel. Sand is pushed in front
of the shrimp´s legs out of the
burrow, past the goby, to
which the shrimp keeps contact with at least one of its
antennae all the time. If anything approaches, the goby dis-
appears in the burrow at an
instant and with it the shrimp.
Only when the fish is back on
its watch - tail inside the burrow - does the busy engineer
resume its part of the work.

Cryptocentrus lutheri   Grande Baie, Mauritius

Sandy partner goby

Le: up to 7 cm. Di: entire area.
De: 4 - 25 m. Ge: with *A. djiboutensis*. Below: **Fan partner
goby** *Flabelligobius latruncu-
larius*, 10 cm, western Indian
Ocean, RS, 20 - 40 m, on sand
and rubble. First dorsal large,
developing filaments in males.
Often singly, with *A. randalli*.

Ctenogobiops feroculus   Ari Atoll, Maldives

Tall-fin partner goby

Length: up to 4.5 cm.
Distribution: western Indian
Ocean; rare, only recently
found at the Maldives.
Depth: 20 - 40 m. General:
this spectacular goby species is
found on sand and fine rubble.
It is readily identified by its tall
first dorsal fin, which is much
higher in males (photo), and
the dark body colour. Found
living together with at least
two species of partner shrimp,
the red-banded *Alpheus randalli*
(its claws are seen in the photo at the entrance of the burrow), and the less conspicuous
A. ochrostriatus.

Vanderhorstia prealta   Ari Atoll, Maldives

Black-ray partner goby

Le: up to 6 cm. Di: Andaman
Sea eastward. De: 8-40 m. Ge:
on sand flats and slopes with
rubble, current prone areas. In
pairs, hovering above burrow,
when feeding on zooplankton.
Below: **Dracula partner goby**
S. dracula, 7 cm, bands may be
red. Both spp. with *A. randalli.*

Stonogobiops nematodes   Similan Islands, Thailand

Inner-spot sand goby

Le: up to 6 cm. Di: W-Indian
Ocean. De: 2 - 15 m. Ge: adults
with extended ray in first dorsal. Below: **Longspine goby**
F. longispinus, 7 cm, 9 - 18 m. In
contrast to the previous spp.,
these two are sand gobies that
live without shrimps on sand
and are much less conspicuous.

Fusigobius inframaculatus   Chagos Islands

205

Gobiodon citrinus   Nosy Be, Madagascar

Lemon coral goby

Le: up to 6.5 cm. Di: entire area, RS. De: 5 - 25 m. Ge: yellow with thin blue lines, body stout compared to other species, unmistakeable by coloration and habitat: it is found exclusively in heads of branching *Acropora* corals. Common in lagoons, sometimes forming colonies. Like its congeners it produces a large amount of thick, sticky mucus that has a strong bitter taste and probably is used to deter possible predators. These two pages show secretive reef gobies; this group comprises the more colourful and the smallest spp.

Trimma haima   Chagos Islands

Chagos pygmy goby

Length: up to 2.5 cm.
Distribution: only known from the Chagos Islands.
Depth: 10 - 30 m.
General: in 1996 the photographer went with a British expedition to the Chagos Islands (see also Chagos, pp.92 - 94). Besides looking for new species, his aim was to also find the fish species, which have been recorded from this island group before during a different expedition in 1989.

Eviota guttata   Richelieu Rock, Thailand

Green pygmy goby

Le: up to 2.5 cm. Di: western Indian Ocean. De: 1 - 15 m. Ge: common in shallow water in diverse mixed rubble, coral, and algae reef habitats. Distinct by large red blotches and (underwater) a greenish sheen. Below: another colourful *Eviota* sp. from Thailand.

Sebree's pygmy goby

Le: up to 3 cm. Di: entire area, RS. De: 6 - 33 m. Ge: found in clear water of reef slopes and walls. Often seen perching on round coral heads, darting out to feed on zooplankton. A widespread and common goby. Below: a similar but distinct *Eviota* sp. from the Maldives.

Eviota sebreei   Ari Atoll, Maldives

Gorgonian goby

Le: up to 4 cm. Di: entire area. De: 5 - 53 m. Ge: genus members live and spawn on gorgonians, whip corals, and certain species of *Acropora, B. tigris* on *Antipathes dichotoma, Juncella fragilis,* and *J. juncea.* Below: **Hovering goby** *B. natans,* 2.5 cm, coloration distinct.

Bryaninops tigris   Raa Atoll, Maldives

Whip coral goby

Le: up to 3 cm. Di: entire area. De: 10 - 40 m. Ge: in pairs on the sea whip *Cirripathes anguinea* along current-swept dropoffs. Below: **Loki whip goby** *B. loki,* 3 cm, 3 - 30 m, common, on smooth whip corals, in pairs or small groups, depending on size of host.

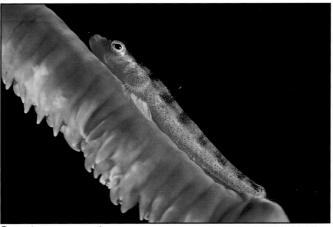

Bryaninops youngei   Gaafu Atoll, Maldives

Bluespotted sleeper goby

Le: up to 16 cm. Di: entire area. De: 3 - 25 m. Ge: on fine sand or silt in lagoons. In pairs, builds a burrow under rocks, sifts sand for food. Below: **Blacklined sleeper goby** V. helsdingeni, 20 cm, 1- 42 m, in pairs, burrows in sand. This page shows sleeper gobies.

Valenciennea sexguttata   **Lhaviyani Atoll, Maldives**

Blue-streak sleeper goby

Le: up to 18 cm. Di: entire area. De: 6 - 25 m. Ge: common, inhabits large patches of coarse sand in outer reefs. In pairs or small groups in burrows under rocks or rubble. Below: **Broad-barred sleeper goby** V. wardii, 12 cm, 10 - 30 m, distinct, but rare and shy.

Valenciennea strigata   **Trinco, Sri Lanka**

White-barred sleeper goby

Le: up to 10 cm. Di: entire area. De: 1 - 22 m. Ge: coloration highly variable, depending on habitat (reef slope, seagrass bed, lagoon, harbour). Below: **False sleeper goby** A. nocturnus, 10 cm, entire area, 1 - 30 m, stripes distinct.

Amblygobius semicinctus   **Chagos Islands**

Purple fire goby

Length: up to 9 cm.
Distribution: Mauritius and
Maldives eastward.
Depth: 27 - 70 m.
General: this beautifully
coloured dart goby is a deep
water species, which is mainly
encountered over rubble and
coral blocks as well as on
patches of sand or fine rubble.
It typically hovers within half a
meter off the bottom, facing
into the current to feed primarily on planktonic crustaceans, particularly copepods.
The species is very shy. The
top large photo shows the
Purple fire goby in an amazing
swimming position while feeding. The centre large photo
shows a pair swimming together as the species usually is
observed. The small photo
below has been shot in the
Maldives, where the species is
rare.

Similan Islands, Thailand

Nemateleotris decora   Surin Island, Thailand

Red fire goby

Le: up to 8 cm. Di: entire area,
not Red Sea. De: 6 - 61 m. Ge:
found over patches of sand,
rubble, or hard bottoms at the
bases of reefs. Hovers above
the bottom to feed on zooplankton, darts into a hole,
when alarmed. Adults in pairs,
juveniles in groups in crevices.

Nemateleotris magnifica   Praslin, Seychelles

Ptereleotris heteroptera   Grande Baie, Mauritius

Tail-spot dart goby

Length: up to 10 cm.
Distribution: entire area
including Red Sea.
Depth: 20 - 40 m.
Ge: usually found over sand
and rubble, well away from
reefs. Swims in pairs well
above the bottom, while feeding on zooplankton. Blue body
and black spot on tail are distinct.

The dart gobies are a family
of 12 genera and about 45
species, some of which were
formerly included in the Gobi-
idae. All are planktivores and
live in habitats with moderate
currents.

Ptereleotris microlepis   Male Atoll, Maldives

Green-eyed dart goby

Le: up to 12 cm. Di: entire
area. De: 1 - 10 m. Ge: in protected lagoons on fine sand.
Swims in pairs or small groups
well above the bottom. Below:
P. grammica melanota, 9 cm, only
known from the Mascarenes,
30 - 70 m.

Ptereleotris evides   Aldabra, Seychelles

Scissortail dart goby

Le: up to 14 cm. Di: entire
area, Red Sea. De: 2 - 15 m.
Ge: adults in pairs, juveniles in
groups. Tends to move away
slowly, when approached
rather than darting immediately into its hole. Hovers a few
metres above the ground to
feed on zooplankton.

Powder-blue surgeonfish

Length: up to 23 cm.
Distribution: entire area, rare in eastern Indian Ocean, not in Red Sea.
Depth: 1 - 30 m.
General: a typical surgeonfish species of the Indian Ocean area. It is found from inshore surge zones to offshore reef flats and slopes, often around rocky peaks breaking the surface. Juveniles may live singly, but adults are often seen in groups; especially near the oceanic islands they form enormous schools as can be seen in the large photos. Even snorkellers can enjoy the whirling blue fish in a depth of only one metre on most house reefs in the Maldives. The small photos below show the regular form and a hybrid with *A. nigricans* (see next page), respectively.

Surgeonfishes are a large circum-tropically family, comprising three subfamilies. The largest are the Acanthurinae, comprising 4 genera and about 50 species. They have a single fixed spine on each side of the caudal peduncle. This spine is not hinged, as erroneously reported in literature, but when used in defense or fighting, the tail is bent which makes the spine stick out. The Nasinae or Unicornfishes comprise about 15 species usually placed in a single genus, featuring one or two bony plates with spines on each side of the caudal peduncle. Some of the species develop horn-like protuberances on the forehead during growth.

Ari Atoll, Maldives

Acanthurus leucosternon   **Aldabra, Seychelles**

Velvet surgeonfish

Le: up to 20 cm. Di: eastern
Indian Ocean. De: 1 - 50 m.
Ge: in groups (large photo,
with a Powder-blue surgeonfish) in shallow surge zones
among large boulders and
along cliff faces with cracks
and ledges, also in outer reef
channels with strong currents.

Acanthurus nigricans   Christmas Island

Epaulette surgeonfish

Le: up to 40 cm. Di: entire
area. De: 2 - 35 m. Ge: singly,
also rarely in groups in clear
coastal reefs and deep lagoons,
grazing algae on rocks. Adults
distinct by dark line behind eye
and strongly lunate caudal.
Able to change coloration
rapidly from dark to light grey.

Acanthurus nigricauda   Ari Atoll, Maldives

Palelipped surgeonfish

Le: up to 35 cm. Di: East Africa
to Andaman Sea. De: 4 - 30 m.
Ge: at drop-offs. White lips
and knifes distinct. White chin
band prominent during threat
and courtship. Singly or in
pairs, not territorial, feeds on
algae. Below: **Brown surgeonfish** A. nigrofuscus, 20 cm.

Acanthurus leucocheilos   Similan Islands, Thailand

Circled-spine surgeonfish

Le: up to 45 cm. Di: East Africa to Sri Lanka. De: 3 - 25 m. Ge: singly or in small groups over shallow reefs with algae-covered coral fragments. Distinct by a light blue elliptic ring around each knife and two short black bands behind eye. Changes coloration (see below).

Acanthurus tennenti   KwaZulu-Natal

Yellowfin surgeonfish

Length: up to 56 cm. Distribution: entire area. Depth: 5 - 90 m. General: one of the largest genus members. Adults usually live in small groups and prefer the deeper water of lagoons and slopes along the base of outer reef drop-offs. Juveniles live singly and are mainly coastal, often found in silty habitats. Feeds (see photo) on the layer of diatoms and detritus on sand or rock, also taking up filamentous algae or even animal matter such as hydroids or pieces of fish. Pectoral fins and eye blotch yellow; changes colour.

Acanthurus xanthopterus   Ari Atoll, Maldives

Pencilled surgeonfish

Le: up to 50 cm. Di: entire area. De: 3 -100 m. Ge: adults (photos) are seen in cave areas and in the open water around seamounts and oceanic islands. Juveniles live in estuaries, grazing on algae-covered rocks. Distinct from similar Yellowfin surgeonfish by white spines.

Acanthurus dussumieri   Mozambique

213

Acanthurus triostegus   Christmas Island

Convict surgeonfish

Length: up to 26 cm.
Distribution: entire area,
not Red Sea.
Depth: 1 - 20 m.
General: this surgeonfish is
encountered singly, in small
groups, or in vast schools of
1,000 or more individuals (see
photo). It feeds on a wide variety of filamentous benthic
algae. Its caudal fin is slightly
emarginate, the corners are
not elongated in adults. A distinct species with little variation from juvenile to adult.
Juveniles are often found in
tidal pools.

Acanthurus mata   Raa Atoll, Maldives

Elongate surgeonfish

Le: up to 50 cm. Di: entire
area, RS. De: 2 - 45 m. Ge:
seen in groups along steep reef
slopes, often in turbid waters,
but also over sandy bottom in
lagoons. Adults feed on zooplankton, juveniles on algae
(often in estuaries). Below:
colour variant from Thailand.

Acanthurus guttatus   Male Atoll, Maldives

Whitespotted surgeonfish

Le: up to 26 cm. Di: Chagos,
Maldives, Sri Lanka. De: 0.5 -
6 m. Ge: mainly seen in the
surge zone, sometimes in large
schools. It grazes on filamentous and certain calcareous
algae, e.g. *Jania*. White spots
on body may conceal it in turbulent water full of air bubbles.

Indian mimic surgeonfish

Le: up to 20 cm. Di: Seychelles, Maldives to Andaman Sea. De: 2 - 40 m. Ge: singly or in groups on mixed sand and rubble bottom. Large photo: adult. Small photo: juvenile, mimics *Centropyge eibli* (p.131). This nearly perfect imitation probably serves in predator avoidance.

Acanthurus tristis   Similan Islands, Thailand

Lined surgeonfish

Le: up to 35 cm. Di: entire area. De: 0.5 - 6 m. Ge: territorial, large males control well-defined feeding territories and harems in the surge zone. Caudal lunate, greatly extended in adults. Below: **Chocolate surgeonfish** *A. thompsoni,* 25 cm, entire area, 5 - 70 m.

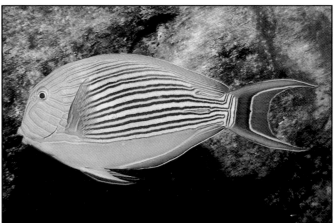

Acanthurus lineatus   Comoros

Palette surgeonfish

Le: up to 30 cm. Di: entire area, not Red Sea. De: 10 - 40 m. Ge: on clear, current-swept terraces of outer reefs, in loose groups about a metre above the bottom, feeding on plankton. Juveniles in groups (below), often near *Pocillopora* coral to wedge into branches.

Paracanthurus hepatus   Flic en Flac, Mauritius

215

Ctenochaetus truncatus   Negombo, Sri Lanka

Goldring bristletooth

Le: up to 18 cm. Di: entire area. De: 2 - 30 m. Ge: from coastal slopes to outer reef lagoons. Juvenile highly variable from drab brown to bright yellow (see small photo below). All genus members have a bristle-like dentition, which they use to graze on algae.

Ctenochaetus binotatus   Praslin, Seychelles

Two-spot bristletooth

Le: up to 20 cm. Di: East Africa to Maldives. De: 2 - 50 m. Ge: singly or in pairs (large photo) in coral and rubble areas on deep lagoon and seaward reefs. Juveniles (below) singly. May concentrate enough ciguatoxin to cause illness in humans in certain regions.

Ctenochaetus striatus   Lhaviyani Atoll, Maldives

Striped bristletooth

Le: up to 26 cm. Di: entire area, RS. De: 1 - 30 m. Ge: singly or in small to very large aggregations, often mixed with other species, on clear coastal to outer reefs. If one encounters a school of dark coloured surgeonfish on a reef in our area, it is often this sp. (below).

Mauritius tang

Length: up to 18 cm.
Distribution: Mascarenes,
Madagascar. Depth: 10 - 60 m.
General: usually found singly in
sandy areas with coral patches.
A rare territorial species. The
photo shows it together with
P. hepatus.
   Members of the genus *Zebrasoma* are distinct from other
surgeonfish species by their
relatively high dorsal and anal
fins. The latter are proportionally even higher in juveniles,
what gives them an almost bat-
fish-like appearance. All tangs
feed on algae, which are
grazed from hard substrates.

Zebrasoma gemmatum   Mauritius

Sailfin tang

Le: up to 40 cm. Di: entire
area, RS. De: 2 - 30 m. Ge:
seen in pairs or groups on
fringing reefs or in lagoons. It
has a sibling species *(Z. velifer-
um)* in the Pacific. Small photo
below: the similarly coloured
juveniles often seek shelter in
branched corals.

Zebrasoma desjardinii   Male Atoll, Maldives

Brown tang

Le: up to 20 cm. Di: entire
area, not Red Sea. De: 1 -
60 m. General: singly or in
small groups in coral-rich
areas of lagoons and seaward
reefs. Juveniles secretively in
rich coral growth (see small
photo below) mainly in coastal
reef and lagoon habitats.

Zebrasoma scopas   Beau Vallon, Seychelles

217

Naso thynnoides   **South Male Atoll, Maldives**

One-knife unicornfish

Le: up to 45 cm. Di: entire area, not RS. De: 20 - 100 m. Ge: adults in large schools (photo), often mixed with other species, at drop-offs near deep water, feeding in open water away from the reef. Return to the reef at dusk, where they seek a nighttime shelter. In contrast to other genus members this one has only one knife on each side of the caudal peduncle.

The fixed defensive peduncular spines of *Naso* species are often pronounced by bright colours, which serve as a warning sign for predators.

Bignose unicornfish

Le: up to 55 cm. Di: East Africa to Sri Lanka. De: 2 - 50 m. Ge: in schools feeding on plankton off deep slopes by day. At night in caves. Only large adults with big nose and long tail filaments. The small photo from the Maldives shows it with blue stripes and spots during courtship.

Naso vlamingii   **Ari Atoll, Maldives**

Humpback unicornfish

Le: up to 70 cm. Di: entire area, not Red Sea. De: 1 - 30 m. Ge: in pairs or small groups in shallow water along edges of steep outer reef slopes. Below: **Sleek unicornfish** *N. hexacanthus*, 75 cm, entire area, RS, 10 - 137 m, common, no "horn," not shy.

Naso brachycentron   **Aldabra, Seychelles**

Orangespine unicornfish

Le: up to 50 cm (excluding very long filaments on tail). Di: entire area, Red Sea. De: 2 - 90 m. Ge: the attractively coloured species is found in coastal areas of clear water on algae-rich rocky reefs, but also seen among coral, rock, or rubble in lagoons and seaward reefs. It lacks the typical bony "horn" of most of its congeners, and feeds primarily on leafy brown algae such as *Sargassum* and *Dictyota*. It feeds singly, in pairs, or sometimes in groups (top large photo), and often joins groups of other algae grazers, including parrotfishes. The small photos below respectively show a juvenile and the characteristic bright orange yellow bony plates on the caudal peduncle, here those of a subadult specimen.

Trinco, Sri Lanka

Naso elegans   **Richelieu Rock, Thailand**

Spotted unicornfish

Le: up to 60 cm. Di: entire area, RS. De: 3 - 50 m. Ge: adults in groups along dropoffs, feeding on zooplankton. Juvenile with white ring around caudal peduncle, feeds on algae. Below: **Bluespine unicornfish** *N. unicornis*, 70 cm, entire area, RS, 2 - 80 m.

Naso brevirostris   **Comoros**

MOORISH IDOLS   ZANCLIDAE

Zanclus cornutus   **Mauritius**

Moorish idol

Le: up to 22 cm. Di: entire area. De: 1 - 180 m. Ge: broad white and black bands distinct, has long white dorsal fin filament. Coastal to outer reefs, often in shallow boulder areas grazing algae, but also venturing to deeper zones, where feeding on sponges. Adults in pairs or small groups, but also schooling in great numbers in some areas. Juveniles expatriate well beyond breeding range into cooler zones. Most widespread coral fish in the Indo-Pacific. Not to be confused with butterfly fishes of the genus *Heniochus* (p.138).

RABBITFISHES   SIGANIDAE

Siganus argenteus   **Beau Vallon, Seychelles**

Forktail rabbitfish

Le: up to 42 cm. Di: entire area, RS. De: 1 - 30 m. Ge: on coral and rubble bottoms or seaward reefs in schools (large photo), also in fields of algae. Night coloration brown with diagonal dark brown zones.

Dusky rabbitfish

Le: up to 25 cm. Di: East Africa, Mauritius, RS. De: 2 - 18 m. Ge: in shallow water, in groups over sandy and weedy areas. Often mingles with other fishes. Below: **Red Sea rabbitfish** S. *rivulatus,* 30 cm, East Africa, RS, 2 - 15 m, often in schools of up to 100 or more.

Siganus luridus   **Comoros**

Andaman rabbitfish

Le: up to 24 cm. Di: Andaman Sea to Sumatra. De: 3 - 25 m. Ge: adults of the most colourful rabbitfish always live in pairs on clear coastal reefs, where they occupy large home ranges. Juveniles are found inshore in rich coral growth. Photo below: night coloration.

Siganus magnificus   Similan Islands, Thailand

Java rabbitfish

Length: up to 53 cm.
Distribution: northern Indian Ocean from Arabian Gulf to Andaman Sea.
Depth: 1 - 25 m.
General: olive green with white spots and stripes, caudal fin dark. Juveniles and adults are found singly or in groups in coastal habitats from shallow estuarine lagoons to adjacent coastal reefs. Prefers murky waters, readily enters brackish water. Feeds on benthic algae, occasionally also on jellyfish and larger zooplankton near the surface.

Siganus javus   Negombo, Sri Lanka

Gold-saddle rabbitfish

Le: up to 40 cm. Di: eastern Indian Ocean, Andaman Sea and western Thailand. De: 3 - 35 m. Ge: spotted, with bright yellow saddle blotch just in front of caudal peduncle. Mainly found in coastal rocky reefs with soft coral growth, inner lagoons, and mangrove areas. Forms small groups, often seen hovering in the shelter of the reef. Replaced by its striped sibling species S. *lineatus* further eastward and in Australia.
   The about 30 species of rabbitfishes are related to the surgeonfishes. With a venomous spine on the pectoral fin.

Siganus guttatus   Surin Island, Thailand

Beard rabbitfish

Praslin, Seychelles

Length: up to 30 cm.
Distribution: Seychelles, Maldives, Similan Islands, Thailand.
Depth: 1 - 15 m.
General: the species is characterised by yellow spots on a bluish background, which may be partially fused in some areas, and a dark blotch below the lower lip that resembles a beard. This blotch extends as a band to just behind the eyes in juveniles (see small photo below), remnants of this band are still present around the eyes in adults (top large photo). The latter occur in pairs or schools (centre large photo) on reef flats and along drop-offs to feed on algae, tunicates, and sponges. The photos from the Seychelles are a considerable extension of the distributional range to the West. The author's impression is that herbivore fishes get more abundant in the course of global warming, which causes coral death and consequently accelerated growth of algae on the dead corals (see also the school of Forktail rabbitfish above).

Siganus puelloides

Beau Vallon, Seychelles

Coral rabbitfish

Le: up to 30 cm. Di: East Africa to Andaman Sea. De: 1 - 25 m.
Ge: very similar to previous species, but with unfused blue spots on yellow ground. Adults on coastal reefs and outer reef lagoons, grazing on algae on dead coral. Juveniles are hiding in *Acropora* corals.

Siganus corallinus

Des Roches, Seychelles

Three-blotch rabbitfish

Length: up to 20 cm.
Distribution: known only from
the isolated coral reefs off the
northwestern coast of Australia.
Depth: 2 - 15 m.
General: very closely related
to the Coral rabbitfish (see
previous page), but differs in
coloration: it has three evenly-
spaced prominent chocolate
brown blotches on upper half
of body below spinous part of
dorsal fin. The species is strictly bound to corals, adults live
in pairs on reefs with a rich
growth of stony corals, particularly *Acropora* (see photo).

Siganus trispilos   North Cape, West Australia

Double-barred rabbitfish

Length: up to 30 cm.
Distribution: Southwest India
and Sri Lanka to northern
Australia.
Depth: 2 - 25 m.
General: this rabbitfish species
is encountered in coastal rock
and coral reef habitats, small
juveniles occasionally also in
pure freshwater. Adults live in
pairs or small aggregations on
coastal, often turbid reefs,
grazing algae on rocky substrate of shallow reef flats or
crests. Sibling species S. *dolia-
tus* in the Pacific. The photo is
from the western margin of
the known distributional range.

Siganus virgatus   Trinco, Sri Lanka

Starry rabbitfish

Le: up to 40 cm. Di: entire
area, RS. De: 3 - 45 m. Ge: in
coral reefs, subadults in small
groups, adults always in pairs
(large photo). Distinct by
close-set dark brown spots on
lighter ground. There is a
colour variant in the Red Sea.
Small photo below: juvenile.

Siganus stellatus   La Digue, Seychelles

WHALES OFF SRI LANKA

Nearing Trinco at daybreak, we detect the bubbles from two Humpback whales. Just as our course has been changed, one of the whales bursts out of the sea with such strength that one can distinctly recognise its overlarge pectoral fins. The water splashes high and wide as its massive body plunges back into the sea again. The author recalls the story.

Two Humpback whales surface in front of the whale watching vessel off Trincomalee at the East coast of Sri Lanka.

Not such a rare spectacle off the port of Trinco, as the fishery town Trincomalee on the East coast of Sri Lanka is called for short. Something in the Bay of Trinco attracts whales, so that they will swim almost up to the shore. A true 'eldorado' for the American and Ceylonese scientists, who over several years have researched the whale population around the large island off the Indian subcontinent. One can regularly meet Sperm whales *(Physeter catodon)*, Bryde whales *(Balaenoptera edeni)*, Humpback whales *(Megaptera novaeangliae)*, and even the huge Blue whales *(Balaenoptera musculus)* there. Over a sensitive hydrophone, below the research ship, the typical 'clicks' of the Sperm whales can be heard. At a guess there are about a dozen of them, hunting for food in the depths of the Bay. Most scientists believe that the regular clicks are a kind of sonar that the Sperm whales use to find their prey. As one listens, it occurs that one of the series of clicks suddenly stops, then becomes faster and

The whale watching vessel *Sudaya* returns after a successful day to the harbour.

224

HELMUT DEBELIUS

A Sperm whale photographed while snorkelling in the close vicinity of Trincomalee.

finally stops again. One can well imagine what is going on underneath. A Sperm whale is closing in on a large squid and the nearer it gets, the faster the clicks become. Just as the prey is snatched, it sounds as if a door has slammed shut and then there is sudden silence - the hunt is over.

The clicks are far more important for the Sperm whale than its eyes. They are actually far more than just a sonar for hunting prey, but are a way of communicating between each other. There are

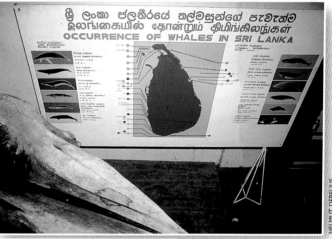

HELMUT DEBELIUS

An educational display of Sri Lankan whales in Colombo. The skull of a baleen whale is seen in the front.

codes for example that are always used, when the creatures swim close together near the surface, usually during the middle of the day. One could almost say that the whales are talking to each other during their siesta.

But what are the whales really up to, so close to the Ceylonese shores? One answer has been provided by the geologists: the measuring of the seabed gave

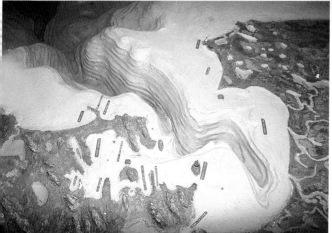

To illustrate the unusual underwater geography of the Sri Lankan coast, this model of the canyon off Trincomalee is also displayed in Colombo.

MARK CONLIN

Even the biggest of all whales, the Blue whale, every once in while shows up over the canyon of Trincomalee.

light to the fact that in front of Trinco, a deep canyon has been worn out of the continental shelf. Whilst whales have not been sighted in the shallow coastal waters of Sri Lanka, here they swim relatively close to the shore, not two kilometres away from the land. It has been surmised that the largest river in Sri Lanka, the Mahaweli Ganga, pushes nutrients into the Bay of Trinco, that could in turn attract food animals for the whales. It must be extremely attractive, since even the Blue whale has been seen there. One question has yet to be answered: in order to be well-fed, all whales must remain at least six months in the polar regions, since that is where the largest concentration of nutrients prevails. This they do particularly during the summer time, normally in the northern polar region from May to September, and in the southern polar region from November to April. Why then is it that the whales appear around Sri Lanka between January and April? At this time they should be in the southern polar region, where there are much better possibilities of finding food. Sri Lanka lies in the Northern Hemisphere. So where do the whales of Sri Lanka come from? An interesting question for marine scientists. But protection of Indian Ocean offshore marine mammals is equally important for them. Like in the Seychelles, the waters around Sri Lanka have meanwhile been declared an absolute protection zone for all marine mammals.

NORBERT WU

An exceptionally rare photograph of one of the fastest-swimming bony fishes in the world's oceans, the Black marlin *Makaira indica* has been achieved while snorkelling! This species has - as its scientific name implies - been discovered in the Indian Ocean many years ago. This magnificent creature is sought after and highly prized by big game fishing enthusiast from all around the world, who visit Sri Lankan waters.

Bigeye trevally

Length: up to 85 cm.
Distribution: entire area
including Red Sea.
Depth: 2 - 90 m.
General: this large trevally is
very common throughout the
Indian Ocean. It is seen in
schools of up to several hundred individuals in deep
lagoons, channels, and near
steep drop-offs. The fishes
move from reef to reef in
search for food, which mainly
consists of small reef fishes.
See also the photo of the
related species *C. melampygus*
in GOING TERRESTRIAL on
p. 50.

Caranx sexfasciatus   Praslin, Seychelles

Black trevally

Le: up to 85 cm. Di: entire
area including Red Sea. De: 2 -
70 m. Ge: widespread in tropical waters. In schools near
coral reefs. Patrols the reef
edges in search for prey. Below:
Yellowspotted trevally
Carangoides fulvoguttatus,
103 cm, entire area, 2 - 100 m.

Caranx lugubris   Christmas Island

Bloch's pompano

Le: up to 65 cm. Di: entire
area, RS. De: 5 - 50 m. Ge:
juveniles in schools in bays and
near river mouths. Yellow
adults (below) in pairs in reefs.
Head profile blunt. Similar:
Black-spotted pompano *T.
bailloni* (54 cm, 2 - 30 m) with
more pointed head profile.

Trachinotus blochii   Burma Banks, Thailand

Ari Atoll, Maldives

Golden pilot jack

Le: up to 110 cm. Di: entire area, RS. De: 2 - 50 m. Ge: juveniles live inshore in deep lagoons, feeding on detritus as shown on the top large photo. They also live as symbionts among the tentacles of jellyfish, or swim below drifting clumps of algae; they even are "piloting" sharks, rays, or groupers. Centre large photo shows an adult with Rainbow runners.

The trevallies (jacks, scads, horse or spiny mackerels) are found in coastal waters of all tropical and subtropical seas, many have a wide range of distribution due to their pelagic eggs and long-lived larvae. The about 140 species show important external similarities. Body laterally compressed, spindle- or torpedo-shaped. Tail strongly forked or lunate. Often with bony scutes on both sides of the caudal peduncle. The typical metallic sheen of the skin is an optical effect caused by numerous tiny mirror-like platelets (guanine crystals) reflecting the light. Anal fin with 2 - 3 spines at its front end ("spiny mackerels").

Gnathanodon speciosus   **Hikkaduwa, Sri Lanka**

Rainbow runner

Length: up to 120 cm. Distribution: entire area, RS. Depth: 1 - 15 m. General: a pelagic species that is usually found at or near the surface, over reefs, sometimes far offshore. It feeds on larvae of crustaceans, and small pelagic fishes. Small schools of juveniles congregate in the vicinity of floating objects at sea. Adults are visiting cleaner fish stations (photo left), and also execute quick runs along the rough skin of reef sharks to get rid of external parasites. See also school in background of centre large photo.

Elagatis bipinnulata   **Ari Atoll, Maldives**

TREVALLIES   CARANGIDAE

Yellowtail jack

Length: up to 170 cm.
Distribution: entire area.
Depth: 5 - 50 m.
General: seen in schools of up
to 300 specimens in coastal
waters. Hunts other schooling
fishes like fusiliers and snappers, but also feeds on pelagic
crustaceans and squid.

Seriola lalandi   **Aliwal Shoal, South Africa**

MACKERELS AND TUNAS   SCOMBRIDAE

Dogtooth tuna

Length: up to 220 cm. Distribution: entire area including
Red Sea. Depth: 3 - 100 m.
General: juveniles are often
seen singly on reef flats or in
shallow coastal waters. Adults
occur singly (photo) or in
small groups along outer reef
drop-offs, and around oceanic
islands. The species is a voracious fish hunter with large
conical teeth - clearly to be
seen in the photo - that preys
on planktivores (smaller trevallies, fusiliers, certain wrasses,
unicornfishes). Not shy.

Gymnosarda unicolor   **Lhaviyani Atoll, Maldives**

Bigmouth mackerel

Length: up to 35 cm.
Distribution: entire area
including Red Sea.
Depth: 5 - 70 m.
General: this elegant swimmer
is mainly encountered in -
sometimes enormously large -
schools, swimming fast along
reefs or over sand and mud
flats, filtering plankton from
the water with mouth wide
open (see photo). It is an
unusual sight to see all fishes
synchronously open their
mouths. Their main food are
decapod and fish larvae, which
are sieved from the water with
numerous gill rakers.

Rastrelliger kanagurta   **Comoros**

229

Striped bonito

Length: up to 90 cm.
Distribution: entire area
including Red Sea.
Depth: 20 - 50 m.
General: this bonito swims in
schools (photo) together with
other tuna species. It prefers
temperatures between 13.5°
and 23°C, and occurs in tropical regions, but does not
appear in the surface waters,
which are often too warm.
The swift swimmer primarily
feeds on herrings and other
small schooling fishes, but also
on pelagic cephalopods and
crustaceans.

Sarda orientalis   **Burma Banks, Thailand**

LEFT-EYED FLOUNDERS   BOTHIDAE

Peacock flounder

Le: up to 45 cm. Di: entire
area. De: 1 - 85 m. Ge: pectoral fin on eyed side large
with greatly elongated filamentous rays (centre large photo).
Eyes far apart in large adults
(bottom large photo). Found in
shallow coastal reefs and
lagoons, mainly on sand, but
often also in rocky areas. Coloration perfectly adapted to
the habitat (below), blind side
unpigmented.

Mauritius

   The Left-eyed flounders are
a very large, primarily tropical
family with 15 genera and
about 90 species in the Indo-
Pacific alone. Their planktonic
larva is bilaterally symmetrical
and has an eye on each side.
When settling on the sub-
strate, the symmetry of the
metamorphosing fish changes
and both eyes become located
on the left side of the head.
Many flatfish species are benthic and nocturnal, and just very
few are strictly diurnal. All are
carnivorous, feeding on various
benthic invertebrates and small
fishes.

Bothus mancus   **Comoros**

Clown triggerfish

Le: up to 35 cm. Di: entire area, not RS. De: 5 - 60 m. Ge: distinct by the large round white spots. Adults primarily along deep drop-offs (see the photo of the specimen under a ledge on the previous page). Juveniles (below) are usually found deeper, also in caves.

Balistoides conspicillum   Ari Atoll, Maldives

Blue triggerfish

Le: up to 55 cm. Di: entire area, Red Sea. De: 1 - 50 m. Ge: inhabits clear lagoons and patch reefs in sandy areas. A very shy species. The small photo below shows a juvenile with a coloration distinct from the adult pattern.

Pseudobalistes fuscus   Chagos Islands

Yellowtail triggerfish

Le: up to 30 cm. Di: entire area, Red Sea. De: 1 - 40 m. Ge: inhabits coral-rich lagoons and coral rubble areas. Like all triggerfish species, it feeds primarily on hard-shelled molluscs and diverse sea-urchins. The juvenile below, however, is shown while preying on spawn.

Balistapus undulatus   Felidhoo Atoll, Maldives

Redtooth triggerfish

Le: up to 40 cm. Di: entire area, Red Sea. De: I - 55 m. Ge: seen in groups feeding on plankton above the reef, even in the company of Manta rays (large photo). Wary, not easily approached, quickly hides in reef crevices. Below: a single specimen in front of a cave.

Odonus niger   Ari Atoll, Maldives

Gilded triggerfish

Le: up to 22 cm. Di: entire area. De: 20 - 150 m. Ge: found at clear outer reef drop-offs. Singly or in pairs, also forming groups in very deep water. Feeds on zooplankton. Males (large photo) distinct from females (below) by blue cheek and orange fin margins.

Xanthichthys auromarginatus   Sodwana Bay, South Africa

Cheekline triggerfish

Le: up to 30 cm. Di: entire area. De: 18 - 60 m. Ge: a very rare species, which is distinct by three lines on the cheek. See also CHAGOS (p.93) for its relative, the **Blue-lined triggerfish** *X. caeruleolineatus*.

Some triggerfish species specialise on eating the long-spined *Diadema* sea urchins, which are blown away from the bottom by a powerful squirt of water from the mouth, and subsequently opened with one bite at their soft and less spiny mouth region while sinking back to the ground.

Xanthichthys lineopunctatus   Durban, South Africa

MONSOONS

Planning a visit to the Indian Ocean? Then you should definitely give some thought to the monsoons. Mention monsoon to most Europeans and they think of lashing rains and howling winds. But that is a misconception. The word monsoon simply means 'season'. As elsewhere in the world, there are good seasons and bad seasons. The photographer provides further explanations.

ALL PHOTOS: CHARLES ANDERSON

Calm conditions during the Northeast monsoon at the Great Basses Reef lighthouse off the south coast of Sri Lanka. This superb, but very exposed diving site can only be visited at the end of this monsoon season.

In the tropical Indian Ocean there are two main seasons. These are named for the prevailing winds. Thus in the central Indian Ocean the northeast monsoon (which lasts from about December to April) has mainly northeasterly winds. During the southwest monsoon (which lasts from about June to October), the winds blow mainly from the southwest.

This reversal of prevailing winds is unique to the tropical Indian Ocean. It is caused by the seasonal heating and cooling of the great landmass of India and central Asia. In the northern summer (starting in about April-May) the Indian subcontinent heats up. Air over the land rises, so moist air is drawn in from the ocean to replace it. As this air blows over the land it too becomes heated and rises. Its cargo of moisture is dropped as rain. This is the rain that gives the monsoons their bad name in Europe. But in the Indian subcontinent their coming is awaited with eager anticipation and celebrated with festivals and merrymaking. For the arrival of the rains, normally in June, brings an end to the oppressive summer heat and regenerates the land for a new crop of life-sustaining rice.

Later in the year, with the approach of the northern winter, the Indian continent cools. This triggers the reversal of the winds, and associated ocean currents. Now winds blow from the relatively cool land out into the ocean. In earlier times, sailing navigators planned their voyages

Manta rays feeding on tiny plankton.

234

across the Indian Ocean to take advantage of the seasonal wind blowing in the direction they wanted to go. Six months later they would return.

Today, for divers and snorkellers, the most important effects of the monsoons are those on sea conditions. The changeover or intermonsoon periods often bring calm conditions. For example, the March-April intermonsoon is the only time to visit the spectacular Great Basses Reef of southern Sri Lanka. However, the strong winds often associated with the start of both monsoons (in December and June-July) can bring rough seas to exposed coasts.

In the central and eastern Indian Ocean the very best diving conditions occur during the northeast monsoon. For Goa in India, the southwest coast of Sri Lanka and also the Andaman Sea coast of Thailand the time to visit is December to March. For Maldives the best season is slightly later: January to May. In the southwest season the west coasts of India, Sri Lanka and Thailand are washed out. But (if the security situation allows) the east coast of Sri Lanka offers good diving from August to October (and also in April). Maldives too has some great diving during August to November.

A tuna purse seiner at Mahé in Seychelles. A fleet of these vessels (mainly from France and Spain) follows the seasonal movements of the tunas around the western Indian Ocean. They fish north of the Seychelles during the Southwest monsoon, around Chagos in November-December.

In the western Indian Ocean the monsoon winds are deflected by the continental land mass of Africa, so wind directions are not the same as elsewhere. Thus, in the Seychelles relatively gentle southeast winds blow from May to October, and the best time for diving is April to November. The stronger and wetter northwest monsoon blows from December to March. The Kenyan coast enjoys similar wind patterns to those in the Seychelles, so diving seasons here are partly related to the coastal exposure. For example, the coast near Malindi faces northeast and is best during July to December. Watamu, just to the south, faces southeast and is best during October to April.

The monsoon seasons affect not only the winds and sea surface conditions, but also the ocean currents. Broadly speaking the currents change with the winds and travel in the same direction as the wind. The main impact that this has for divers is on visibility. If the current is coming straight from the ocean it is likely to bring very clear water. If the current has passed by some land it is likely to be a bit murky. This may not be as bad as it sounds, because murk means nutrients, which plankton needs to grow. And plankton is the food of manta rays and whale sharks.

As a result mantas (and the occasional whale shark) are found on the west coast of the Maldives during the northeast monsoon (December to April), and on the east coast during the southwest monsoon (June to October). They are also seen off Watamu in Kenya during December to February. For a better than average chance of seeing a whale shark try Seychelles in November, the west coast of Thailand in March-April, Christmas Island in December and of course Ningaloo during March to May.

Wet and windy conditions during the Southwest monsoon. Its strong gusts bend the palms and make the water spray.

Indian triggerfish

Le: up to 25 cm. Di: entire area. De: 5 - 35 m. Ge: on steep outer reef slopes, and in current-swept surge channels. Very shy species, readily hiding in crevices. The small photo below from the Maldives shows a specimen displaying its bright courtship coloration.

Melichthys indicus   Similan Islands, Thailand

Halfmoon triggerfish

Le: up to 20 cm. Di: East Africa to Sri Lanka. De: 1 - 30 m. Ge: a common, but shy species, which inhabits shallow lagoons and seagrass beds. Solitary, territorial, often seen at oceanic islands. Below: a colour variant (Andaman Sea) with two cheek lines.

Sufflamen chrysopterus   Lhaviyani Atoll, Maldives

Scythe triggerfish

Le: up to 20 cm. Di: East Africa to Sri Lanka. De: 3 - 45 m. Ge: in outer reefs below the surge. Distinct scythe mark crossing the pectoral base is yellowish-tan to green in juveniles and subadults. Below: **Bridled triggerfish** S. *fraenatus*, 38 cm, entire area, rare in the South.

Sufflamen bursa   South Male Atoll, Maldives

TRIGGERFISHES

BALISTIDAE

Picasso triggerfish

Le: up to 25 cm. Di: entire area. De: 0.5 - 5 m. Ge: pattern distinct. In seagrass beds, on subtidal reef flats. Common over sand in shallow water. Territorial, but shy, feeds on various marine animals. Below: **Wedge Picassofish** R. rectangulus, 25 cm, entire area, 1 - 20 m.

Rhinecanthus aculeatus   Astove, Seychelles

Strickland's triggerfish

Le: up to 25 cm. Di: Mauritius and Maldives to Andaman Sea. De: 5 - 25 m. Ge: rare, little known, only recently photographed in the Andaman Sea by Mark Strickland. Below: **Yellowmargin triggerfish** *Pseudobalistes flavimarginatus,* to 60 cm, south. IO, 2 - 50 m.

Rhinecanthus cinereus   Burma Banks, Thailand

Giant triggerfish

Le: up to 75 cm. Di: entire area including Red Sea. De: 5 - 35 m. Ge: found on open sandy areas with scattered coral patches. It is not advisable to approach the male guarding its nest in a shallow crater dug in the sand or rubble ground. The fish attacks at once, and painfully bites with its large teeth.

All triggerfish species have a distinct way of propelling themselves through the water by "waving" their symmetrically arranged dorsal and anal fins simultaneously from left to right and back.

Balistoides viridescens   Felidhoo Atoll, Maldives

Cantherhines pardalis   Beau Vallon, Seychelles

Wire-net filefish

Le: up to 25 cm. Di: entire area, Red Sea. De: I - 25 m. Ge: wary, secretive in seagrass beds and algae fields. Pattern of dark brown polygons on body (popular name).
 All file- and triggerfishes have a stout dorsal fin spine that can be locked in an upright position. At night or when in danger the fishes wedge them-selves head-first into narrow holes in the reef, the locked spine serving as an anchor to prevent being pulled out by a predator. The scales of filefish-es have small spines, and are thus rough like a file (name).

Cantherhines fronticinctus   Des Roches, Seychelles

Spectacled filefish

Le: up to 23 cm. Di: entire area. De: I - 35 m. Ge: adults on protected reefs, usually below 20 m. Juveniles shallow. Secretive, camouflaged. Below: **Barred filefish** *C. dumerilii*, to 35 cm, entire area, I -35 m, adults in pairs, male with yellow spines on tail base (see photo).

Ear-spot filefish

Le: up to 13 cm. Di: entire area. De: 0.5-15 m. Ge: verti-cal gill blotch distinct. Singly or in pairs on shallow reef flats or in rocky estuaries. Very secre-tive. Below: **Orangetail filefish** *P. aspricauda,* to 12 cm, only around the oceanic islands in our area, 3 - 30 m.

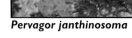

Pervagor janthinosoma   Male Atoll, Maldives

Scribbled filefish

Length: up to 100 cm
(including the long tail).
Distribution: entire area
including Red Sea, circumtropical.
Depth: 1 - 80 m.
General: in coastal reefs,
'script' pattern distinct (see
below). Largest family member.
A shy and solitary species, only
rarely seen in groups. Small
juveniles are yellow with black
spots and develop bright blue
ornaments while growing. The
juveniles are pelagic up to a
large size, form schools, and
associate with floating weeds.
Like some of the triggerfishes,
this filefish species sometimes
feeds on medusae, as can be
seen in the large photo.

Aluterus scriptus   Similan Islands, Thailand

Longnose filefish

Length: up to 10 cm.
Distribution: East Africa,
Seychelles, Madagascar,
Mascarenes, Chagos, Maldives,
Sri Lanka.
Depth: 1 - 30 m.
General: this spectacular little
filefish inhabits clear lagoons
and seaward reefs. It is common, wherever *Acropora* corals
occur, the polyps of which are
its main diet. The pointed
snout is used to snip the
polyps from their cup-like
skeletal calices. Adults are usually encountered in pairs (see
large photo). Juveniles swim in
small groups between or over
the tips of the corals, and are
also feeding primarily on the
polyps.

Oxymonacanthus longirostris   Ari Atoll, Maldives

Cube boxfish

Le: up to 45 cm. Di: entire area including Red Sea. De: 1 - 45 m. Ge: small juveniles (top large photo) are bright yellow with black spots nearly as large as the pupil. Their body is cube-shaped (dice fish), becoming more elongate with age. The caudal fin increases in size with age and the caudal peduncle becomes long and thick. Females (centre large photo, adult) are yellow and have many regularly rounded, black-rimmed white spots on the carapace. Large adults (small photo of male below) are variable in colour, ranging from ochre to purplish brown, the round spots on the carapace of the smaller female phase being more or less prominent (may be absent), the fins have small black spots. A solitary species, always seeking shelter under overhangs in the reef.

The body of boxfishes is covered with hexagonal bony plates, fused into a rigid case with holes for the moving parts (fins, caudal peduncle, mouth, eyes, and gills).

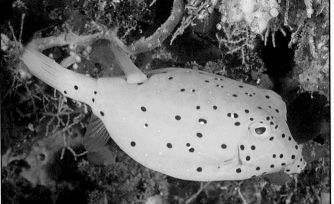

Male Atoll, Maldives

Ostracion cubicus   Comoros

Mauritius boxfish

Le: up to 11 cm. Di: only known from Mauritius. De: 15 - 45 m. Ge: similar to *O. mele-agris* (see opposite), but white spots larger. Mainly seen below 20 m among the rocks typically found around Mauritius, also in small groups. Large photo: female; small photo: male.

Ostracion trachys   Mauritius

Pyramid boxfish

Le: up to 30 cm. Di: entire area, RS. De: 3 - 110 m. Ge: solitary in seagrass beds or sandy areas with blocks of rock. Below: **Longhorn boxfish** *Lactoria cornuta,* up to 50 cm, entire area, RS, 1 - 100 m. These boxfish species are characterised by horn-like spines.

Tetrosomus gibbosus   **Ari Atoll, Maldives**

Thornback boxfish

Le: up to 15 cm. Di: East Africa to Sri Lanka. De: 1 - 30 m. Ge: singly or in pairs over coral rubble and sand with corals patches. Green to brown with blue spots and scribbles. Best identified by prominent spine in middle of back. Below: juvenile.

Lactoria fornasini   **Pemba, Tanzania**

Whitespotted boxfish

Le: up to 16 cm. Di: entire area, not Red Sea. De: 1 - 30 m. Ge: common in southern Indian Ocean, pairs often swimming together, but in a distance of up to 20 m. Similar to *O. trachys* (see opposite), but white spots smaller. Large photo: female; below: male.

Ostracion meleagris   **Shimoni, Kenya**

Starry pufferfish

Beau Vallon, Seychelles

Le: up to 50 cm. Di: entire area, not RS. De: 3 - 25 m. Ge: singly in coral-rich clear lagoons and outer reefs. Feeds on the tips of staghorn corals, but also on molluscs and crabs. Swims occasionally together with other puffers. Top large (pair) and small photo: usual coloration; centre: yellow colour variant, distinct by spots on dorsal (see also *A. nigropunctatus* below).

Pufferfishes are a large family comprising about 20 genera and at least 100 species that are placed in two distinct subfamilies: the short-nosed (Tetraodontinae) and the sharp-nosed pufferfishes (Canthigasterinae). Their common name reflects their unique ability to inflate themselves like a balloon with water or air to deter predators. Many species are also prickly or spiny, making them even more hazardous to consume when inflated. To top the list of defensive mechanisms of these slow-moving fishes all are poisonous: skin and reproductive organs contain the lethal tetrodotoxin.

Arothron meleagris   Mauritius

Blackspotted pufferfish

Le: up to 30 cm. Di: entire area, not in Red Sea. De: 3 - 35 m. Ge: large photo shows normal coloration, small photo shows yellow colour variant, very similar to yellow *A. meleagris* (see above), but lacks spots on dorsal. Sibling *A. diademata*, common in Red Sea.

Arothron nigropunctatus   Felidhoo Atoll, Maldives

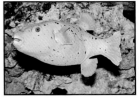

Mappa pufferfish

Le: up to 65 cm. Di: entire area. De: 2 - 30 m. Ge: shy, solitary, found in deep caves of outer reef drop-offs. Feeds on benthic invertebrates. Shows sexual dimorphism. Shown in large photo together with a Trumpetfish (see also A TRUMPET SOLO, p.64 - 65).

Arothron mappa Beau Vallon, Seychelles

Bluespotted pufferfish

Le: up to 80 cm. Di: Reunion, Mauritius, Maldives eastward. De: 2 - 50 m. Ge: similar to the other species on this page, but distinct by alternating brown and blue lines around eye, and many blue spots on head and body. Described only recently. Small photo: Mauritius.

Arothron caeruleopunctatus Baa Atoll, Maldives

Giant pufferfish

Le: up to 120 cm. Di: entire area, RS. De: 5 - 60 m. Ge: a large family member, shy, usually singly in coastal reefs. Feeds on invertebrates, mainly echinoderms. Below: **Seagrass pufferfish** A. *immaculatus*, 28 cm, entire area, RS, 5 - 15 m, found in seagrass beds.

Arothron stellatus South Male Atoll, Maldives,

243

Canthigaster coronata   **Hikkaduwa, Sri Lanka**

Crowned toby

Le: up to 13 cm. Di: entire area, RS. De: 5 - 80 m. Ge: singly or in pairs over rubble and sand. Often seen in the vicinity of caves and crevices.

The species of this genus belong to the sharp-nosed pufferfishes of the subfamily Canthigasterinae, all of which are small compared to their short-nosed relatives.

All pufferfishes produce globular eggs, less than 1 mm in diameter, which are sticky and demersal. Their larvae are pelagic, and up to 6 mm long, when they get ready to settle on the substrate.

Canthigaster tyleri   **Male Atoll, Maldives**

Tyler's toby

Le: up to 8 cm. Di: southern Indian Ocean. De: 12 - 35 m. Ge: singly or in pairs (see photo of 'dancing' pair) in crevices, also seen in a wreck. Below: **Smith's toby** *C. smithae,* up to 15 cm, East Africa to Mascarenes, 25 - 52 m. Lives in deeper waters, not common.

Canthigaster solandri   **Kilifi, Kenya**

Solander's toby

Le: up to 11 cm. Di: East Africa to Sri Lanka, rare in southern Indian Ocean. De: 3 - 30 m. Ge: singly or in pairs on coral rubble. Below: **Bennett's toby** *C. bennetti,* 9 cm, entire area, 1 - 30 m, adults often in pairs, found in coastal bays, coloration varies with habitat.

244

Valentin's toby

Le: up to 10 cm. Di: entire
area. De: 1 - 55 m. Ge: common on shallow reefs, often in
pairs. Feeds on algae and a
variety of small invertebrates.
Males have blue lines radiating
from the eye. Model for non-
poisonous mimics (a filefish
and a juvenile grouper).

Canthigaster valentini   Ari Atoll, Maldives

Masked porcupinefish

Le: up to 50 cm. Di: entire
area, not in Red Sea. De: 3 -
90 m. Ge: a shy species, which
hides under rocks and in
crevices during the day. Only
seen in coral reef areas, avoid-
ing open sand flats.
   Porcupinefishes are similar to
pufferfishes (they can inflate
and are poisonous), but are
covered with short to long
spines, which normally are
lying flat on the body and erect
only when the fish inflates.
Prey are diverse shelled invertebrates, also medusae.

Diodon liturosus   Similan Islands, Thailand

Common porcupinefish

Le: up to 70 cm. Di: entire
area, Red Sea. De: 5 - 65 m.
Ge: the species inhabits coral
or rocky reefs, and mainly
feeds on gastropods and
bivalved shells. Below: **Freck-
led porcupinefish** D. holocan-
thus, up to 30 cm, entire area
including Red Sea, 3 - 100 m.

Diodon hystrix   Myanmar

245

The crustaceans are one of the truly dominant groups living in coral reefs. Due to the tiny size and cryptic habits of many species, however, it is easy to under-estimate their impact on the reef's ecology. The group is incredibly diverse with regards to size, shape, colour, and life style. Not only does it include well known representatives such as lobsters, shrimps, and crabs, but also a wealth of microscopic organisms that form a large portion of both the zooplankton and the interstitial fauna.

The class Crustacea belongs to the phylum Arthropoda, which includes the land-dominating insects, spiders, scorpions, millipedes, and centipedes. The phylum is huge, outnumbering all other animal groups combined by a ratio of at least three to one. It is estimated that three quarter of a million species have been scientifically described and named, of which crustaceans account for only about 30,000 species. About two thirds of these are put in the 14 orders of higher crustaceans. Most members of the order Decapoda, comprising the two suborders Natantia (shrimps) and Reptantia (lobsters and crabs), live in shallow water, in reach of diver and camera. Photographers should be familiar with this group to portray its beauty.

Crustaceans live in a wide variety of habitats, feed on almost everything, and occupy important niches in the ecology of the oceans, especially as food for others. They are the 'insects of the sea,' the most speciose group of marine animals except molluscs. Crustaceans are typified by the presence of a rigid, calcium carbonate-based external skeleton called carapace. Because growth is nearly continuous throughout the life cycle, the animal periodically outgrows its armour coating. Therefore the shell is shed (molted) and replaced at regular intervals. Before molting the calcium component of the carapace is partly absorbed and recycled, while the new shell begins to form. When the shell is finally shed and the new coat is still relatively soft, the animal is particularly vulnerable to predators and therefore seeks the shelter of a burrow or other hiding place.

Crustaceans are also characterised by a segmented body, although individual segments may be hidden by the external shell. In general the body can be divided into two major sections, front and back that are referred to as the cephalothorax and abdomen. Another typical feature is the jointed limbs with internal muscular attachment, capable of movement in all directions. These serve a variety of functions that include locomotion, touch and chemical reception, respiration, and feeding. The most conspicuous of these are the walking legs, antennae (two pair in contrast to the single pair of other arthropods), and pincer-like claws or nippers typical of crabs and shrimps.

The gills are protected by the carapace, but at the same time their contact with fresh, oxygenated water is hampered. Therefore crustaceans have a special pumping limb, the scaphognathite (gill bailer), that fans the gills providing a constant stream of oxygenated water to the gill chamber. Like vertebrates, crustaceans have an oxygen-binding blood pigment (the blue hemocyanine), which transports this vital element to the organs. The heart lies dorsally in the carapace, and pumps the blood from the gills into two main arteries, which support the head region and the tail musculature. The circulatory system is open, so a significant part of the blood does not flow in vessels but must find its way back through sinuses. This calls for an integral, undamaged body envelope, otherwise blood would leak out. This problem is solved by a mechanism called autotomy (self-dismembering): each joint of the leg segments can quickly be cut and sealed in case of injury, e.g. by a predator. The missing part is regenerated during growth and reappears after the next molting. Sexes are separate, sexual dimorphism occurs. Crustacean development includes large numbers of planktonic eggs, metamorphosis through several larval stages, most of which are also planktonic and contribute a major part to the plankton's biomass.

The majority of crustaceans encountered in coral reefs are decapods. Decapod literally means "ten legs". These are four pair of walking legs and the first pair, which is often strongly developed and in many species has terminal claws. Such clawed legs are called chelipeds. Shrimps (often called prawns), lobsters, and crabs are all prominent members of this group. For the most part of their life they are secretive creatures that remain hidden for long periods in burrows, crevices, under dead coral slabs, or inside empty mollusc shells. They form an integral part of the food chain, being hunted by larger predators, mainly fishes. They have evolved a largely inconspicuous life style in response to this pressure. Generally the best time to observe crustaceans is at night, when many species emerge from their retreats to feed. The largest of the about 10,000 decapod species has a carapace length of 0.5 m and its legs span up to 3 m. But size alone is not everything. Observing and photographing the multitude of colourful crustaceans in tropical reef environments will always yield new insights into the complex interactions of crustaceans with their hosts, friends, and foes.

Scarlet cleaner shrimp

Le: up to 5 cm. Di: Maldives, Sri Lanka, Andaman Sea. Ge: this scarlet red cleaner shrimp species is usually found in depths greater than 20 m. It lives in pairs or small groups and defends territories against conspecifics. There is no externally visible sexual dimorphism. Although not the most important invertebrate cleaner in the reef, the species readily cleans fishes. The coloration shows some variation throughout the species' wide range of distribution: the small photo below from the Line Islands in the Central Pacific shows a colour variant with the white confined to a few spots on the carapace, the legs are entirely red. Maldivian specimens, however, have partly white legs and white spots also on the abdomen (photo right).

Cleaning shrimps are found mainly in tropical coral reefs and belong to the families Hippolytidae (cleaner shrimps) and Palaemonidae (partner shrimps, see further below). Other than parasites and skin particles, they also take detritus and even small fish as food. However, not all species signal their offer to perform a cleaning service as explicitly as the territorial Whitebanded cleaner shrimp *Lysmata amboinensis* (see further below) does with characteristic waving movements of its white antennae. Once the problem has been successfully communicated, even large fish will allow a cleaner shrimp to clean the insides of its gills. Never will the fish's jaws close over one of the symbiont helpers in order to eat it. Just like the gentle waving and touching of the shrimp's antennae, also the fish has its ways of telling the shrimp, when it is satisfied with the work and wants to retreat. See also BREEDING SCARLET CLEANER SHRIMP on the following pages.

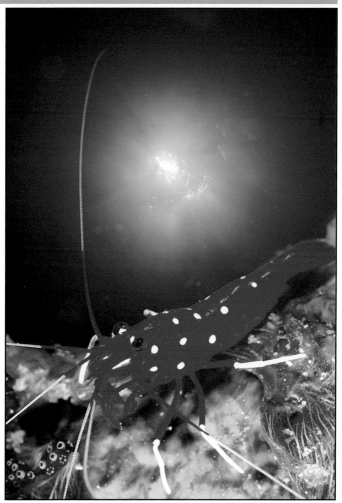

Baa Atoll, Maldives

Lysmata debelius   **Ari Atoll, Maldives**

CORAL CASTLE

Most snorkellers and divers see coral reefs as huge underwater aquaria, filled with many different colourful fishes. Indeed, sessile animals such as corals and sponges, and actively swimming fishes are of course the most conspicuous inhabitants on coral reefs. However, there are a multitude of smaller and easily overlooked animals which live inside the living corals. Hundreds of species of small crustaceans live in these coral cities, either occasionally or in a life-long association on corals. The author provides an insight into the secret life within hard corals.

ROGER STEENE

The distinctly coloured palaemonid shrimp *Coralliocaris graminea* associates with diverse hard corals.

Reef-building (hermatypic) corals are among the most fascinating animals on the planet. Most people have no idea how important these animals are. Corals are able to form entire islands and thus make living space available to plants and animals, including humans. Even more important their particular morphology and often large size create numerous microhabitats and are thus responsible for an endless number of slightly different ecological niches occupied by other organisms. To illustrate how fine-tuned these niches can be, we imagine a large stag-horn coral colony *(Acropora)* with organisms dwelling deep inside the branches, crawling on the tips or close to the basal dead portion of coral, or just swimming between the branches. Coral polyps also are an important food source for many animals, either in the form of the living coral tissue, parts of the skeleton or the mucus secreted by the polyps.

Crustaceans are particularly numerous on corals, but are rather difficult to see. Many dwell deep between the branches or in cavities, and come out at night and only for a short period of time. Beautifully coloured shrimps such as *Saron* come out at night to forage or to search for a mate. *Saron* species, many of which are still undescribed, are not symbiotically associated with corals, but simply use the cavities and narrow spaces between coral branches where they are relatively safe from most predators. At night, however, they have to be very careful because many predators such as squirrel fishes (Holocentridae) are notorious nocturnal hunters of reef-dwelling crustaceans.

Paguritta species are tiny and funny-looking hermit crabs which use small holes made by coral-boring worms or molluscs for a home. They often look out of their "windows" filtering plankton brought by the current with their feather-like antennae. The photo shows a coral portion with a particularly large "colony" of these hermits.

Other crustaceans live in so-called mutualistic associations (with mutual benefits for each partner) with corals. Many shrimps from the palaemonid subfamily Pontoniinae (commensal shrimps) and the family Alpheidae (snapping shrimps) are obligate coral associates. Corals are not only safe domiciles but also free canteens for these shrimps.

Pocillopora species are among the corals which are most frequently inhabited by shrimps, squat lobsters, porcellanids and crabs. At close inspection a single large colony of *Pocillopora damicornis* can yield dozens of these small decapods and of course many other animals such as other crustaceans, fishes and worms. How do they live together? How strong is the competition for living space? How do they share the food resources? Are all of them "gentle" to their coral hosts or, if not, to which

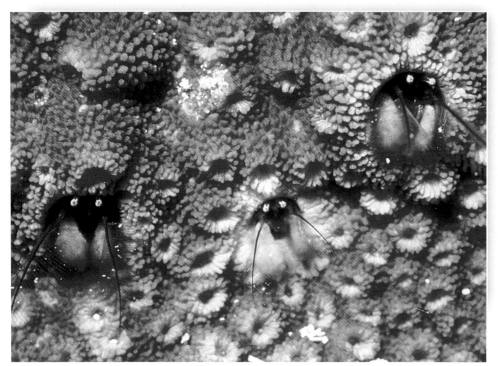

Residence of *Paguritta* hermit crabs. Each has a small "flat" with a "window".

degree do they damage the coral colony? We are actually only at the beginning of understanding the function of this complex community. Behavioural studies on the snapping shrimp *Alpheus lottini* and a crab of the genus *Trapezia* show how fascinating this can be. *Trapezia* crabs have powerful claws and are slightly larger and more robust than snapping shrimps. The shrimps know that they would probably loose a direct fight with the highly territorial *Trapezia* crabs, and for this reason they developed a completely different technique making possible a peaceful cohabitation with the crabs. Male and female *Trapezia* communicate with each other using very specific signals. Each encounter between the male and the female starts with the exchange of specific behavioural patterns, such as gentle pushing, claw rubbing and - finally - body contact. These patterns are part of the so-called appeasement behaviour, *Alpheus lottini* has apparently "learned" to imitate these patterns, it can speak "crabese language".

The shrimp tries to transmit a kind of message like "I'm not an intruder, we can peacefully live together" to the crab, and in most cases it works. Crabs, which initially reacted reacted aggressively towards the shrimp, suddenly become very gentle and relaxed! Then what do all the other coral symbionts in order to live with their dominant neighbours? We don't know yet.

One of the most conspicuous members of the genus *Trapezia* is *Trapezia rufopunctata*.

249

Similan Islands, Thailand

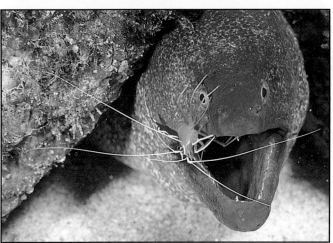

Des Roches, Seychelles

White-banded cleaner shrimp

Length: up to 6 cm.
Distribution: entire area.
General: one of the most important invertebrate cleaners of reef fishes. The distinct coloration is very similar to that of the Atlantic species *L. grabhami,* the synonymy of which is still being discussed. The white line on the red back is broken at the tail fan in *L. amboinensis,* continuous in *L. grabhami.* Often seen in pairs, groups of up to 100 have been encountered in the reef.

The cleaner shrimps of the family Hippolytidae are known to free especially large, stationary reef fishes such as morays and groupers from parasites and infected skin. Additionally, they do not only pick parasites off the outside of these fishes, but they may even stroll into the mouth of their predatory customers to remove food remains from between their teeth. Consequently, they have become known by the generic term "cleaner shrimp" and are recognised by uw-photographers as well as crustacea enthusiasts by this name. However, there are species of cleaner shrimp in other families, too.

Members of the genus *Lysmata* are not only found in tropical seas, but also in temperate and cold waters. Two, for example, live in the Mediterranean Sea. Almost all are known to be cleaners.

Lysmata amboinensis Mentawai, Sumatra

Marble shrimp

Le: up to 4 cm. Di: entire area. Ge: carapace short, abdomen with hump (all fam. members), rostrum large and spiny, a row of tufts of bristles down the back. Nocturnal, singly or in pairs in protected lagoons and fringing reefs. Adult males (below) with first pair of legs longer than in females (right).

Saron marmoratus   Ari Atoll, Maldives

Tapestry shrimp

Length: about 10 cm including the chelipeds.
Distribution: until now known only from the coast of Myanmar.
General: this yet undescribed species with its unique colour pattern was discovered by the photographer during a midnight dive at the largely unexplored coast of Myanmar. He reports that it showed principally the same behaviour as its more common congener *S. marmoratus*. After the photo flash it immediately disappeared into the coral reef thicket. Photo shows a male.

Saron sp.   Myanmar

Squat shrimp

Le: up to 2 cm. Di: entire area. Ge: commensal on corals and anemones, e.g. *Heteractis*. Abdomen held up almost vertically. Females almost twice the size of males. Usually seen in pairs on their host, also in groups. Not a cleaner, but found on mantis shrimp (eyes in left half of large photo).

Thor amboinensis   Similan Islands, Thailand

251

Ghost boxer shrimp

Le: up to 3 cm. Di: entire area. Ge: found in its natural reef habitat from 10 m downward. The Ghost boxer shrimp is shy and hides in caves and crevices by day. It is seen singly or in pairs. There is no external sexual dimorphism. The species is relatively rare in nature, where it has been observed cleaning fishes. This boxer shrimp leads a significantly more secretive life than other cleaning species of *Stenopus*. The photo was taken in 55 m while searching for an undescribed angelfish. See also preceeding page.

Stenopus pyrsonotus　　　　　Flic en Flac, Mauritius

Blue-legged boxer shrimp

Length: up to 3 cm. Distribution: entire area. General: this boxer shrimp is found singly or in pairs in the reef, where it hides in caves. No external sexual dimorphism. Described only in 1984.

Stenopus cyanoscelis　　　　　Kilifi, Kenya

Devaney's boxer shrimp

Length: up to 6 cm. Distribution: from the Maldives eastward to the Andaman Sea. Not known from East Africa or the Mascarenes. General: this boxer shrimp species shows a distinct mating behaviour. However, there is no external sexual dimorphism, both sexes have two red spots on the back. Reproducing females carry yellowish-white eggs under the abdomen. The eggs hatch after 14 days. The extremely shy species has been described only in 1984.

Stenopus devaneyi　　　　　Negombo, Sri Lanka

Banded boxer shrimp

Length: up to 5 cm.
Distribution: entire area.
General: a common cleaner shrimp with spiny, bristly body and chelipeds. The base of the chelipeds is blue. The species is always found in pairs. Sexual dimorphism: males are smaller. Found in crevices from 3 m downward.

Stenopus hispidus   Ari Atoll, Maldives

Zanzibar boxer shrimp

Length: up to 3 cm.
Distribution: entire area.
General: abdomen and chelipeds of this boxer shrimp species show a repetitious white and red pattern, characteristic for all members of the genus. Antennae red, body and first leg segments yellow.

Stenopus species have small first two pairs of legs, the third pair is enlarged to form clawed chelipeds. Probably all are cleaners, waving antennae at the entrance of their cave to attract fish customers. These are searched for parasites after they have been pacified with gentle strokes of the antennae.

Stenopus zanzibaricus   Shimoni, Kenya

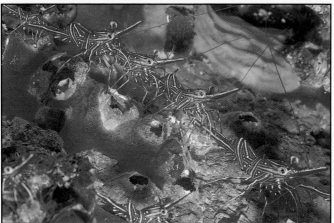

La Digue, Seychelles

Rhynchocinetes durbanensis   Surin Island, Thailand

Durban dancing shrimp

Length: up to 4 cm.
Distribution: South Africa to
Thailand. General: the Durban
dancing shrimp is similar in
colour pattern and often
incorrectly reported as *R. uritai*, but differs in having a very
long, toothed rostrum. Another difference is concerning the
coloration: the white inner
lines are as bold as the red
ones, and not of different
width as in *R. uritai*. It lives
deep in crevices and holes,
usually in large numbers.
   Large bulging eyes and the
humpback are obvious mor-
phological characteristica that
differentiate members of this
family from other decapods. A
less obvious, but very important morphological detail is
their hinged rostrum that can
be folded down. In other
decapods the (often serrated)
appendage extending forward
from the head is usually a fixed
part of the cephalothorax. The
significance of this moveable
appendage for dancing shrimps
is seen during the molting
process: the folded-down rostrum facilitates shedding the
old carapace.
   Rhynchocinetids are called
dancing shrimps because of
their unusual way of moving
on the ground: they strut
around carefully, only to pause
after a few movements. This
abrupt stop is reminiscent of a
tango dancer.

Dancing shrimp species

The photos show two unde-
termined and very probably
yet undescribed species of
dancing shrimp; the small photo below is also from Thailand.
   Dancing shrimps are gregari-
ous and often encountered in
their natural habitat in groups
of up to 100 individuals.

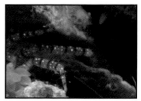

Rhynchocinetes sp.   Burma Banks, Thailand

PARTNER SHRIMPS — PALAEMONIDAE

Bruun's cleaning partner shrimp

Le: up to 3 cm. Di: entire area including Red Sea, eastward to Japan. Ge: this partner shrimp is nearly totally transparent with red and white markings on carapace and legs. It is encountered in holes and caves, where it seems to float motionless in the water. This species is often incorrectly reported as *Leandrites cyrtorhynchus*. Like the species of the Cleaner shrimp family it is an important invertebrate cleaner of diverse reef fishes. The top large photo shows several individuals cleaning the body surface and the interior of the mouth cavity of a Redmouth grouper *Aethaloperca rogaa*. The centre large photo shows another customer of the serranid family, the Window grouper *Gracila albomarginata*, also cleaned especially in the head region and the mouth cavity. The small photo below (Andaman Sea) shows the shrimp resting on a fan coral. See also **Harlequin shrimp** *Hymenocera picta* (Hymenoceridae) on back cover.

Felidhoo Atoll, Maldives

Urocaridella antonbruunii — Astove, Seychelles

Emperor partner shrimp

Length: up to 2 cm. Distribution: entire area including Red Sea, eastward to Hawaii. General: the broad lamina of the antennal scales of this partner shrimp species give it a duck-billed appearance. Its overall coloration is always excellently adapted to its invertebrate host. The shrimp is regularly found on the Spanish dancer *Hexabranchus sanguineus*, where it feeds on fecal pellets and mucus near the nudibranch's gills. It is also found on diverse species of sea cucumbers (see photo).

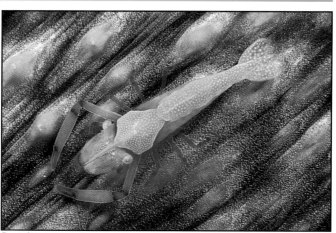

Periclimenes imperator — Similan Islands, Thailand

Magnificent partner shrimp

Le: up to 2 cm. Di: Andaman Sea eastward. Ge: with coral *Catalaphyllia* and tube anemone *Dofleinia armata* (photo). Below: **Clown shrimp** *P. brevicarpalis*, 4 cm, entire area, 5 dark 'ocelli' on tail fan. With anemones, especially *C. adhaesivum*.

Periclimenes magnificus   Richelieu Rock, Thailand

Ornate partner shrimp

Le: up to 4 cm. Di: entire area, RS. Ge: transparent body with fine red reticulate pattern. Legs and tail fan with deep purple and white specks. Associated with *Entacmaea* spp., and *Heteractis magnifica*. Below: **Inornate partner shrimp** *P. inornatus*, 3 cm, with anemones.

Periclimenes ornatus   La Digue, Seychelles

SNAPPING SHRIMPS
ALPHEIDAE

Djedda snapping shrimp
Length: up to 4 cm. Distribution: entire area, RS. General: coloration is a diffuse light greenish mottling. There is also a distinctive white saddle on the back and a black blotch on both sides of the caparace. The antennae are yellowish. Found on bottoms covered with coral rubble, living in association with species of the goby genus *Amblyeleotris* (here *A. steinitzi*). About 140 family members are known in tropical seas, most of which are not symbiotic. See further symbiotic species on pp.203-204.

Alpheus djeddensis   Praslin, Seychelles

Similan Islands, Thailand

Painted spiny lobster

Length: up to 40 cm.
Distribution: entire area including Red Sea.
Ge: the antennae of this species are white, its carapace is black and yellowish-white, the abdomen green with black and white transverse bands. The tail fan appears green to blue. See also photo on previous page taken at noon at the house reef of Elaidhoo, Ari Atoll.

Spiny lobsters are among the most beautiful and impressive crustacea. The absence of claws separates them from other lobsters, their first pair of walking legs is still in a primitive stage of development. The second to last leg segment, however, bears a thorn that - when enlarged proportionally - distinctly resembles the propus, the non-moveable finger of the crustacean claw. Scientists assume that lobsters with large claws evolved from spiny lobsters. Another difference concerns the rostrum: spiny lobster have two, while other lobsters have only one rostrum.

Panulirus versicolor

Ari Atoll, Maldives

Ornate spiny lobster

Length: up to 40 cm.
Distribution: entire area including Red Sea.
General: all species of spiny lobster are able to swim backwards with strong and rapid flapping movements of their abdomen and tail fan. The abdominal segments have sharp spines and edges for defence. Handle with care, if one has to. The long antennae are the main sensory organ. As nocturnal animals they rely on their sense of touch. Broken antennae are regenerated after the next molt.

Panulirus ornatus

Mafia, Tanzania

Common spiny lobster

Le: up to 35 cm. Di: entire area including Red Sea. Ge: the most common spiny lobster in our area. Antennae not white, series of dark-ringed white spots on the spotted dark abdomen. Legs dark with white longitudinal lines. Broad tail fan. No claws on legs.

Panulirus penicillatus   Lhaviyani Atoll, Maldives

Scalloped spiny lobster

Length: up to 33 cm.
Distribution: entire area.
General: by day spiny lobsters hide in crevices, antennae showing, often in groups. At night they are scavenging and preying on worms, shells, and echinoderms all over the reef. Many species of spiny lobsters migrate into shallow water during summer. They are regionally of commercial importance, and caught in traps baited with carrion.

Panulirus homarus   Myanmar

Long-legged spiny lobster

Length: up to 30 cm.
Distribution: entire area.
General: the first antenna of spiny lobsters is not whip-like as in lobsters, but forked close to the tip. The second antenna is long and has a strongly developed basal segment. By rubbing the antennae segments against each other, spiny lobsters can produce audible creaking noises. A peculiarity concerning the reproductive behaviour can occasionally be watched under water: some spiny lobster species congregate in long queues to march to their mating grounds.

Panulirus longipes   Thailand

Red reef lobster

Length: up to 12 cm.
Distribution: entire area.
General: reef lobsters are
spending the day hidden in the
deepest parts of caves and
crevices. Consequently, they
can be encountered only at
night. If a specimen or a pair
have been found, they will be
in the same area night after
night as long as they are not
molested. The external sexual
organs of reef lobsters can
only be seen on the ventral
side of the abdomen. There is
no further (more obvious)
external sexual dimorphism.
   The small photo below
shows a surprised specimen
found after a dead piece of
coral had been turned over.

Enoplometopus occidentalis　　　　**Ari Atoll, Maldives**

Voigtmann's reef lobster

Le: up to 10 cm. Di: Maldives,
probably Sri Lanka. Ge: this
attractive species has been
described in 1989, and has yet
been found only in some locations at the Ari and Male
Atolls in the Maldives. There
are yet unconfirmed reports of
this species from Sri Lanka.
Below: **Daum's reef lobster**
Enoplometopus daumi, up to 11
cm, eastern Indian Ocean and
West Pacific. Despite the fact
that reef lobsters are relatively
widespread and common, they
are rarely found during nocturnal dives due to their highly
secretive way of life. Very shy,
exposed to light they immediately retreat into hiding places.

Enoplometopus voigtmanni　　　　**Male Atoll, Maldives**

White-spotted hermit crab

Le: up to 25 cm, usually 10 cm.
Di: South Africa and Madagascar to Australia and Pacific.
Ge: large sp., sometimes with tiny red and white shrimp as commensal inside shell.
 Hermit crabs are walking decapods with their fourth and fifth pair of legs reduced in size, and a soft abdomen, which is put into an empty snail shell for protection. A hermit crab has to move to a new, larger shell every now and then as it grows. Availability of shells is a major point for discussion between hermits.

Dardanus megistos   Ari Atoll, Maldives

Blue sock hermit crab

Le: up to 2 cm. Di: entire area.
Ge: coloration of antennae and tips of walking legs distinct for *Calcinus* spp., which use a wide variety of shells. Below: undescribed *Calcinus* sp. (Maldives).
 Many hermit crabs are nocturnal predators, feeding on diverse living and dead animals.

Calcinus latens   Male Atoll, Maldives

Feather star squat lobster

Le: up to 2 cm. Di: Indo-Pacific to Australia, RS. Ge: lives on the arms of feather stars. First pair of legs about twice as long as carapace, strong, clawed. Coloration variable, depending on that of the feather star host, often with white longitudinal band on back. Tips of claws and legs white. Steals plankton food from host. Male smaller than female. The pontoniid shrimp *Allopontonia iaini* closely resembles this species, but lives on a sea urchin.

Allogalathea elegans   Praslin, Seychelles

PORCELAIN CRABS   PORCELLANIDAE

Anemone crab

Le: up to 3 cm. Di: entire area.
Ge: carapace rounded, crab-
like, surface smooth. Chelipeds
broad, strong, with large claws.
Colour creamy white, many
small red spots. Among tentacles
or under rim of large sea anemones (Cryptodendrum, Entacmaea). Bel.: N. alobatus (Kenya).

Neopetrolisthes maculatus   **Aldabra, Seychelles**

Anemone crab species

Le: up to 1.5 cm. Di: Mauritius.
Ge: undescribed species.
Below: *Petrolisthes cinctipes*. All
family members have the third
maxillipeds lined with many
long bristles: these fans move
rhythmically to and fro to filter
plankton from the water, which
is brushed in by the mandibles.

Neopetrolisthes sp.   **Mauritius**

CORAL CRABS   TRAPEZIIDAE

Red-spotted coral crab

Le: up to 1.5 cm. Di: entire
area, RS. Ge: yellowish with
about 200 red dots on carapace and legs. On branching
corals. Feeds on mucus and
detritus. Below: *Tetralia cavima-
na,* 1.2 cm, on *Acropora* corals.

Trapezia rufopunctata   **Des Roches, Seychelles**

262

Peacock mantis shrimp

Le: up to 17 cm. Di: entire area. Ge: very colourful, uses tail fan in threat display (centre large photo), guards eggs (small photo below). Feeds on shrimps, fishes, and worms.

Mantis shrimps (Stomatopoda) are elongate crustaceans characterised by a very short carapace, only three pairs of walking legs, and a long flattened tail. Most conspicuous is a pair of praying mantis-like raptorial claws, folded under the sides of the carapace. In Gonodactylids the claws have an inflated terminal segment, an adaptation to crush prey with a strong blow (smashers; this sp. is the largest smasher, able to destroy aquarium glass! Members of other families (see next sp.) have slender, toothed claws to spear prey (spearers). Mantis shrimps are living solitarily in simple burrows with two openings. They hunt from the burrow or leave it to forage.

Trinco, Sri Lanka

Odontodactylus scyllarus   Felidhoo Atoll, Maldives

Banded mantis shrimp

Le: to 38 cm. Di: entire area. Ge: distinctly banded, also swimming in open water. All family members have T-shaped eyes and slender raptorial claws (below), used to spear prey in praying mantis fashion.

Lysiosquillina maculata   Ari Atoll, Maldives

COMBAT FOR TERRITORY

That space is a limited commodity in the ocean's most densely populated environment, the tropical coral reef, is obvious to every observant skin diver. There are many ways in which organisms can assert themselves against neighbours of the same or of a different species. Sedentary invertebrates like corals and sea anemones use chemical defense mechanisms, while moving organisms such as fishes tend to resort to outright violence. Here are a few examples:

MARK STRICKLAND

Two Spotted hawkfishes *Cirrhitichthys oxycephalus* having a heated argument over the best place to lie in ambush for prey.

As is the case in every other natural environment, reef organisms have only two basic needs: to feed and to reproduce. These two fundamental necessities of life provide ample cause for territorial competition between reef fishes of the same species.

Hawkfishes, for instance, hover motionless over a coral head or branch and wait for some unsuspecting prey to swim by. If the passerby happens to be a member of the same species, there is bound to be trouble because the intruder is obviously looking for new feeding grounds and the present "proprietor" is not about to give up his territory without a fight. Waiting in ambush means investing a lot of time and being dependent upon chance. Therefore, good places are rigorously defended. The fish push and shove each other with their snouts until the weaker combatant finally abandons the field.

The same basically applies to the larger groupers, even though they chase down their prey rather than wait in ambush. Each one of these solitary predators has its own limited hunting territory, which provides just enough nourishment for one specimen. Consequently, intruders have to be chased away immediately and with as little expenditure of energy as possible. By the way, these confrontations are not really always as violent as they appear to be. Active predators can hardly afford serious wounds, and so it

Large fishes like the Malabar grouper *Epinephelus malabaricus* are also willing to start a fight over the least incursion into their territory because they need a lot of space to hunt in.

HELMUT DEBELIUS

Two male Two-spot splendour wrasses *Oxycheilinus bimaculatus* contend for a female and a spawning place.

usually remains a matter of matching strength. Among some of the more colourful denizens of the reef, such as a few species of butterflyfishes, the entire conflict is reduced to a mere display of strength without any body contact at all. Behavioural scientists refer to this as ritualised fighting.

The other major cause for territorial conflict within the species is the sexual drive. Many species of fish (e.g. several groupers, wrasses, gobies, and trigger fishes) don't simply spawn in the open water (as pelagic spawners like surgeon fishes, mackerel, and tunas are in the habit of doing), but watch over their eggs until they hatch. This task begins with the process of finding an appropriate spawning place. Depending upon the species, either the male or the female will choose a suitable spot and thereby lay claim to a certain spawning territory that both partners will fiercely defend against all intruders, even giant ones like curious divers and underwater photographers. In the case of those fishes that are better equipped to defend themselves, such as large trigger fishes or poisonous lion fishes, it is highly advisable to maintain a certain distance in order to avoid serious consequences.

There is a simple way to test the aggressiveness of territorial fishes: whereas primates and humans are able to recognise their own reflection, fishes will automatically regard it as a rival that has to be chased

A quick bite from behind and the enemy takes to his heels: Common bigeyes *Priacanthus hamrur* in a territorial dispute.

The Bicolor cleaner wrasse *Labroides bicolor* mistakes its reflection in the mirror for a rival that needs to be driven off.

away. However, such experiments should be terminated before the "real McCoy" dies of sheer exhaustion....

Pairs or entire families of anemone fishes are in the habit of occupying a very special kind of territory, namely nettling sea anemones. This symbiosis is vital for the anemone fish, which is why it signals its territorial claim with a cracking sound that carries over 2 metres. An absolutely unique phenomenon in the world of fishes. This ritualised acoustic defense mechanism enables the fish to remain near its protector and

thereby reduce the chances of being devoured by a predator. Only when the rival proves to be obstinate, will the fish reduce the distance to a few centimetres. Then minimal but still quite apparent changes in coloration will occur, such as a streak above the eye, to denote the heightened aggressiveness of the fish. If all these rituals should fail to scare away the intruder, then the tiny pugilist will deal out a series of sharp blows with its snout, which many a diver has felt on the reflecting surface of his mask. A word to the wise: one should not carry such underwater experiments too far because, as was mentioned previously, not all territorial fishes are harmless.

Anemone fishes (in this case *Amphiprion clarkii*) defend their host anemone against anything and anyone, regardless of size. Here the tiny fellow is about to attack the camera lens with gaping "jaws."

The message is absolutely clear: the outspread fins and gaping mouth of the Zebra dwarf lionfish *Dendrochirus zebra* leave little room for doubt.

Molluscs are characterised by a muscular mantle (the outer part of the soft body), a radula (a tooth-covered rasping "tongue" working much like a conveyor belt), and a muscular foot that originally serves in locomotion but may be modified for diverse uses. Molluscs are adapted to live almost anywhere in barren, lifeless zones, where food is non-existent or inaccessible. Thus, sandy areas are heavens for molluscs with long siphons and bodies adapted for burrowing, such as a majority of bivalves, and many gastropods. A mixture of sand and mud will provide an even better habitat for burrowers because it contains more food. This is the ideal environment for numerous bivalve groups, particularly those with delicately constructed shells. Molluscs with stronger shells are associated with rocky shores and their rough conditions. The phylum Mollusca comprises several classes, covered are snails and slugs (Gastropoda), bivalves (Bivalvia, Lamellibranchiata), and cephalopods like octopus and squid (Cephalopoda).

Gastropoda fall into several subclasses, two of which are covered here: Prosobranchia (gills by body torsion during evolution in front of internal organs; Turbinidae p.266 - Conidae p.271), including the popular shelled species, and Opisthobranchia (gills at posterior end of the body; Aplysiidae p.271 - Phyllidiidae p.277), including sea slugs. Prosobranchs contain two orders of different evolutionary level: Archaeogastropoda (primitive), and Caenogastropoda (conservative to modern). The Turbinidae belong to the first group. Other prosobranch families in this book belong to the more advanced caenogastropods.

Opisthobranchia have reduced or no shells, a soled foot for creeping or lobes for swimming, and dorsal protuberances called cerata, often used in defence as deposit for active stinging cells of their cnidarian prey. Vulnerable as they are, most sea slugs are poisonous, advertising this fact by bright and colourful warning patterns. All are voracious carnivores, consuming slower or sessile organisms. Among others the group includes the orders sea hares (Anaspidea), sap-sucking slugs (Saccoglossa), and the numerous nudibranchs (Nudibranchia, literally "naked gills", in most species the gills or branchial plumes are external). They are found in most habitats of all oceans, diversity being greatest in the Indo-Pacific. For more information see another volume in the series of marine identification guides: NUDIBRANCHS AND SEA SNAILS.

Bivalves (p.278-279) are found from the tidal zone down. All have two shells (left and right), connected by a group-specific type of hinge and flexible bands (ligaments). Most of them are sessile filter-feeders, buried in soft (sand), or fixed to hard (rock) substrate by byssus (threads secreted from a gland) or one cemented shell. A few can swim.

The highly specialised Cephalopoda (p.280-283) have a head with the molluscan foot modified into eight (octopuses) or ten (cuttlefish and squid) prehensile tentacles, equipped with suckers and/or hooks and arranged in a circle. In its centre lies the mouth with a strong parrot-like beak, used to crack the shells of molluscs and crabs, their main prey. They can swim fast by contracting the mantle and thus squirting a jet of water. A dark "ink" is used in defence.

Taxa above family level are listed in the contents section at the beginning of this book.

Turbo petholatus

Mentawai Islands, Sumatra

Cat's eye turban

Le: up to 12 cm. Di: entire area. Ge: the calcareous operculum of turbans is called cat's eye. Below: **Silvermouth turban** *T. argyrostomus*, 7 cm, entire area, shallow. Popular name refers to the aperture.

Common spider conch

Le: up to 18 cm. Di: entire
area, Red Sea. Ge: large, locally
common, collected and eaten,
on coral sand, in lagoons.
Aperture smooth, nodules of
spire relatively small. Females
with longer "fingers."
Below: *L. chiragra*, 15 cm, sub-
spp. in W- and E-Indian Ocean.

Lambis lambis   Cocos Keeling Islands, West Australia

False Arabian cowrie

Le: up to 7 cm. Di: entire area.
Ge: the shell of this cowrie
shows a brown reticulate pattern on a lighter bluish-grey
background.
  Characteristic for living
cowries is the bilobed mantle,
which can cover the whole
shell when it is fully extended.
It keeps the outer shell shiny
as long as the animal is alive.
An empty shell will soon loose
its porcelain-like appearance
and become dull due to chemical (acidic) and mechanical
(abrasion) influences.

Mauritia histrio   Ari Atoll, Maldives

Tiger cowrie

Length: up to 10 cm.
Distribution: entire area, not
in Red Sea. General: this large
cowrie is a well-known shell,
common in shallow coastal
reefs. Its coloration is very
variable throughout its range
from heavily mottled and spotted to almost entirely white.

Cypraea tigris   Beau Vallon, Seychelles

267

Carnelian cowrie

Length: up to 6.5 cm.
Distribution: entire area, Red
Sea. General: a common
species found under coral slabs
in shallow water. Below: similar, but larger is the **Leviathan
cowrie** *L. leviathan,* 8 cm,
regarded as subspecies of *L.
carneola* by some authors.

Lyncina carneola   Male Atoll, Maldives

Mole cowrie

Length: up to 6 cm.
Distribution: entire area
including Red Sea.
General: a common species,
closely resembling the much
rarer Exusta cowrie *T. exusta,*
which is found around the
Arabian Peninsula. The shell
can be distinguished by finer
teeth and a more curved aperture. The animal itself looks
quite spectacular with its black
mantle that is covered with
white specks and finger-like
papillae.

Talparia talpa   Trinco, Sri Lanka

Tiger egg cowrie

Le: 1.5 cm. Di: Thailand. Ge:
mantle coloration distinct, lives
in 1 - 75 m, feeds on gorgonians *(Euplexaura).* Below: **Umbilical ovula** *Calpurnus verru-
cosus,* feeds on leather corals
(Sarcophyton), imitates host.

Crenavolva tigris   Mergui, Myanmar

Maldives sponge snail

Le: up to 4 cm. Di: Maldives only. Ge: nocturnal, shallow. Mantle has thick appendages and resembles a sponge. Thin shells overgrown by mantle, eyes located on base of tentacles, thus mistaken for opisthobranchs even by specialists. Feeds on ascidians (sea squirts).

Coriocella hibyae Lhaviyani Atoll, Maldives

Horned helmet

Le: up to 22 cm. Di: East Africa eastward. Ge: largest family member, shoulder knobs distinct, common in sand areas in depths of 1 - 20 m. The small photo below shows the aperture.

Cassis cornuta Praslin, Seychelles

Partridge tun

Le: up to 12 cm. Di: ent. area. Ge: animal can be 50 cm long, too large for its shell. Only after shrinking by releasing water from its tissues, does it fit into its shell. Sipho serves as olfactory organ to detect prey (see below: *Tonna* sp.).

Tonna perdix Flic en Flac, Mauritius

Chicoreus ramosus   **Praslin, Seychelles**

Ramose murex

Length: up to 20 cm.
Distribution: Red Sea, Arabian
Sea, Indo-Pacific.
General: a very common shallow water species, found on
coral reefs. Probably THE sou-
venir shell, hence exploited by
heavy collecting.
The family of Murex shells
belongs to the caenogastropod
suborder Stenoglossa (with a
narrow radula), containing the
most advanced sea snails.
These comprise a large number of families with about
20,000 species. Most are carnivorous or feed on carrion,
some are parasitic.

Colubraria sp.   **Hin Daeng, Thailand**

Vampire pygmy triton

Le: up to 4 cm. Di: Andaman
Sea. Ge: all genus members
lack the typical feeding organ
of molluscs, the radula. Moreover, they have a specially
modified proboscis, a tube-like
part of the snout, which is
extendable and retractable,
and looks like a lump of spagh-
etti, when stored inside the
animal. *Colubraria* spp. are ectoparasites sneaking up sleeping
fishes to suck their blood as in
the Nurse shark on the photo.
See NUDIBRANCH GUIDE
for more info.

Harpa davidis   **Similan Islands, Thailand**

David harp
Length: up to 8 cm.
Distribution: Maldives to Thailand.
General: found in a few metres
depth, often partially buried in
sand near coral patches and in
shallow lagoons. Large creeping foot, long sipho. Eyes are
located on long stalks, tentacles are long and pointed.
Feeds on crabs that are first
covered with mucus and sand
to stun and suffocate them,
before they are eaten. Able to
autotomise part of foot when
threatened by predatory snail.
Photo shows a mating pair.

CONE SHELLS CONIDAE

Map cone shell

Length: up to 10 cm.
Distribution: entire area.
General: a common, wide-spread shallow water species.
The shell is relatively thin-walled, and has convex sides in contrast to most other cone shells. The venom of the Map cone shell is highly toxic to fishes and mammals. Very probably it is the most danger-ous family member, responsi-ble for several dozen human deaths. The photo shows the voracious proboscis of the liv-ing animal.

Conus geographus Grande Baie, Mauritius

SEA HARES APLYSIIDAE

Lemon sea hare

Length: up to 4 cm.
Distribution: Maldives to Andaman Sea, probably more widespread. General: found on algae-covered substrates. Look for them in *Halimeda* fields! Below: congregating group.

Stylocheilus citrina Ari Atoll, Maldives

ELYSIIDS ELYSIIDAE

Moebius' elysia

Length: up to 3 cm. Distribu-tion: western Indian Ocean. General: all genus members are greenish due to the chlo-roplasts taken up with the algae that they feed on. Below: *E. expansa*, 3 cm, E- to S-Africa.

Elysia moebii Mabibi, South Africa

Lined neon slug

Length: up to 4.5 cm.
Distribution: Seychelles to western Australia. General: brown lines or blotches on body distinct, moves relatively fast, feeds on tunicates. Below: this colour pattern from the Seychelles resembles the nominal form most closely.

Nembrotha lineolata   Chagos Islands

Mauritius neon slug

Length: up to 5 cm.
Distribution: southern Indian Ocean.
General: this nudibranch is living in the tropics, where it is mainly found from the subtidal zone to the base of reef slopes. A Japanese expert found differences between this species and the well-known *T. morosa* and thus described as new species.

Tambja kushimotoensis   Flic en Flac, Mauritius

Variable neon slug

Length: up to 6 cm.
Distribution: South Africa to Micronesia.
General: the surface of the body is covered with small green pustules, the thin red margin around the foot and the head is present in all specimens from throughout the species' range of distribution. The photo depicts the nominal colour pattern mainly found in the Indian Ocean, while western Pacific specimens tend to be more variable in coloration. The facing page (Ari Atoll, Maldives) shows *N. cristata* feeding on colonial ascidians.

Nembrotha kubaryana   Flic en Flac, Mauritius

NOTODORIDIDS   NOTODORIDIDAE

Gardiner's neon slug

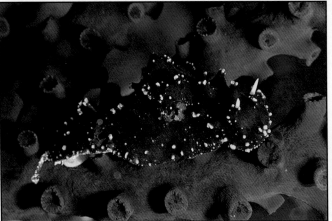

Length: up to 8 cm.
Distribution: Maldives to Australia. General: intensity of
brown colour and distribution
of blotches very variable. Body
rigid and motionless, when
handled. Below: *N. minor,*
9 cm, East Africa to West
Pacific, feeds on sponges.

Notodoris gardineri   **Ari Atoll, Maldives**

HEXABRANCHIDS   HEXABRANCHIDAE

Spanish dancer

Le: up to 40 cm. Di: entire
area, Red Sea. Ge: many divers
are familiar with this exquisite,
mainly red and white patterned snail. Shown is the typical Indian Ocean colour pattern. The common name
refers to its amazing ability to
swim with graceful undulations
of its mantle margins. The
species feeds on sponges that
provide noxious substances
making it distasteful. Accompanied by a pair of the shrimp
Periclimenes imperator, matched
in colour for protection.

Hexabranchus sanguineus   **Mozambique**

CHROMODORIDIDS   CHROMODORIDIDAE

Loch's magnificent slug

Length: up to 3 cm.
Distribution: East Africa to
West Pacific. General: feeds on
sponges. Below: *C. elizabethina,*
4.6 cm, Seychelles to West
Pacific. This family comprises
the most attractive nudibranchs.

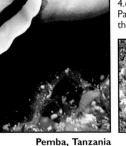

Chromodoris lochi   **Pemba, Tanzania**

Twin magnificent slug

Length: up to 6 cm.
Distribution: eastern Indian
Ocean, Red Sea. General: several similar species occur in
the range of distribution.
Below: *C. tritos*, 4.5 cm, Maldives, Seychelles, coloration
similar, but distinct from that
of the previous species.

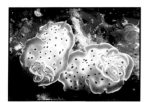

Chromodoris geminus   Praslin, Seychelles

Joshi's magnificent slug

Length: up to 6 cm.
Distribution: Thailand eastward. General: only recently
described, black and yellow
colour pattern distinct. Below:
C. gleniei, 4.5 cm, East Africa to
Sri Lanka, patterned central
colour patch distinct, waves
mantle margin when disturbed.

Chromodoris joshi   Similan Islands, Thailand

Beau Vallon magnificent slug

Length: up to 3 cm.
Distribution: Seychelles eastward. General: one of four
similarly coloured species in
the wide range of distribution,
difficult to separate. Below:
Glossodoris hikuerensis, 8 cm,
entire area, RS, pattern distinct.

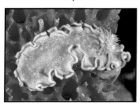

Mexichromis multituberculata   Beau Vallon, Seychelles

Black and white jorunna

Length: up to 5 cm.
Distribution: entire area, Red Sea.
General: the two-tone colour pattern is distinct for the species as is the rough surface texture for all genus members. Its rhinophores and gills are always jet black. A comparison of both specimens in the photo - feeding on their favourite food, a blue sponge (*Haliclona* sp.) - nicely shows that the brownish pustules on the surface of the body may be concentrated in circular patches or dispersed over almost the entire body.

Jorunna funebris   **La Digue, Seychelles**

HALGERDIDS   HALGERDIDAE

Iota slug

Le: up to 1.5 cm. Di: Maldives to Thailand. Ge: described from the Maldives, not common, shown immediately after laying its eggs (left). Below: *H. willeyi*, 7 cm, entire area, RS, deep water sp. (Mozambique).

Halgerda iota   **Mergui, Myanmar**

DENDRODORIDIDS   DENDRODORIDIDAE

Tuberculated dendrodoris

Le: up to 17 cm. Di: entire area, RS. Ge: on intertidal mud flats and muddy reefs, irritates eyes and skin, when carelessly handled. Below: *D. denisoni*, 6 cm, South Africa eastward.

Dendrodoris tuberculosa   **Beau Vallon, Seychelles**

Reticulated wart slug

Length: up to 7 cm.
Distribution: Thailand eastward.
General: not to be confused
with the doridid genus *Halgerda*, this wart slug - like all family members - lacks external gill
plumes. There are similarly
coloured species of this genus
in our area, however, with a
different coloration of the
mantle margin. The wart slugs
are among the most attractive
objects for underwater photographers keen on nudibranch
sea snails.

Reticulidia halgerda   Hin Daeng, Thailand

Krempf's wart slug

Le: up to 7 cm. Di: Sri Lanka
eastward. Ge: a very elongate
genus member with brightly
pink tubercles that fuse to
form ridges on the body.
Below: **Ocellated wart slug**
Phyllidia ocellata, 6 cm, entire
area, RS, very variable species.
Photo from the Seychelles.

Phyllidiopsis krempfi   Praslin, Seychelles

Varicose wart slug

Le: up to 7 cm. Di: entire area,
RS. Ge: all wart slugs are mas-
ters of chemical defence.
When stressed in any way,
they produce a pungent toxin.
No marine organisms are
known to prey on this species.
Below: **Pustulose wart slug**
P. pustulosa, 6 cm, ent. area, RS.

Phyllidia varicosa   Comoros

Burrowing giant clam

Le: up to 30 cm. Di: entire area. Ge: relatively small, embedded in corals. Mantle coloration variable (blue, green, brown), mantle shows to collect sunlight for symbiotic algae, is rapidly withdrawn when disturbed. Below: *T. crocea,* 12 cm, one of the smallest giant clams.

Tridacna maxima   Mozambique

Squamose giant clam

Le: up to 40 cm. Di: entire area, RS. Ge: locally common in shallow reefs to about 10 m. Embedded hinge-down in corals, shell with rows of flanges. Below: a field of giant clams.

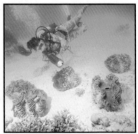

Tridacna squamosa   Beau Vallon, Seychelles

TRUE OYSTERS   OSTREIDAE

Zig-zag oyster

Le: up to 30 cm. Di: entire area, Red Sea. Ge: a locally common oyster, found from 5 m down. The left shell is fixed by strands of byssus to hard substrates at exposed places in the subtidal zone.

Lopha folium   Praslin, Seychelles

THORNY OYSTERS   SPONDYLIDAE

Thorny oyster

Le: up to 25 cm. Di: entire area, RS. Ge: shells heavy, almost circular, edge smooth. Right shell cemented to substrate, moveable left shell as lid. Both with radial ribs and spines on outer surface. margin of mantle colourful (white, blue, yellow, brown, red), with rows of small stalked eyes (a relative of scallops, not oysters!). Shell rapidly closes when shadowed. Heavily overgrown by various invertebrates, here a **Cock's comb oyster** *Lopha cristagalli,* 10 cm, with distinct, sharp-angled zig-zag folds, and an orange sponge.

Spondylus squamosus   Ari Atoll, Maldives

FILE CLAMS   LIMIDAE

Annulated file clam

Le: up to 4 cm. Di: entire area, Red Sea. Ge: file clams are not attached to the substrate and able to move freely by rapidly closing their shell and squirting out a jet of water, thus 'jumping' away from predators (crabs). The filter feeders cannot retract into the shell, have distinct rows of long, pointed tentacles at mantle margin with specific colour and pattern. Common in the subtidal on sand down to 20 m. Build a 'nest' of stones, shell and coral bits, glued together with mucus.

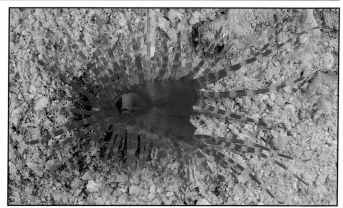

Limaria fragilis   Mulaku Atoll, Maldives

WINGED OYSTERS   PTERIIDAE

Penguin winged oyster

Le: up to 10 cm. Di: entire area. Ge: shells symmetrical, hinge long and straight, one small and one long process at each end. Juv. with processes considerably longer than width of shell. Shell often overgrown by epibionts.

Pteria penguin   Negombo, Sri Lanka

PRIVATE SEPIA

"We were the first living men, who were allowed to look into the peculiar light outside in front of the window, and it was even more peculiar than any fantasy could dream about." This was written by William Beebe over fifty years ago after he had looked out of his diving sphere. Since thirty-five years and much more humble, but with the same fascination, the photographer and narrator looks through the window of his diving mask at the life in the sea. This time he is after "his" cuttlefish again.

ALL FOTOS: HERWARTH VOIGTMANN

Competition in the reef: paired Pharaohs cuttlefish *Sepia pharaonis* and rival males.

Meanwhile I know my cuttlefish quite well. I know on which side of the reef, in which current, and in which depth they are. But only when they are involved in mating and spawning, one can approach them closely. Spawning has such a dominant position in their life that they hardly show any tendency to flee, and one could even catch them by hand. When I meet a single individual in the reef, I watch it from a safe distance. Only in this way I can be sure that it leads me to a spawning pair. After having arrived there I slowly approach the scene, where I am able to watch the most interesting activities from nearby. If the pair is alone and not molested by another courting male, the male stays right beside its chosen female. The female eagerly searches the rubble for empty spaces to deposit its eggs there. The male has raised its two median tentacles like an elephant's proboscis. It looks, as if it were taking up a scent. Its coloration is perfectly adapted to the surroundings and only its marginal fins are moving. If another male approaches, it moves on top of its female partner to signal: she is mine! It spreads all tentacles, assumes an intensive coloration with a zebra pattern, and synchro-

"This girl is mine!" A male Pharaoh cuttlefish keeps contact with its chosen one.

nously follows all movements of the female. She is still searching for egg deposition sites. She does not care at all what is going on around her. Meanwhile, the other male is waiting for its chance. If it approaches the pair too closely, a fight between the males is inevitable. Fast as lightning both opponents stick together with their suckers. Now they try to bite and push away each other. The separation of both sounds like the opening of a bur-type zipper. I have seen wounds from bites on many males, mainly on big ones, who were constantly accompanying females. Once a male

The aroused female assumes a reddish-brown coloration.

obviously took my extended hand and fingers for a competitor. The male quickly grabbed and strongly bit it with its "parrot beak". The wound was small, but real and bleeding profusely. If one leaves cuttlefish alone, however, they will never bite a human being.

Females are smaller than males in most cases, their coloration is less conspicuous than that of courting or fighting males. During spawning the females become reddish-brown, and put their tentacles together to form a point. After having found a small, safe crevice inaccessible for predators, they glue their eggs to its interior wall. These are white, 15 to 20 millimetres long. and resemble grapes. I wanted to know more, and

This male cuttlefish is ready to mate and covering its partner almost completely.

became an egg thief. Exactly after 19 days the 10-millimetres-long, fully developed cuttlefish hatched from their eggs in the aquarium. Immediately they acquire the coloration of their surroundings. They also already have an ink reservoir, which they use in case of disturbance. After a female has deposited about 15 eggs, the climax approaches. The male has to fertilise all eggs that are still inside the female, not those glued to the cave wall. Both partners face each other head to head. They embrace each other with ten tentacles each. Now the male deposits sper-

Copulating cuttlefish with tentacles entwined.

matophores in a pouch under the females mouth within the arm crown. She then passes each egg over this mass of sperm as she transfers them into caves or ledges. New males will sometimes use jets of water to try to flush the sperm of previous suitors out of this pouch before depositing his own.

Meanwhile I know eight pairs in the reef. Two thirds of the year one can meet them in depths from 5 to 30 m. The cuttlefish are long since acclimatised to spotlights, flashlights, film and

After copulating the female hides the fertilised eggs inside a crevice.

photo cameras, and their owners. They are not disturbed by them. Every uw-photographer will be rewarded for a tender approach. Then he or she can be a spectator of one of the most beautiful events in marine life.

After a few days one can see the tiny cuttlefish developing in its egg.

La Digue, Seychelles

Bigfin reef squid

Le: up to 35 cm (mantle). Di: entire area, Red Sea. Ge: body elongate, cigar-shaped, with fins all along its margin. Head small, eyes large. Eight short arms with two rows of suckers, two long tentacles (ending in clubs with suckers), which can be thrown forward to catch fish and shrimp prey. Found in open water of coastal habitats, over reefs, in lagoons, and seagrass beds, from the surface down to at least 100 m. Nocturnally active. Small groups (see centre photo) are often encountered swimming slowly in parallel or staggered formations.

Squids and sepias (see the two previous pages) are decapod (ten-armed) cephalopods. They have two elongated, thin arms called tentacles that end in a club full of suckers. The suckers of squids are equipped with horny rings bearing tooth-like spikes, which are ideal for catching slippery prey. Cephalopods are famous for their ability to change colour patterns extremely fast. Below: a translucent juvenile squid.

Sepioteuthis lessoniana   **Kilifi, Kenya**

Marbled octopus

Le: up to 30 cm. Di: entire area. Ge: mantle with fine papillae in a reticulate pattern, a permanent single cirrus over each eye, found down to a depth of at least 40 m.

All cephalopods have the molluscan foot modified into highly flexible, sensitive arms, which have a multitude of purposes such as locating and catching prey, transfer of sperm, cleaning of eggs etc. Octopuses have a large brain and are regarded as the most highly developed invertebrates.

Octopus aegina   **Male Atoll, Maldives**

Big red octopus

Le: up to 140 cm. Di: entire area, Red Sea. Ge: basic coloration purplish-brown, but variable. Two more or less prominent ringed dark blotches in front of the eyes on the umbrella-like skin that connects the eight arms. By day hidden in a permanent home (a crevice in the reef), the entrance of which is marked by empty mollusc and crab shells, leftovers of meals. Arms may protrude from the cave. Active at night, adults seen by day only when courting (then a second individual is not far away). Juveniles live less secretively in shallower waters. See also SEX ON THE REEF, page 196.

Octopus cyanea   Des Roches, Seychelles

Paper nautilus

Le: up to 20 cm. Di: entire area. Ge: argonauts are related to octopuses; they have eight arms, the two dorsal ones of females bear expanded webs at their ends, which secrete a brittle white shell, the "paper nautilus" shell. This spiralled shell serves as an egg case, in which the eggs are brooded. It is a secondary shell, not a primary one like that of the true Nautilus, which is secreted by the mantle. Argonaut males are dwarves compared to their females, being only about a tenth in size. They lack an external shell. Their third left arm is stored in a pouch and modified as detachable 'hectocotylus' used for sperm transfer to the female. The unique photo shows a female attached to a pelagically drifting medusa ('jellyfish'). Jellies or Scyphozoans are related to corals and basically a free-swimming single polyp turned upside down; they are not covered in this guide.

Argonauta argo   Andaman Sea

283

Pseudoceros bifurcus   **Pemba, Tanzania**

Bifurcated flatworm

Le: up to 6 cm. Di: Madagascar and Comoros eastward. De: 4 - 26 m. Ge: this flatworm is found only on reef slopes. Colour bluish lavender to cream, with distinct white stripe down midline, this stripe orange anteriorly, posteriorly bordered by thin, deep purple edge. Eyes apparent just anterior to the midline. The worm feeds on colonial tunicates.

Flatworms belong to the phylum Platyhelminthes, which also comprises many parasitic species, e.g. tapeworms. Colourful marine species resemble toxic nudibranchs (mimikry).

Pseudoceros susanae   **Baa Atoll, Maldives**

Susan's flatworm

Le: up to 3 cm. Di: Seychelles, Maldives. De: 5 - 30 m. Ge: probably the commonest pseudocerotid flatworm on Maldivian reef slopes, described only very recently.
Below: *P. dimidiatus*.

Pseudoceros lindae   **Sodwana Bay, South Africa**

Linda's flatworm

Le: up to 5 cm. Di: East and South Africa eastward. De: 3 - 34 m. Ge: details (tint, size of spots) of colour pattern variable. Active at night, found under ledges on reef slopes. Flatworms move by sliding on a self-secreted mat of mucus.
Below: from Zanzibar (15 m).

Glorious flatworm

Le: up to 9 cm. Di: Maldives eastward. De: 2 - 30 m. Ge: large, velvety black with three marginal bands. Found under ledges on reef slopes. Flatworm colour patterns may indicate toxicity to deter predators.

Pseudobiceros gloriosus   South Male Atoll, Maldives

Yellowspot flatworm

Le: up to 3 cm. Di: Maldives eastward. De: 2 - 20 m. Ge: dorsal surface black, covered with short papillae, which are tipped yellow. Prominent white line around edge of body. A very similar *Pseudobiceros* sp. lacks the white margin. Found on reef slopes. Genus distinct by two male genital pores.

Flatworms are hermaphrodites, which usually reproduce sexually (see next pp.), but are also able to regenerate an entire animal from a detached fragment of the thin, leaf-like body. They feed on small crustaceans and molluscs via a proboscis.

Thysanozoon nigropapillosum   Raa Atoll, Maldives

Orsaki flatworm

Le: up to 3.5 cm. Di: Maldives eastward. De: 2 - 19 m. Ge: margin strongly ruffled. With 3 to 5 female and 2 male genital pores. Polyclad (many-branched gut without anus) flatworms have a pair of true tentacles or pseudotentacles, which are only folds of the body margin.

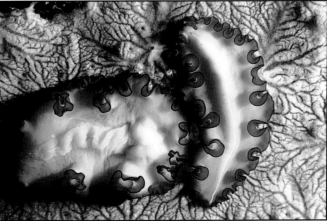

Maiazoon orsaki   Ari Atoll, Maldives

ABSOLUTELY FABULOUS FLATWORMS

Worms have an image problem. Think of worms and you probably think of rather disgusting, dirty, furtive little creatures. But not all worms were created equal. Marine flatworms are aristocrats: magnificently colourful, worms with attitude. The photographer lightens up the general image of an amazing group of marine animals.

Flatworms (*Pseudobiceros* sp.) swim by undulating their body margins (Chagos).

Dive on Indian Ocean coral reefs and you will find a galaxy of flatworm species. You will have to look closely though, for they are small. Put your nose to the reef and turn your back on all those sharks and manta rays! Diving at night helps too, because many flatworms are nocturnal.

Not only are flatworms easily missed, but even when spotted they are often misidentified. Many divers confuse them with sea slugs (which are nudibranch molluscs, relations of garden slugs and snails). This confusion is compounded by the fact that many flatworms (particularly the larger, frillier ones) can swim, with flamboyant undulations of their bodies. This leads some divers to think that they are Spanish Dancers, but that name properly applies to the giant red or orange sea slug, *Hexabranchus sanguineus*.

What is the difference between a flatworm and a sea slug? No prizes for the first one: flatworms are flat! They are only a few cell layers thick, while sea slugs tend to be quite chunky little things. In addition, flatworms have just a couple of sensory folds (pseudotentacles) on their front margins, while sea slugs have a fully developed pair of sensory tentacles (rhinophores) on their heads. Finally, flatworms are so thin that they can survive without gills, relying instead on diffusion of oxygen into their tissues directly from the sea water. Sea slugs, however, have gills for respiration (although these are sometimes tucked away underneath and so not immediately apparent).

Thysanozoon nigropapillosus shows its sensory folds or pseudotentacles (Chagos).

Marine flatworms belong to the Platyhelminthes, a major group of worms that also includes such nasties as liver flukes and tapeworms. Fortunately for divers, marine flatworms (also known as polyclad worms) have little interest in our internal anatomy. That is not to say that they are without importance. Although they are often overlooked, marine flatworms are ecologically important members of coral reef ecosystems. Some are significant predators of colonial ascidians, while others are pests of commercial clams and oysters (these species being known as 'wafers'). Several are mimics of toxic nudibranchs, and yet others live symbiotically on a variety of reef invertebrates.

Many flatworms are brightly coloured, in most cases as a warning. Many flatworms are believed to be toxic or at the very least bad-tasting. Their gaudy patterns warn fishes and other potential predators to leave well alone. These colours and patterns also make them a firm favourite with underwater photographers. As a keen underwater photographer myself, I like to be able to put names to my

A yet undescribed species of *Pseudoceros*, photographed in the Maldives.

ALL PHOTOS: CHARLES ANDERSON

snapshots. Unfortunately, very few tropical marine flatworms have common English names, let alone scientific names.

There are two main reasons why so few flatworms have been named. First, many flatworms live subtidally on coral reefs and only come out at night. They were not the easiest of targets for the Victorian and other early naturalists, who provided us with so much information on most other animal groups. Indeed, it is only within the last few years, with the growth of diving and the spread of dive resorts and liveaboards throughout the tropics that is has become feasible for scientists to collect coral reef flatworms on a broad scale.

Another undescribed *Pseudoceros sp.* (Maldives).

Secondly, flatworms are particularly delicate creatures. They are only a few cell layers thick and do not take kindly to rough handling. Drop one into a collecting jar of normal preservative such as formalin and they self-destruct. Most of the old Victorian collectors were unable to preserve the specimens that they did find, and so museum collections (which scientists rely on for describing new species) are very poorly endowed with marine flatworm specimens. Again, only very recently have researchers concocted a special brew that allows a better than average chance of ending up with an intact specimen instead of a glob of slime.

The common and frequently seen *Pseudobiceros bedfordi* (Maldives).

Despite being so delicate, when it comes to sex, marine flatworms are anything but gentle. To start with, they are hermaphrodites, each worm having both male and female sex organs. So when two mature worms of the same species meet, they both want to fertilise the other. In a further twist, some flatworms have two penises. The penises have needle-sharp ends, with which the worms carry out 'h y p o d e r m i c impregnation'. Sex by stabbing can leave both partners with numerous cuts and gashes, but flatworms have amazing regenerative powers. Within 24 hours all is healed, and another generation of absolutely fabulous flatworms is on its way.

Named after an unusual lady: *Pseudoceros susanae* (Mal.).

Sex by stabbing: a pair of *Pseudobiceros gloriosus* mate on a Maldivian reef.

There is no better place to find different members of the phylum Cnidaria than a coral reef. All are characterised by tentacles armed with myriads of nettling or stinging cells (nematocytes). Each of these cells is equipped with a minute 'safety pin' (cnidocil), which acts as a trigger mechanism. Whenever potential prey like a fish, shrimp, or larger plankton touches the tentacles it cannot avoid bending cnidocils, which in turn leads to an instantaneous avalanche of nematocytes being ejected. This process happens within a few milliseconds, and leaves no chance for escape. Each stinging cell is turned inside out: at first a cover-like flap flips open, then a bundle of knife-like appendages extend, which cut into the prey's skin. Immediately thereafter a long filament from inside the cell penetrates the cut and bores into the victim's tissues while unrolling like a glove's finger. The filament exudes a toxin to paralyse or even kill the prey. Keep in mind that all this is microscopically small and happening a billion times in a few seconds, so there is no chance to get away. One can place a finger on the tentacles of an anemone and feel that they stick to it a little bit. This is caused by the penetration of the filaments into the skin. But make sure before conducting the experiment that it is a harmless species! Two classes of cnidarians are covered here: Hydrozoa (body cavity of polyp without folds) and Anthozoa with the subclasses Octocorallia (number eight symmetry of the polyp) and Hexacorallia (number six symmetry). The following pages show representatives of the hydrozoan families Milleporidae and Stylasteridae, and the octocorallian orders Alcyonacea (Alcyonariidae, Nephtheidae), Gorgonacea (Subergorgiidae to Ellisellidae), and Helioporacea (Helioporidae).

FIRE CORALS

MILLEPORIDAE

Fire coral

Wi: up to 80 cm. Di: entire area. De: 2 - 20 m. Ge: strongly nettling plankton feeder with fragile calcareous skeleton and endosymbiontic algae. Fast-growing colonies in main current and sun-lit areas of reef.

Millepora tenella   Astove, Seychelles

FILIGRANE HYDROCORALS

STYLASTERIDAE

Violet hydrocoral

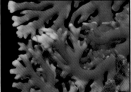

Wi: up to 25 cm. Di: entire area, Red Sea. Ge: grows transversal to strong current in places protected from sunlight on the reef edge and upper slope. Feeds on microplankton. Below: *D. nitida.*

Distichopora violacea   Male Atoll, Maldives

Gray's carrot coral

Length: up to 5 cm.
Distribution: eastern Indian Ocean.
Depth: 30 - 75 m.
General: mainly found in deeper water, growing on rubble. The colonies are elongate and finger-shaped, often curved and tapering towards the tip. The entire surface of the colony is covered with one type of polyp. Colonies are red or orange, the white polyps may have yellow bases. They are preyed upon by the arminid nudibranch *Dermatobranchus gonatophora*. Over a dozen genus members are known.

Eleutherobia grayi   Mozambique

Alderslade's carrot coral

Le: up to 5 cm. Di: Maldives eastward. De: 2 - 25 m. Ge: common in caves. Finger-shaped colonies bear two types of polyps, which retract completely into the colony and do not form mounds. Larger ones extend to feed on microplankton at night. Below: *Minabea* sp.

Minabea aldersladei   Lhaviyani Atoll, Maldives

Mushroom leather coral

Wi: up to 40 cm. Di: ent. area. Ge: one of the commonest and most widespread of about 35 spp. of the genus. Found on shallow reef flats. With polyps retracted surface looks smooth and leathery. Bel.: *Sarcophyton* sp.

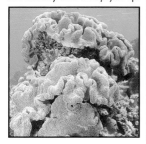

Sarcophyton trocheliophorum   Aldabra, Seychelles

Hemprich's soft coral

Le: up to 70 cm. Di: entire area, common in Red Sea . Ge: pioneer settler, colony tree-shaped, stem branches close to substrate. Shrinks several times per day to a small heap, extends fully at night. Host to many commensals (egg cowries, spider crabs, brittle stars).

Dendronephthya hemprichi   **Ari Atoll, Maldives**

Leafy soft coral

Length: up to 45 cm. Distribution: entire area, RS. General: the genus has some of the most variable and brightly coloured species of reef-dwelling soft corals. Tree soft corals are profusely branched with the branches being long and slender. The colonies have a prickly appearance due to the sharp bundles of sclerites supporting each polyp. Adjacent polyps are united into distinct bundles that are conspicuously separated. Polyps cannot totally withdraw into the branch.

Below: **Klunzinger's soft coral** D. *klunzingeri*, 100 cm, entire area, RS, 15 - 40 m. Red calcareous sclerites show as loosely distributed spines in the translucent body wall. Pink to violet. On hard substrate, nocturnal plankton feeder.

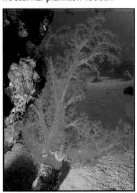

Dendronephthya mucronata   **Gaafu Atoll, Maldives**

TREE SOFT CORALS   NEPHTHEIDAE

Soft coral species

Le: up to 9 cm. Di: Mauritius
to Seychelles. De: 10 - 35 m.
Ge: forms stiff, spiny colonies,
polyps armed with supporting
sclerite bundles. Numerous
species of the genus have been
described, most of which are
not brightly coloured (compare
small photo of a different sp.).

Stereonephthya sp.   Grande Baie, Mauritius

GORGONIAN FAN CORALS   SUBERGORGIIDAE

Giant fan coral

Le: up to 200 cm. Di: entire
area. De: 10 - 60 m. Ge: this
type of gorgonarians has a
flexible uni-plane skeleton.
Normally found growing on
drop-offs, reaching far out into
the open water. The one
shown here closes the strong-
current gap between two
rocks.

The species has been called
Subergorgia hicksoni for a long
time, but today two genera of
reef-dwelling gorgonarians are
recognised: *Subergorgia* comprises the species with free
branches and exclusively spin-
dle-shaped skeletal elements
(sclerites), and to *Anella* belong
species forming a closely anastomosing network of branches
and entirely different sclerites
(double-heads, double-discs).
The small photo below shows
a group of red specimens of
Anella mollis, being the home of
a group of soldierfishes.

Annella mollis   Flic en Flac, Mauritius

291

Subergorgia suberosa   Ari Atoll, Maldives

Medium fan coral

Width: up to 150 cm.
Distribution: Mauritius eastward.
Depth: 15 - 30 m.
General: the fans of this species are dichotomously branched, a medial longitudinal groove is visible on the surface of each branch. The polyps are arranged on the branches in two rows opposite one another. Coloration rusty orange to reddish brown.

The axis of subergorgiids is composed of a meshwork of branched and fused calcareous sclerites that additionally is held together by a small amount of horny material (gorgonine). In that way the axis is both rigid and flexible at the same time, while the youngest terminal branches may be delicately thin. When fan corals sway in and are bent by the currents, they hardly look like gorgonians with a calcareous axis, but more like those with a flexible horny axis.

Melithaea ochracea   Pemba, Tanzania

Knotted fan coral

Width: up to 100 cm.
Distribution: entire area, RS.
Depth: 20 - 40 m.
General: the colonies are fan-shaped, a thick main stem dichotomously branches many times in one plane. The polyps are distributed over the entire surface, preferably in the main plane. Coloration is variable, mainly deep red with white polyps. Sexes are separate on different colonies. Grows on steep slopes and drop-offs, also on deeper terrace reefs. Feeds on microplankton. Best known of about 30 species.

Family members are distinct by having the sclerites tightly fused in certain segments of the branches, and the intermediate parts being thickened nodes of horny material, which are lacking fused sclerites; the sclerite parts provide stability and the flexible nodes elasticity when the fans sway in the current. Home to various epibiontic invertebrates (see photo).

WHIP CORALS ELLISELLIDAE

Delicate whip coral
Le: up to 110 cm. Di: entire area. De: 5 - 30 m. Ge: whip-like gorgonians with heavily calcified horny axis. Found in groups on reef slopes. Sexes are separate, but also asexual reproduction by budding, buds fall down and grow to become neighbours of the parent. Below: *Menella* sp. (Maldives).

Junceella fragilis Andaman Sea

BLUE CORALS HELIOPORIDAE

Blue coral
Wi: up to 150 cm. Di: patchy, ent. area, not RS. De: 2 - 18 m. Ge: form variable, living colony olive (zooxanthellae), skeleton bright blue (bilirubine). Unique octocoral with massive, but brittle carbonate skeleton. Sole sp. of the order Helioporacea.

Heliopora coerulea Mentawai Islands, Sumatra

ANEMONES ACTINIARIA

The cnidarian order Actiniaria belongs to the subclass Hexacorallia (with a number six symmetry of the polyp), and comprises many types of anemones found on coral reefs, but relatively few are readily visible. Most are well hidden in cracks or underneath rocks or coral slabs. The most conspicuous ones are those occupied by anemonefishes. These host anemones belong to different families and range in diameter from a few centimetres to over a metre. The body of all anemones is a hollow muscular tube (column), the closed end of which (pedal disc) usually serves in attaching to a hard substrate, the other one (oral disc) has a mouth opening surrounded by the tentacles. Actually the hollow centre of the body tube has several thin-walled partitions, making a cross section look like a wheel with spokes. These partitions serve to increase the area active in respiration, digestion, and excretion. An anemone is basically built like a single hexacorallian polyp lacking the skeleton. Its crown of tentacles is often the most obvious part. Some anemones have short, knobby tentacles, others long, slender ones. They contain myriads of stinging cells or nematocytes, and are used to catch, kill, and handle prey ranging in size from plankton to fishes. They also serve to deter predators, e.g. butterflyfishes. The nettling capacity depends on the species and in many cases is to weak to harm a human, but there are exceptions and again one should follow the simple rule 'do not touch'. Like the closely related stony corals, some anemones contain symbiotic algae (zooxanthellae).

Mertens' anemone

Wi: up to 150 cm. Di: entire area, Red Sea. De: 4 - 35 m. Ge: in cracks, column warty with orange spots, oral disc carpet-like, tentacles sting. Below: *S. gigantea,* up to 70 cm, similar, but column smooth, without spots, carpet-like tentacles strongly stinging.

Stichodactyla mertensii   Ari Atoll, Maldives

Magnificent anemone

Wi: up to 30 cm. Di: entire area, RS. De: 1 - 10 m. Ge: colour variable, tentacles greyish with yellowish tip. Exposed on hard substrates of drop-offs and slopes, may change location. Below: **Leather anemone** *H. crispa,* 30 cm. Both spp. host various *Amphiprion* spp.

Heteractis magnifica   Lhaviyani Atoll, Maldives

Bubble anemone

Wi: up to 40 cm. Di: ent. area, RS. De: 2 - 30 m. Ge: very common, column smooth, tentacles swollen at tip, hidden in cracks on hard substrates. With zooxanthellae (colour variations). Below: *Heteractis aurora,* fam. Stichodactylidae.

Entacmaea quadricolor   Male Atoll, Maldives

Knob-edged anemone
Wi: up to 55 cm. Di: entire area, RS. De: 0.5 - 5 m. Ge: singly, body hidden in rock crevices. Oral disc very broad and wavy, with many short, sticky, multi-branched tentacles. Coloration extremely variable. Host to *Amphiprion, Thor, Periclimenes* spp. Below: **Hemprich's anemone** *Heterodactyla hemprichi,* ent. area, RS, 40 cm, small tentacles in groups.

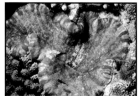

Cryptodendrum adhaesivum   Similan Islands, Thailand

Club anemone

Wi: up to 12 cm. Di: Maldives, but generally rare. There are more genus members in the Atlantic Ocean. De: 20 m. Ge: living solitary. Body column long, lower part with 'bark' and small false tentacles. Oral disc wider than pedal disc. Relatively few, short, but strong, club-shaped tentacles surround the mouth in circles of six; they catch zooplankton and small invertebrates for food. Coloration variable.
   Below: an unknown species of anemone from the Maldives, which most probably belongs to the family Thalassianthidae (see above).

Telmatactis clavigera   Raa Atoll, Maldives

DISC ANEMONES   DISCOSOMATIDAE

Disc anemone species

Width: up to 10 cm. Distribution: entire area including Red Sea. Depth: 10 - 30 m. General: disc anemones belong to the hexcorallian order Corallimorpharia or False corals. Tentacles are short or absent, column very short, individuals disc-like. Able to reproduce asexually by budding, thus covering large areas of the substrate in a short period of time and overgrowing even living substrate settlers like corals and giant clams. The large photo also shows the extended tentacle spirals of annelid tubeworms (Polychaeta), abundant and often colourful distant relatives of the earthworm. Below: close-up of another *Discosoma* sp., and a *Metarhodactis* sp., respectively.

Discosoma sp.   Ari Atoll, Maldives

BLACK CORALS   ANTIPATHIDAE

Spiral black coral

Le: up to 150 cm. Di: entire area. De: 15 - 50 m. Ge: one polyp row, often misidentified as *Cirripathes spiralis,* which grows only to 30 cm in length. Below: *Antipathes* sp., a typical bush of black coral.

Stichopathes sp.   South Male Atoll, Maldives

The stony or hard corals of the hexacorallian order Scleractinia are by far the most important reef builders. Millions upon millions of tiny coral polyps live in close symbiosis with even more numerous brownish, unicellular algae (zooxanthellae) embedded in their tissues. It is this symbiosis that enables the polyps of these so-called hermatypic corals to shed calcium carbonate at such a high rate that their skeleton can grow up to 15 cm per year. The algae need sunlight and carbon dioxide for photosynthesis and provide up to 98% of the nutritional requirements of the polyps, which in turn thrive only at sufficiently warm water

A healthy coral reef off Christmas Island in the eastern Indian Ocean.

temperatures. This restricts the range of living coral reefs to the tropics, and from the surface down to only a few dozen metres; farther down the light intensity is not high enough to allow for photosynthesis, and average water temperatures below about 20°C will kill the polyps. Unfortunately also a temperature rise of only a few degrees in the annual mean has the same effect: as can be seen in many regions today, global warming is the cause for the bleaching of vast areas of coral reef. But there are also ahermatypic corals without zooxanthellae, which rely on capturing animal prey with their tentacles. Much of their food consists of zooplankton, but some species also able to capture worms, sea urchins, and even small fishes.

Hundreds of species of stony corals are known from the Indian Ocean, diversity being greatest in its eastern part. Many have wide distributions, ranging from the Red Sea and East Africa to the remote islands of the Central Pacific. Although there are solitary types such as the mushroom corals (Fungiidae), the vast majority of species are colonial forms. In the latter category the members of the genus *Acropora*, frequently referred to as table and staghorn corals, are especially abundant. Coral colonies mainly grow by asexual division of polyps, but there is also sexual reproduction with separate sexes delivering eggs and sperm, and hermaphroditism (both sexes on a polyp).

Protected by *Tubastraea micrantha* Fairy basslets feel safe.

Individual polyps resemble fleshy sacks topped by a ring of tentacles around a central mouth opening, very similar to miniature anemones. They sit in calcareous skeletal cases, which are secreted by the polyp itself. Colony members are connected by living tissue, so nutrients available in one section can be shared around. Major groups of corals can be readily identified underwater, but recognition of species often is the task of trained specialists, as this calls for microscopic examination of skeletal characteristics.

The least attractive way to look at corals: as dead souvenirs.

Acropora robusta — **Male Atoll, Maldives**

Robust staghorn coral

Distribution: Chagos Is. eastward into Pacific Ocean. General: this species is restricted to shallow reefs, where it is common on reef margins exposed to strong surf action. Colonies are irregularly shaped, with thick colonial branches at the centre and with thinner prostrate branches with upturned ends at the periphery. Radial corallites are of mixed sizes and shapes, but are generally rasp-like. Bright green with deep pink branch tips, also pinkish-brown, yellowish-brown, or cream in colour.

Acropora formosa — **Praslin, Seychelles**

Formosa staghorn coral

Di: Madagascar eastward. Ge: very common, often the dominant sp. of lagoons and fringing reefs. Colonies arborescent, usually forming thickets. Radial corallites similar or varied in size, uniformly or erratically distributed. Cream, brown, or blue. Branch ends often pale.

Acropora cytherea — **Similan Islands, Thailand**

Fine table coral
Di: Mascarenes eastward. Ge: thin wide flat tables, one of the most abundant corals of upper reef slopes, polyps often show by day. Below: *A. nasuta*, entire area, RS, in all *Acropora* assemblages, very common on upper reef slope. Radial corallites look like inverted noses. Cream with purplish tips.

Table coral species

Distribution: Maldives.
General: this view onto a Maldivian house reef at early dusk shows a healthy growth of diverse species of *Acropora*. When trying to identify the species of the large colony at the centre, even Charly Veron's bible of corals "Corals of Australia and the Indo-Pacific" did not lead to a satisfactory solution.

Small photo below: another *Acropora* table coral that grows in an unusual upright position, very probably to optimally utilise the local current, which brings the zooplankton food to the tiny coral polyps. The intricate network of branches is nicely to be seen in this photo.

In all Indo-Pacific reefs we find species of *Acropora* growing in many forms and shapes ("staghorns", bushes, thickets, plates, columns, tables). They are so successful because most species have light skeletons, which allow them to grow quickly and overcome their neighbours. Also the corallites of a colony are connected and can grow in a coordinated way.

Acropora sp.   Ari Atoll, Maldives

Solid table coral

Di: Madagascar eastward. Ge: anastomosing branches form an almost solid plate. Below: diving tank as artificial mini reef.

Acropora clathrata   La Digue, Seychelles

BUSH CORALS   POCILLOPORIDAE

Warty bush coral

Di: entire area and Red Sea.
Ge: common, in most shallow
reef habitats. Uniform upright
branches covered with "warts"
(verrucae) of irregular size.
Colour cream, pink, or blue.
Below: *Seriatopora hystrix,* common in all shallow reefs, cream
branches tapering to a point.

Pocillopora verrucosa   Comoros

RIDGE CORALS   AGARICIIDAE

Maze coral

Di: RS to Central Pacific. Ge:
common, colonies rarely wider
than 200 cm, consist of usually
horizontal unifacial laminae,
but may develop columns.
With more than one row of
corallites between the ridges.

Pachyseris speciosa   Aldabra, Seychelles

Ridge coral

Distribution: Red Sea to Australia and Palau.
General: the species is rarely
common, except on vertical or
overhang faces, especially of
lower reef slopes. The
colonies are composed of unifacial laminae, which may be
horizontal with entire or lobed
margins, or contorted and
partly upright. Corallites are
widely spaced and inclined
outward. Covered with fine,
but conspicuous radiating
ridges. Coloration is brown or
yellowish-brown, often with
white margins, as can be seen
in the specimen on the photo.

Leptoseris explanata   Mulaku Atoll, Maldives

Lobed pore coral

Di: Central Indian Ocean eastward to Galapagos. Ge: very common, frequently dominant on reef margins, in lagoons, and fringe reefs. Large colonies hemispherical or helmet-shaped. Usually cream or pale brown, but may be bright blue, purple, or green in shallow water. Corallites evenly distributed, 1.5 mm wide. *Porites* can grow to a height of 8 m, and at a growth rate of 9 mm per year such giants may be nearly 1,000 years old! The upper two photos also show the colourful tentacles of embedded *Spirobranchus* tube worms.

Porites lobata   Trinco, Sri Lanka

Yellow pore coral

Di: Red Sea eastward to Tuamotu. Ge: very common, with *P. lobata* on reef margins, in lagoons and fringing reefs. May become very large, surface usually smooth. Coloration variable. Below: *P. solida,* RS to Hawaii, common, massive, up to several metres in diameter.

Porites lutea   Similan Islands, Thailand

Djibouti flower coral

Di: East Africa to West Pacific. Ge: distinct polyps extended. See small photo below for ball-shaped colonies with retracted polyps. The author was not able to overlook the vast field of *Goniopora* balls growing on a sand flat in a depth of 30 m! Below: *G. columna,* Red Sea to Fiji (photo from the Maldives).

Goniopora djiboutensis   Male Atoll, Maldives

Mushroom coral

Distribution: Red Sea to Tuamotu.

General: colonies are attached or free (like the specimen in the photo), encrusting or laminar, unifacial, and can grow to 150 cm in width. The diver nicely serves to demonstrate the size of this specimen. A central corallite is sometimes distinguishable. The ridges on the colony are similar to those of some species of *Fungia* (see below). Polyps may be extended day or night.

First small photo below: *Fungia scutaria*, up to 17 cm long, RS to Hawaii (photo Seychelles). Common, not attached, on upper reef slopes exposed to surge. Second: *F. fungites*, up to 28 cm wide, RS to Tuamotu (photo Chagos). Very common, ridges with triangular teeth.

Podabacia crustacea   Ari Atoll, Maldives

Lichtenstein's bubble coral

Di: Madagascar eastward. Ge: polyps extended at night, by day covered with grape-sized bubbles (photo), which retract when disturbed. Below: *Plerogyra sinuosa*, RS to Pacific, bubbles retract only slowly, if at all.

Physogyra lichtensteini   Baa Atoll, Maldives

Leafy crater coral

Distribution: Red Sea to Fiji. General: very common, may be dominant in shallow turbid water habitats. Colonies are usually less than 1 m in diameter, but may be much larger on fringing reefs. They are composed of unifacial laminae, highly contorted and anastomosed in subtidal habitats, upright or tiered fronds on upper reef slopes (photo), and horizontal fronds in deeper water, according to light availability (contains zooxanthellae, which are responsible for the yellowish green coloration). Polyps only on the upper faces.

Turbinaria mesenterina   Aldabra, Seychelles

Column crater coral

Di: East Africa to Pacific. Ge: common in a wide range of habitats, columns or flat plates, may reach several metres in diameter, large polyps often extended by day. Photo: young colony. Below: *T. frondens,* East Indian Oc. to Fiji, juv. (photo) cup-shaped, later upright fronds.

Turbinaria peltata   Grande Baie, Mauritius

Green cup coral

Di: entire area. Ge: the commonest cup coral seen by divers because it grows in areas exposed to currents (see also p.297), and not in caves like the other genus members. See small photo below of the **Orange cup coral** *Tubastraea coccinea.*

Tubastraea micrantha   Des Roches, Seychelles

SARDINE RUN OFF SOUTH AFRICA

The annual movement of sardines *Sardinops sagax* up the Wild coast, eastern Cape Province, is a phenomenon that is anticipated by both humans and marine predators. Known as the "Sardine Run," scientists are unsure of how and why the migration occurs, but one thing is for certain: it is probably the single most important biological event along this coast, bringing in critical nutritional value to these otherwise impoverished waters. The photographer, a marine predator specialist, describes an unusual truce.

ALL PHOTOS: VIC PEDDEMORS

1. Sardine frenzy: the annual winter sardine run is the cause of much excitement amongst the people of KwaZulu-Natal, South Africa, as people of all sizes and ages loose their decorum in the frenzy to collect this plentiful fish. Using seine nets and cast nets, the more serious fishermen collect enough to sell at exorbitant prices, but other "fishermen" use anything that will entrap the little fish - even nuns have been seen in the breaker zone scooping fish into their habits!

2. Marine predators: however, out at sea the real marine predators are also using this opportunity to replenish their energy reserves. Although both Humpback whales *Megaptera novaeangliae* and Bryde's whales *Balaenoptera edeni* feed on the sardines, the most spectacular activity results from the over 15,000 Common dolphins *Delphinus delphis*, 3,000 Bottlenose dolphins *Tursiops truncatus,* and hundreds of thousands of Cape gannets ploughing into the sardine shoals.

3. Common dolphins: generally, the Common dolphins can be seen following the 70 m isobath, while they spread out searching for the sardines. While snorkel diving to observe the feeding behaviour of Common dolphins, one had to be careful not to land on the back of a Copper shark *Charcharhinus brachyurus*. It appeared as if the sharks were travelling below the dolphins. Although they showed no interest in the dolphins, the Copper sharks would often follow divers to the surface. It is a rather un-nerving experience having an interested 3.5-m-shark on your tail! Almost every time we entered the water we encountered this apparent relationship between the dolphins and sharks, something that astounded us as it requires almost full throttle on an inflatable boat to keep up with the dolphins.

4. Bull shark: the Bottlenose dolphins move up the coast just beyond the surf zone while feeding on both the sardines and other predatory fishes *(Sarpa salpa, Pomatomus saltatrix)* that associate with the migration. Although the water is green with the faeces of all these predators, dives with the Bottlenose dolphins showed that on several occasions their arch-enemy, the Bull shark *Carcharhinus leucas*, swam in loose formations below the dolphins. Fortunately, these potentially dangerous sharks ignored both diver and dolphin! Usually, dolphins and sharks are mortal enemies off this coast, with up to 28% of Humpback dolphins and 10% of all Bottlenose dolphins exhibiting healed shark bite wounds. Do the sharks use the superior foraging capabilities of the dolphins to locate their prey? Is a truce between the predators called during this bounty of sardines? For the first time both predators have been seen swimming apparently ignoring each other and it begs further research into such unusual predator/prey relationships.

The echinoderms are an exclusively marine phylum with a long fossil record and five major living classes: feather stars (Crinoidea, this page) are plankton filterers; brittle stars (Ophiuroidea) skim the surface for bacteria, specialised forms like *Astroboa* (this page) filter plankton at night; sea stars (Asteroidea, p.306) are predators; sea urchins (Echinoidea, p.307) graze algae and animal epibionts from hard substrates; sea cucumbers (Holothurioidea, p.308) sieve the substrate for microorganisms and organic matter. All have in common a more or less flexible external calcareous skeleton: it is fused into a rigid case in most sea urchin species, forms a flexible, but entire armour in sea, brittle, and feather stars, but is reduced to microscopically small skeletal elements, loosely embedded in a tough, leathery skin in sea cucumbers. All echinoderms share a complex and elaborate, so-called ambulacral system, consisting of interconnected water-filled tubes, which start at the madreporal plate (a perforated 'intake sieve,' nicely to be seen on top of many sea stars) and terminate in rows of many small feet. These feet may or may not have a sucker-like disc at the end. Feet, spines, and diverse 'tools' (e.g. tweezer-like pedicellaria, in some sea urchin species equipped with poison glands) serve in locomotion, handling food, camouflaging by carrying pieces of seagrass or algae, etc. But most important of all is the basic symmetry of five that rules all extant echinoderm constructions. Even the intricately divided arms of basket stars or the armless sea cucumbers reveal that symmetry, when given a closer look. Of course there are exceptions from the rule like the colourful feather stars with hundreds and sea stars with dozens of arms, but these are of secondary nature.

FEATHER STARS   MARIAMETRIDAE

Long-arm feather star

Wi: up to 40 cm. Di: Maldives eastward. De: 5 - 20 m. Ge: up to 30 arms, variable patterns of white and red, seen filtering plankton. Below: cirri of *Lamprometra palmata;* used to cling to and move along substrate.

Dichrometra flagellata   Hikkaduwa, Sri Lanka

BASKET STARS   GORGONOCEPHALIDAE

Naked basket star

Wi: up to 120 cm. Di: entire area. De: 5 - 120 m. Ge: five multiple-branched arms, forming a filter basket at night, curl up when lighted. Bel.: another mariametrid; feather stars can swim by undulating their arms.

Astroboa nuda   Male Atoll, Maldives

SERPENT SEA STARS   OPHIDIASTERIDAE

Blue sea star

Wi: up to 30 cm. Di: East Africa to Hawaii. De: 1 - 25 m. Ge: among algae-covered coral debris and in seagrass beds. Adults often in shallow water by day. Below: a single arm of *L. multiflora*; it will grow via a 'comet form' to a complete animal (asexual reproduction).

Linckia laevigata   **Praslin, Seychelles**

NAIL SEA STARS   MITHRODIIDAE

Nail sea star

Wi: up to 40 cm. Di: patchy, entire area, RS. De: 10 - 35 m. Ge: arms with widely-spaced conical thorns, nocturnal detritus feeder. Below: *Fromia milleporella* (Ophidiasteridae), 6 cm, Maldives east, from 1 m down.

Mithrodia clavigera   **Comoros**

CUSHION SEA STARS   OREASTERIDAE

Indian cushion sea star

Wi: up to 25 cm. Di: East Africa to Sri Lanka. De: 1 - 33 m. Ge: resembles a sea urchin without spines, colour pattern very variable (see below), feeds on detritus and epibionts. Often with *Periclimenes* partner shrimps.

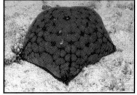

Culcita schmideliana   **Beau Vallon, Seychelles**

LEATHER SEA URCHINS   ECHINOTHURIIDAE

Toxic leather sea urchin

Wi: up to 18 cm. Di: entire area, not RS. De: 3 - 30 m. Ge: coloration white and red to orange. Body consists of plates loosely connected by leathery tissue, thus its form is variable. Found all over the reef, not abundant, but common. Distinct from the very similar Red Sea *Asthenosoma marisrubri,* described in 1998. Nocturnal omnivore, feeds on algae, sponges, and sea squirts. Spines often laid together in bundles. The white bubbles at the tips of the spines are very poisonous! Stings are painful and take days to heal, avoid!

Asthenosoma varium   Richelieu Rock, Thailand

TOXIC SEA URCHINS   TOXOPNEUSTIDAE

Poison claw sea urchin

Wi: up to 12 cm. Di: entire area, RS. De: 1 - 35 m. Ge: spines blunt, short; poisonous pedicellaria with 3 large claws longer. Feet long, fix debris for camouflage. In lagoons, beds of seagrass, reefs; avoid touching!

Toxopneustes pileolus   Beau Vallon, Seychelles

DIADEMA SEA URCHINS   DIADEMATIDAE

Black diadema sea urchin

Wi: up to 10 cm. Di: entire area, RS. De: 5 - 25 m. Ge: mainly found on hard sub-strates, where feeding on algae, detritus, and coral polyps. May be locally very abundant. Its black spines are long, thin, hollow, and very fragile. Almost all underwater enthusiasts have made an unpleasant experience with the spines of this sp. or another family member (harmful, but not poisonous). Juveniles have thicker spines with alternating dark and white rings.

Echinothrix diadema   Negombo, Sri Lanka

COMMON SEA CUCUMBERS

Graeffe's sea cucumber

Le: up to 50 cm. Di: entire area, RS. De: 5 - 45 m. Ge: mouth surrounded by 25 black tentacles (see photo), ending in discs, used to pick up detritus and small organisms from the substrate. Below: *Bohadschia* sp., with a characteristic pattern of ocellated dark spots.

Bohadschia graeffei   Beau Vallon, Seychelles

PAPILLATE SEA CUCUMBERS

STICHOPODIDAE

Greenish sea cucumber

Le: up to 30 cm. Di: entire area, RS. De: 1 - 30 m. Ge: with double rows of conical papillae with orange tips, mouth with 20 tentacles facing downwards. Bel.: *S. variegatus*, 50 cm, entire area, mainly on sand.

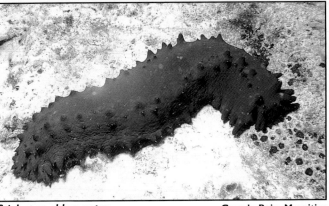

Stichopus chloronotus   Grande Baie, Mauritius

WORM SEA CUCUMBERS

SYNAPTIDAE

Godeffroy's sea cucumber

Le: up to 150 cm. Di: RS to Hawaii. De: 1 - 26 m. Ge: uses 15 feathery mouth tentacles to wipe detritus from the ground, shrinks to a third of length when disturbed. Bel.: *Opheodesoma spectabilis*, in same wreck.

Euapta godeffroyi   Beau Vallon, Seychelles

COVER-UP STORY

Even though enchanting, coral reefs are no paradise. These constructions built by myriads of tiny coral polyps offer opportunities to settle for such an enormous variety of plant and animal life that they are exceeded in their complexity only by the tropical rain forests. Offspring and newcomers do indeed prefer the calcareous skeletons of dead coral as the first choice for settlement and growth, but the supply of such surfaces is considerably smaller than the demand. This condition promotes two characteristics of the harsh survival game: on the one hand, the natural death rate is markedly increased by overgrowing those individuals whose resistance starts to dwindle; on the other hand, it is the own expansion that easily leads to war with the neighbours. Between individuals of the same species this is quite a peaceful process in most cases. But between different species there is no mercy.

1. Admittedly stony corals are often the winners in the displacement competition - otherwise how could the coral reefs of the Indian Ocean have grown to such a size? Nevertheless, on many occasions stony corals have to fight their kin - but of different species that grow towards them. The winner is determined right from the start. The assumption that fast-growing species like staghorn corals have an advantage, is wrong. The slower a colony expands, the better the effect of its strategy: the stomach of the coral polyp is turned inside out on top of the neighbouring competitor for space, who is consequently digested. Thus, a balance of forces has been established in the reef community slowing down the fast-growers and offering a chance for all. But stony corals are menaced by members of other classes of the animal kingdom: an orange sponge has overgrown not only the large table coral, but also the brain coral growing on top of it. Only the soft coral is still thriving there.

2. Lateral protection is very important for the giant clams of the genus *Tridacna*. Therefore, they literally "dig" themselves into a substrate of stony corals. This specimen, however, will soon be the victim of a specialist in overgrowing, a discoid anemone of the family Discosomatidae. Each and every surface worth settling on has already been occupied by these coelenterates. Only their ability to reproduce vegetatively by budding daughter specimens makes possible such a fast and complete coverage of the substrate.

3. For many organisms the most important prerequisite for survival is to secure a space where to live. But exactly that may be scarce and thus fought over violently. Sea squirts of the family Didemnidae are among the first pioneers to settle on dead coral. These relatively large dead coral tables are covered with innumerable specimens of the hermaphroditic ascidians. A major contribution to such a high population density is the short period of time (a few days in most species) needed for the development of their larvae. *Didemnum molle* is extraordinarily quick: its larvae settle on their final position in the reef after only ten minutes.

309

Leathery turtle

Sole species of family, largest turtle (over 500 kg). No horny scales or claws, seven ridges along back, upper beak with tooth-like projections. Only a few nesting sites in our area (below, Mozambique). Feeds on medusae, makes long migrations. Left: with remoras.

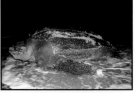

Dermochelys coriacea   Andaman Sea

Hawksbill turtle

Easily identified by two pairs of scales between the eyes. Most common turtle in area. Left: magnificent shot of a Hawksbill and a Whale shark. Below left: mating (note barnacles).

Turtles and tortoises are considerably older than dinosaurs, but today's populations of the evolutionary highly successful sea turtles are severely endangered by man's hunting for eggs and meat, by accidental drowning in huge drift nets (small photo) actually set to catch tuna, mackerels, and other pelagic fishes, by swallowing spilled oil or drifting man-made debris, and especially by nesting site denaturalisation. The latter is the cause when new tourist hotel complexes are built right on the beaches to where the turtles return to lay their eggs, driven by natural instincts including fantastic navigational abilities. It is a shame that today all turtle species are found on the Red List of the IUCN (International Union for Conservation of Nature).

Richelieu Rock, Thailand

Eretmochelys imbricata   Mentawai Islands, Sumatra

Green turtle

Of seven species of marine turtles the five pantropical ones occur in our area, two of which are common. All are aquatic except for brief periods of time, when - often after long migrations in the sea - the females come ashore on the same beach where they were born to deposit their eggs, on average every 2 years. Batches of 50 to 150 eggs are laid into a hole laboriously excavated with the hind flippers, and at once covered with sand (see below). They are incubated for 2 months, the sun's heat is responsible for their development. Mortality of eggs and hatchlings is extremely high due to predators (sea birds, lizards, man). Sea turtles are carnivores preying on medusae (bottom photos), sponges, tunicates, crabs, squid, and fish. Only adult Green turtles (the second most common species in our area, with one pair of scales between eyes) feed on seagrass and algae.

During a visit at the Seychelles, the author on several occasions found the unusual relationship of Green turtles swimming permanently together with a single batfish. Why they associate, is yet completely unknown (right and below).

Beau Vallon, Seychelles

Beau Vallon, Seychelles

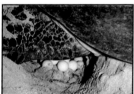

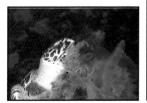

Chelonia mydas　　　　　　　　　　**Ari Atoll, Maldives**

Pelagic sea snake

The commonest sea snake, most likely to be encountered in our area. It is easily recognised by its banded tail. Huge aggregations, pelagically drifting and holding on to each other, have been observed from ships.

Sea snakes are a family of reptiles, breathing air with lungs, able to dive excellently and continuously for at least 30 minutes. Adapted to locomotion in the water, the posterior part of their body is laterally strongly flattened, their rudder-like tail serving in propulsion. Adults grow to between 0.5 and 2 m long, and reach an age of a few to over 10 years.

There are 54 marine species in the subfamily Hydrophiinae, which give birth to about 12 live young underwater after gestation periods of up to 9 months. Whereas the 5 amphibious sea cobras (*Laticauda* spp., subfamily Laticaudinae) deposit eggs on land like most terrestrial snakes do.

Sea snakes prey on benthic fishes (gobies, morays, garden eels) and on fish eggs.

Pelamis platurus   **Ari Atoll, Maldives**

Banded sea snake
Sea snakes are extremely poisonous, *E. schistosa* for example produces up to 15 mg of a toxin, 1.5 mg of which can kill a human adult. But they are not aggressive, as there are no confirmed reports of attacks on divers or reef waders. Below: **Olive sea snake** *Aipysurus laevis,* 150 cm, off West Australia.

Enhydrina schistosa   **Negombo, Sri Lanka**

Spinner dolphin

The popular name refers to its habit of jumping out of the water and spinning around its axis. Worldwide distributed in tropical and temperate waters. Snout sleek, feeds mainly on small fishes. Unites with tuna schools to hunt, but unfortunately often drowns in tuna nets.

Stenella longirostris   **Flic en Flac, Mauritius**

Spotted dolphin

This distinctly spotted dolphin is one of the commonest dolphin species encountered in our area, where it is mainly found between 22°N and the equator. In coastal waters it is seen either singly or in groups of 10 to 50 animals, but far offshore there are also large schools of up to 2,500 individuals. Like most family members it feeds on squid and a variety of small schooling fishes, primarily at the surface. Besides incidental takes in fishing nets, dolphins are endangered by chemical pollutants, disturbance, and habitat modification.

Stenella attenuata   **La Digue, Seychelles**

Striped dolphin

This dolphin species lacks spots, and is distinct by longitudinal stripes on the body. Its main colours are shades of blue and white, a perfect adaptation to its pelagic habitat. Its skull and snout are relatively wide, indicating that it is the generalist feeder of the genus: preys on many species of cephalopods and fishes. Dolphins are highly social, travelling in huge schools of up to several thousands. Mothers with young, subadults, and adults often form own groups that do not mix with the others. See also SARDINE RUN on p.304.

Stenella coeruleoalba   **Andaman Sea**

TROPHY HUNTER

Almost nothing is known about the hunting behaviour of killerwhales - especially in tropical waters. Sometimes a little bit of it is revealed during a chance meeting. The photographer and eye-witness recalls such a dramatic encounter.

The beautiful sailfish *Istiophorus platypterus,* one of the fastest creatures in the sea, raises its high dorsal fin in threat display.

ALL PHOTOS: MARK STRICKLAND

We are on our way to the Similan Islands off the coast of Thailand. As usual, everybody is watching the surface of the sea from the deck of the liveaboard. Suddenly Suzanne points at a peculiar black rectangle that is cruising in zig-zag fashion only a hundred metres from our vessel. Very close to it a dozen of large, dolphin-like dorsal fins appear. As we approach, we realise that the rectangle is the erected black dorsal fin of a sailfish. It is extremely difficult to approach this shy pelagic predator while diving. After the engines of our vessel have been shut down, we take the opportunity to snorkel towards the scene. Naturally, we also want to find out what is going on between the dolphins and the sailfish.

In the water, we are amazed by the size of the "dolphins" because they are three to five metres in length. Judging from their head shape, they have to be toothed whales. Obviously interested in us, they do not swim away, but circle beneath us, sometimes even belly-up. Our eyes meet. While we use all our fin-power trying to keep pace, it seems as if they wait for us to approach. How amusing it has to be for them to watch us humble creatures in the water. They swim in groups of three, but sometimes there are up to 15 individuals together. When one of the whales opens its mouth, I see its large teeth and realise that we are surrounded by a school of False killerwhales *Pseudorca crassidens.* They are predators, which - unlike dolphins - do not hunt for sardines and fusiliers, but utilise their strong dentiti-

on to prey on large pelagic fish and marine mammals.

As if it were not fantastic enough to swim along with these whales that are hardly known from the Indian Ocean, we then approach the sailfish. With its fully erected dorsal fin, it obviously tries to impress the killerwhales. Although the whales are able to kill the fish any time, they seem to delight in terrorising it. A group of ten False killerwhales totally controls the sailfish: when it speeds up, it is immediately surrounded. A sailfish could certainly outswim a single killerwhale, but it cannot cope with their group strategy. The fish shows strong signs of

Cornered by killerwhales, the sailfish clearly shows signs of stress: its normally brilliant blue coloration has become almost white on the body, and black on the dorsal fin.

stress: while sailfish normally display wonderful shades of blue striped with bronze, it now is totally pale. It looks, as if it is fighting for its life. Underwater photographs of sailfish are quite rare, but I succeed in shooting some of the terrified animal on its zig-zag course.

Breathless, one after the other of our snorkelling group gives in. Especially my legs are hurting, as I have to carry the additional weight of the heavy camera housing. Then the sailfish gets out of sight. I signal to Suzanne, who is swimming with me, to return to the liveaboard. Some of the False killerwhales are still swimming around us. Suddenly

A group of False killerwhales *Pseudorca crassidens* pursues the sailfish. One of these toothed whales alone would have no chance to catch the speedy sailfish.

eight of them come out of the blue and swim towards us. I can clearly see that the largest of the group is holding something in its mouth. Suzanne and I dive towards the marine mammals to get a closer look. Puzzled, we are watching from a distance how the whale drops

After the meal: one of these False killerwhales holds a trophy of the hunt in its mouth. The object remains unidentified at this distance.

something and another individual immediately picks it up again. I have just reached the surface to get fresh air, when the killerwhale with the object in its mouth leaves the group in a depth of about six metres. It smoothly approaches Suzanne, who is diving in the same depth, and "spits out" the unknown object right in front of her. She instinctively grabs it, and brings it up with her. The object is the pectoral fin of a sailfish that has just been removed from the body! The whales must just have killed the surrounded sailfish. But what about this action? Was the fin a gift for Suzanne? Was it an invitation to play? Or was it just an unintentional move? I am, after all, happy not to have been a sailfish in the company of killerwhales!

Only after the whales have given the object as a "gift" to Suzanne, it can be identified: it is one of the pectoral fins of the sailfish!

315

RORQUALS

BALAENOPTERIDAE

Blue whale

Meeting the largest and heaviest of all animals underwater is most impressive. Adult males reach a length of over 30 m and a weight of 150 tons. Young (7.5 m, 2.2 tons) are born after 11 months of gestation (see also pp.224-226). Below: **Bryde's whale** *B. edeni,* 14.5 m.

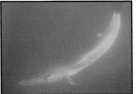

Balaenoptera musculus Burma Banks, Thailand

Minke whale

The smallest of the rorquals, reaching "only" 10 m in length. Easily recognised by a white band across the flippers. Seen singly in temperate waters near the coast, rarely far offshore, where jumping entirely out of the water. In our area rorquals feed on small fishes.

Balaenoptera acutorostrata Arabian Sea

Humpback whale

The famous singing whale is distinct by its long flippers adorned with barnacles. It reaches a length of 19 m and a weight of 48 tons. Migrates in winter in groups of 4 - 12 individuals into tropical seas, where young are born. Feeds on krill during summer in polar waters.

Megaptera novaeangliae Trinco, Sri Lanka

INDEX: SCIENTIFIC NAMES

INDEX: COMMON NAMES

319

BIBLIOGRAPHY

Abbott, R. T. & Dance, S. P. (1986) Compendium of Seashells. American Malacologists, Melbourne, FL.

Allen, G. R. & Steene, R. (1995) Riff-Führer Indopazifik. Conchbooks, Hackenheim.

Anderson, R. C. (?) Living reefs of the Maldives. Novelty, Maldives.

Branch, G. M., Griffiths, C. L., Branch, M. L. & **Beckley, L. E.** (1994) Two Oceans. David Philip, Cape Town & Johannesburg.

Briggs, J. (1974) Marine zoogeography. McGraw-Hill Inc.

Collette, B. B. & Nauen, C. E. (1983) Scombrids of the world. FAO Species Catalogue Vol. 2.

Compagno, L. J. V. (1984) Sharks of the world. FAO Species Catalogue Vol. 4/1+2.

Debelius, H. (1984) Armoured knights of the sea. Kernen Verlag, Germany.

Debelius, H. (1994) Marine Atlas. Tetra Press, Blacksburg.

Debelius, H. (1996) Fischführer Indischer Ozean, 2nd ed. UW-Archiv-Ikan, Frankfurt.

Debelius, H. (1998) Red Sea Reef Guide. UW-Archiv-Ikan, Frankfurt.

Debelius, H. (1998) Nudibranchs and Sea snails. 2nd ed. UW-Archiv-Ikan, Frankfurt.

Gosliner, T. M., Behrens, D. W. & Williams, G. C. (1996) Coral Reef Animals of the Indo-Pacific. Sea Challengers, Monterey, California.

Grüter, W. (1990) Leben im Meer. Ott Verlag, Schweiz.

Heemstra, P. C. & Randall, J. E. (1993) Groupers of the world. FAO Species Catalogue Vol. 16.

King, D., (1996) Reef fishes and corals. East coast of Southern Africa. Struik, Cape Town.

Kuiter, R. H. (1998) Photo Guide to the Fishes of the Maldives. Atoll Editions, Australia.

Lorenz, F., Jr. & Hubert, A. (1993) A guide to worldwide cowries. Verlag Christa Hemmen, Wiesbaden.

Randall, J. E. & Heemstra, P. C. (1991) Revision of Indo-Pacific groupers (Perciformes: Serranidae: Epinephelinae) with descriptions of five new species. Indo-Pacific Fishes 20. B. P. Bishop Museum, Hawaii.

Roper, C. F. E., Sweeney, M. J. & Nauen, C. E. (1984) Cephalopods of the world. FAO Spec. Cat. Vol. 3.

Smith, M. M. & Heemstra, P. C. (1986) Smiths' Sea Fishes. Springer, Berlin.

Van der Vat, D. (1984) The last corsair. The story of the Emden. Panther Books, London.

Veron, J. E. N. (1986) Corals of Australia and the Indo-Pacific. Angus & Robertson, Australia.

DO YOU KNOW THE OTHER VOLUMES OF THIS SERIES?

World Atlas
of Marine Fishes

RUDIE H KUITER – HELMUT DEBELIUS

World Atlas
of Marine Fauna

RUDIE H KUITER – HELMUT DEBELIUS

**Nudibranchs
of the World**

HELMUT DEBELIUS
RUDIE H KUITER

**Red Sea
Reef Guide**

Helmut Debelius

Egypt
Israel
Jordan
Sudan
Saudi Arabia
Yemen
Arabian
Peninsula

To be ordered directly from
conchbooks@conchbooks.de

INDIAN